A Primer on Crime and Delinquency Theory

D1715045

A Primer on Crime and Delinquency Theory

FOURTH EDITION

Robert M. Bohm

Brenda L. Vogel

CAROLINA ACADEMIC PRESS

Durham, North Carolina

Library of Congress Cataloging-in-Publication Data

Bohm, Robert M.
  A primer on crime and delinquency theory / Robert M. Bohm and Brenda
L. Vogel. -- Fourth edition.
      pages cm
  Includes bibliographical references and index.
  ISBN 978-1-61163-685-7 (alk. paper)
  1. Criminology. 2. Crime. I. Vogel, Brenda, 1938- II. Title.

HV6018.B645 2015
364--dc23

                              2014042075

Carolina Academic Press
700 Kent Street
Durham, North Carolina 27701
Telephone (919) 489-7486
Fax (919) 493-5668
www.cap-press.com

Printed in the United States of America
2020 Printing

Dedicated to Bob's mom and dad, Elizabeth and Jack Bohm,
and Brenda's husband Ron and their remarkable daughter Hailey

Contents

Preface

The primary purpose for writing this book has not changed since the first edition: to provide both undergraduate and graduate students with a relatively brief but comprehensive exposition of crime and delinquency theories. The book should prove useful either as a primary text (with instructor supplements) or as a supplement to other texts, anthologies, or collections of journal articles.

As noted in the first three editions of this book, although many fine criminological texts are on the market, none of them precisely provides the material in a manner that we believe students of crime and delinquency theory ought to receive. For example, some texts contain much more material than can ever be covered satisfactorily within the time constraints of an academic semester or quarter. Consequently, instructors are forced to ignore some theories or offer a superficial rendering of some of the theories that they do present. With this relatively slim volume, instructors need not worry about such time constraints but still can be confident that they are presenting a reasonably comprehensive description. Some texts focus only on one or another theoretical perspective and thus ignore the rich multidisciplinary nature of crime and delinquency theory. For example, many criminological texts present only sociological theories, or, when other theories are examined, they are given short shrift. This text, though brief, is comprehensive and multidisciplinary in its scope.

Few of the available criminological texts provide an adequate introduction to theory. For example, conspicuously missing from these texts are discussions of the critically important issues of the philosophical assumptions on which all theories are based, and how theories can be evaluated in relation to each other. This book rectifies each of those omissions. Also, although other texts present descriptions of the theories, few of them identify the policy implications that are either explicit or implicit in all theories. A major feature of this book is the description of the policy implications of the theories. Other texts fail to present results of empirical tests of a theory or to otherwise comment on the empirical validity of a theory. For many theories, particularly positivist theories, this book does both. Perhaps most importantly, very few of the available texts incorporate a comprehensive critique of the theories. Again, a principal feature of this book is a thorough critique of most of the theories.

In sum, the first three editions of *A Primer on Crime and Delinquency Theory* provided in a very manageable format (1) an introduction to theory with a special focus on the philosophical assumptions of theories, and how the theories can be evaluated in relation to each other, (2) descriptions of philosophical and social scientific crime and delinquency theories, (3) the presentation of the policy implications of each of the theories, (4) results of empirical tests of a theory or comments about a theory's empirical validity (added in the third edition), and (5) a comprehensive critique of most of the theories. In addition, the second edition added study questions to the end of each chapter. Study questions are included in this edition and are intended to promote class discussion and also can be used for examination purposes.

This fourth edition of *A Primer on Crime and Delinquency Theory* has remained faithful to the previous three editions in both intent and organization. However, its content has been increased, though it remains a relatively thin volume. New material has been added to several chapters to clarify or expand explanations in the first three editions, include material omitted, or describe developments since the third edition was completed about five years ago. In addition, numerous subheadings have been added to the chapters to help the reader better navigate the material. This addition has reduced the density of the material in the first three editions.

Following is a list of some of the fourth edition's new or expanded topics or issues (with the chapter in which the addition is found in parentheses):

- Changed title of section on Testing Theories to Evaluating Theories and revised section for greater clarity (Chapter 1)
- Added new criticisms of classical theory, regarding social contract, free will, and deterrence (Chapter 2)
- Added new problems with twin studies (Chapter 4)
- Added new material on epigenetic factors and their influence on gene activity (Chapter 4)
- Added new material on the effects of hormones on antisocial behavior (Chapter 4)
- Added new material on impulsivity and criminality (Chapter 5)
- Added new material on corporate tax loopholes (Chapter 8)
- Added new material on developments in feminist criminology (Chapter 8)
- Added a new section on green or environmental criminology (Chapter 8)

- Added a new section on rural criminology (Chapter 8)
- Added a new section on convict criminology (Chapter 8)
- Added a new section on queer criminology (Chapter 8)
- Added new material on Hagan's power-control theory (Chapter 9)
- Added new material on Agnew's general theory of crime and delinquency and his unified criminology (Chapter 9)

Another change to *A Primer on Crime and Delinquency Theory* is a new publisher: Carolina Academic Press. We are excited about this new affiliation with CAP and look forward to a long and productive relationship.

In sum, our hope is that students who read this book come to appreciate the diversity of crime and delinquency theories as well as the policy implications, empirical evidence, and problems associated with each of them. As mentioned in the preface to the first three editions of this book, ultimately, we hope that the knowledge gained by studying this relatively thin volume will lead to the significant reduction in the harm and suffering experienced by both crime victims and offenders and to the improvement of everyone's quality of life.

Robert M. Bohm
Brenda L. Vogel

A Primer on Crime and
Delinquency Theory

1

An Introduction to Theory

What Is Theory?

A *theory* is an explanation. It tells why or how things are related to each other.[1] A theory of crime explains why or how a certain thing or certain things are related to criminal behavior. For example, some theories assume that crime is a part of human nature, that human beings are born evil. In those theories, human nature is the thing explained in relation to crime. Other theories assume that crime is caused by biological things (for example, chromosome abnormalities, hormone imbalances), psychological things (such as below-normal intelligence, satisfaction of basic needs), sociological things (for instance, social disorganization, inadequate socialization), economic things (such as poverty, unemployment), or some combination of all four kinds of things. In the chapters that follow, a variety of things associated with crime are examined. (Note that, unless indicated otherwise, the term *crime* includes delinquency.)

Scientific theories are comprised of (1) concepts, (2) definitions of concepts, (3) propositions, and (4) philosophical assumptions.

Concepts

Those "things" mentioned in the previous paragraph, including criminal behavior, are called concepts. *Concepts* are words or phrases that represent some phenomenon in the world. The object of theory is to explain the interrelationship of concepts, that is, how concepts are related to each other. For example, through theory, we might attempt to explain how the concepts of crime and poverty are interrelated. Does poverty cause crime? Does crime cause poverty?

Definitions of Concepts

Definitions of concepts refer to both nominal and operational definitions. *Nominal definitions* are "dictionary definitions" assigned to concepts to clarify what the concepts mean to a researcher and to make possible general discussions about them. The generally accepted nominal definition of the concept of crime, for example, is a violation of the criminal law. *Operational definitions* describe how concepts are or will be measured for research purposes. Standard operational definitions of the concept of crime include the category of "offenses known to the police" as reported in the Federal Bureau of Investigation's (FBI's) uniform crime reports or data on victimizations as reported in the U.S. Justice Department's national crime victimization surveys. *Offenses known to the police* refer to crimes that are sometimes discovered by the police, but more generally are reported to the police and officially recorded by the police and sent to the FBI. Data from the national crime victimization surveys are based on interviews in which respondents are asked whether they have been victims of certain crimes during the past six months, and if they have, they are asked to provide information about the experience. Most crime theories assume those nominal and operational definitions; however, interactionist, radical, and some critical theories question their usage. Alternative definitions of crime and their implications are discussed later in the chapter.

Propositions

Interrelated concepts are called *propositions*. An example of a proposition that interrelates the concepts of poverty and crime is: "As poverty increases, crime increases." This particular relationship is referred to as a *positive linear relationship*. A positive linear relationship is one in which concepts increase or decrease together in a relatively straight-line fashion. Using the concepts of poverty and crime as examples, a positive linear relationship would be one where both poverty and crime increase or decrease together in a relatively straight-line fashion.

A *negative linear relationship* is one in which concepts vary in opposite directions in a relatively straight-line fashion. Thus, using the concepts of poverty and crime again, a negative linear relationship would be one where poverty increases while crime decreases or poverty decreases while crime increases.

Possibly no relationship exists between the concepts. For example, poverty and crime may be completely unrelated to each other. In other words, increases or decreases in poverty may have no relationship to crime whatsoever.

Finally, not all relationships are linear. An example of a nonlinear relationship, using the concepts of poverty and crime, is that as poverty increases to a point, crime also increases, but after poverty reaches that point, crime decreases. This is called a *curvilinear relationship*, and some criminologists believe that it describes the relationship between poverty and crime during the height of the Depression in the United States during the 1930s.[2]

Philosophical Assumptions

All theories are based on certain philosophical assumptions or ideas that cannot be tested scientifically or empirically.[3] A *scientific* or *empirical test* uses human senses (seeing, hearing, smelling, tasting, and touching) to discover some aspect of the world. Philosophical assumptions, which are also referred to as *background* or *domain assumptions*, are like religion in a way—they are either believed or they are not, but they cannot be supported empirically or scientifically. For example, despite some arguments to the contrary, it cannot be supported scientifically or empirically that God or some other supreme being exists. The existence of God or a supreme being is either believed or it is not.

Though they often are ignored and thus are sometimes considered the "hidden agenda" of theories, the philosophical assumptions on which all theories are based should be considered another component of all theories. Three types of philosophical assumptions are important to all theories: ethical, epistemological, and metaphysical.

Ethical Assumptions

Ethical assumptions or *normative implications* are ideas about what is "good" and "bad," "right" and "wrong," and what we ought to do. Thus, implicit in each theory about crime are certain value judgments and policy implications that follow logically from the theory. For example, if someone believes that criminal behavior is caused by poverty, then that person is probably making an implicit value judgment that crime and poverty are "bad." A policy implication would be to reduce poverty in an effort to reduce crime. Likewise, if someone believes that criminal behavior is caused by poor parenting, then that person is probably making an implicit value judgment that crime and poor parenting are "bad." A policy implication of the theory would be to reduce crime by improving parenting skills.

Policy implications, whatever they may be, generally can be linked to conservative, liberal, or radical political views. In this way, all crime theories are "political." As conventionally defined, *conservative policies* aim to preserve traditional social institutions, methods, customs, and so forth; *liberal policies* seek reform or change by means of existing social institutions; and *radical policies* favor fundamental or extreme change by abolishing existing social institutions and creating new ones. Examples of social institutions are the family, organized religion, schools, the media, the political system, and the economic system. Politically conservative criminal justice policies generally focus on the individual offender, leaving social institutions untouched. Examples of such policies are most bio- or psychotherapeutic interventions, "three strikes and you're out" laws, and the death penalty. Politically liberal criminal justice policies, on the other hand, generally attack crime using existing social institutions, especially agencies of the state. Examples include educational and vocational programs, community policing, and after-school programs. Politically radical criminal justice policies, by contrast, seek the fundamental transformation of social institutions or their abolition. An economic system based predominately on socialist rather than capitalist principles, a redefinition of crime, greater attention to corporate and government crimes, and community-based strategies for controlling crime are examples of politically radical criminal justice policies. In the examination of crime theories throughout this book, the value judgments and policy implications of the theories are described too.

Epistemological Assumptions

The second type of philosophical assumption is epistemological. Epistemology is the branch of philosophy that investigates the origins, structure, methods, and validity of knowledge. *Epistemological assumptions* address the question of how knowledge is obtained. Most crime theories are based on the epistemological assumption that the world can be understood through science, that is, the human capacity to observe and to reason. A related assumption is that once the world and its functioning are understood, then the world can be controlled or changed. With respect to crime, the assumption is that once the causes of crime are understood, then those causes can be effectively controlled or, perhaps, even eliminated.

Some theories of crime, however, are based on the epistemological assumption that a single, objective reality does not exist. In this social-constructionist view, each person creates his or her own unique social reality. In this view, concepts are sometimes referred to as constructs. Still other theories of crime are based on other epistemological assumptions. Other ways of knowing, besides science and social constructionism, include authority, instinct, introspection, intuition, mysticism, spiritualism, extrasensory perception, anamnesis (recollection from previous lifetimes), supernatural revelation, occult sources such as astrology, pragmatism, and linguistic analysis.[4] In the examination of the theories in this book, the epistemological assumptions of each theory or group of theories are described as well.

Metaphysical Assumptions

Finally, implicit in all theories are *metaphysical assumptions*. Metaphysical assumptions address the question of what is the nature of reality. For purposes of this analysis, the important metaphysical assumptions involve human nature (*ontology*) and the nature of society (*cosmology*). All crime theories are based on two ontological assumptions. The first addresses whether human behavior, including criminal behavior, is freewilled or determined. The second considers the inherent condition of human beings, or the condition of human beings in a hypothetical "state of nature."

Some theories assume that human beings are free to do whatever they please, while other theories assume that human beings are determined by forces largely beyond their control. An important corollary of the first assumption is that if humans are freewilled, then they are responsible for their behavior, unless, as is the case in many legal systems, they can provide an acceptable defense or excuse. A corollary of the second assumption is that if behavior is determined, then people ought not to be held liable, or at least not fully liable, for their crimes. If people freely choose to commit crimes and, thus, are responsible for them, then a normative implication is that people should be deterred from committing crimes. However, if criminal behavior is a product of factors (whether biological, psychological, or sociological) largely beyond an individual's control, then an ethical implication is that those factors should be changed or eliminated. Ontological assumptions about free will and determinism will be discussed more fully when specific theories are examined in later chapters of this book.

The inherent condition of human beings, or the condition of human beings in a hypothetical "state of nature," is the second important ontological assumption implicit in all crime theories. Three competing conceptualizations differentiate those theories. The first and oldest is that human beings are inherently bad or evil and, thus, likely or expected to commit crime. This view probably originated with the Christian belief that everyone is born into original sin. The seventeenth-century English philosopher Thomas Hobbes

(1588–1679), who wrote "the life of man [is] solitary, poor, nasty, brutish, and short," promoted the idea. This view of human nature is also found in Freudian psychoanalytic theory and some versions of social control theory. If, indeed, human beings are inherently bad or evil, then the general policy implication is that society must devise methods to constrain or control such behavior.

The second conceptualization is attributed to the seventeenth-century English philosopher John Locke (1632–1704), who believed that human beings were born with a "tabula rasa" or blank slate. Such individuals are neither inherently good nor bad, but rather a product of their experiences. Learning theories are based on this assumption. The general policy implication is to structure society to promote experiences conducive to law-abiding behavior rather than criminal behavior.

The third conceptualization portrays human beings as inherently good. This view is associated with the eighteenth-century French philosopher Jean-Jacques Rousseau (1712–1778) and forms the basis of most critical theories. If, in this view, human beings are inherently good, then society, or something about society, makes human beings bad and prone to commit crime. The normative implication is to change society so that human beings will not be subjected to corrupting influences.

As for cosmological assumptions, some theories assume that the world is characterized primarily by a consensus about moral values, whereas other theories assume that the world is characterized primarily by conflict about moral values. In the first view, it is assumed that most people agree most of the time about what is right and wrong or good and bad. In the second view, the assumption is that most people disagree most of the time about what is right and wrong or good and bad. If a moral consensus in society exists, then an important ethical issue is how to control conflict. On the other hand, if conflict better characterizes social relations, then building consensus, better appreciating diversity, or repressing dissent and conflict are critical social goals implied by the assumption. Note that ethical assumptions or normative implications are derived directly from metaphysical assumptions. Put differently, beliefs about human nature and the nature of society inevitably guide public policy decisions. As was the case with the other philosophical assumptions, the metaphysical assumptions of each theory or group of theories will be described also.

Philosophical Assumptions Are Important

Understanding the philosophical assumptions on which theories are based is important! Theories frequently are accepted or rejected because of one's be-

lief in a theory's philosophical assumptions rather than on the scientific support (or lack of support) for the theory. This is because scientific research into
the causes of crime almost never offers conclusive results that support one
competing theory over another. Focusing on philosophical assumptions, then,
if it is believed that human beings are freewilled and thus completely responsible for their behavior, then it may be difficult to accept theories that posit
that crime is determined by factors largely beyond the individual's control.
Even when the scientific evidence is compelling, the theory still may be rejected because it is not based on the philosophical assumptions in which one
believes.

Paradigms

Philosophical assumptions are often grouped together in organizing schemes
called *paradigms*. A paradigm is:

> a fundamental image of the subject matter within a science. It serves
> to define what should be studied, what questions should be asked,
> how they should be asked, and what rules should be followed in in-
> terpreting the answers obtained. The paradigm is the broadest unit
> of consensus within a science and serves to differentiate one scientific
> community (or sub-community) from another. It subsumes, defines,
> and interrelates the exemplars, theories, and methods and instruments
> that exist within it.[5]

In this book the theories presented are grouped into three general paradigms: (1) the classical/neoclassical, (2) the positivist, and (3) the critical. The
philosophical assumptions associated with each of the paradigms are described as each paradigm is introduced.

Evaluating Theories

Numerous theories will be presented in the following chapters, and they will
offer different, sometimes contradictory explanations of crime, which begs the
question: How does one choose among the many competing theories of crime?
To begin, theories must be evaluated *in relation to each other*. The goal is to determine which theory or theories is the most *compelling, believable*, or *convincing* in relation to the other theories. It is possible that two or more theories may
be compelling explanations of crime, in which case an appropriate question is
how much influence on crime does each theory's key concept or concepts exert?

In the previous section, the importance of clearly defined concepts and clearly specified relationships among concepts (propositions) to the evaluation of theories was emphasized. Also stressed was the need to critically scrutinize the philosophical assumptions upon which a theory is based. In this section, the focus is on explanatory power, parsimony, testability, and empirical validity.

Explanatory Power

Explanatory power, as a standard by which to evaluate crime theories, is a multidimensional concept that consists of criteria such as generalizability, scope, or breadth; comprehensiveness; and precision. More compelling theories have greater explanatory power than less compelling theories.

Generalizability, scope, or *breadth* refers to the ability of a theory about crime to explain and predict various types of crime (for example, street crime, corporate crime, government crime, organized crime, and so forth) in different places at different times. Generalizability, scope, or breadth of a theory also denotes a crime theory's ability to explain crime at different levels of analysis. A theory with greater explanatory power provides compelling explanations not only for why individuals commit various crimes but also for rates of crime among various groups or social structures. Theories of why individuals commit crimes are sometimes referred to as *microtheories* or *process theories.* Theories that explain rates of crime among various groups or social structures are sometimes called *macrotheories* or *structural theories.* Put somewhat differently, a theory with greater explanatory power provides compelling explanations that integrate dispositional, situational, and systemic factors or biological, psychological, and sociological factors. A theory with less explanatory power, by contrast, may provide an explanation at only one level of analysis (for instance, at the individual level, the group level, or the social structural level or with only biological or dispositional factors or only sociological or situational factors). All things being equal, a crime theory with greater explanatory power explains more than just one type of crime in one place at one time and at one level of analysis.

Comprehensiveness, as applied to crime theories, refers to the inclusion of all possible variables, especially those dealing with motivation, opportunity, ability, constraint, and absence of alternative motivation.[6] Variables are operationalized concepts that have at least two attributes, e.g., the variable pregnancy has the attributes of yes or no. If a concept does not have at least two attributes, it is a constant. (See the discussion of operational definitions earlier in this chapter.)

Precision is the ability of a crime theory to specify the operation, form, and contingencies of the causal relationships, such as the time interval between cause and effect, the influence of extraneous or intervening variables, and the direction of the causal relationship.[7] The time interval between cause and effect refers to the amount of time it takes the independent variable (the presumed cause) to affect the dependent variable (the presumed effect). For instance, in a hypothetical relationship between a new policing philosophy and crime, the new policing philosophy may not affect crime for several months or possibly years following its implementation. Not specifying the time interval of a relationship may result in the premature rejection of a theory (and, in this example, the rejection of a potentially successful new policing philosophy).

An extraneous variable is any variable other than the independent variable that may influence the dependent variable. For example, in a hypothetical relationship between testosterone (the male sex hormone) and crime, the percentage of young males in the population could be an extraneous variable. Attempts are made to control extraneous variables because they may cause misinterpretation and false conclusions.

An intervening variable is a variable that occurs between the independent and dependent variable. It is caused by the independent variable and is a cause of the dependent variable. For instance, in a hypothetical relationship between social disorganization and crime, family stability could be an intervening variable. Failure to consider intervening variables may result in missed nuances in causal relationships and premature rejection of a theory.

Causal relationships may be unidirectional or reciprocal. A reciprocal relationship is one in which the independent and dependent variable are both cause and effect of each other. For example, in a hypothetical relationship between poverty and crime, poverty may cause crime and crime may cause poverty. Knowing the direction of a relationship adds greater complexity and understanding to a theory.

Parsimony

Another common standard by which theories are evaluated is parsimony. *Parsimony* refers to simplicity. All things being equal, the simplest theory, with the fewest concepts and propositions, that has the greatest generalizability, scope, or breadth is generally considered the more compelling theory. However, a problem with parsimony as an evaluation criterion is that a parsimonious theory may not provide as great an understanding of crime as a more elaborate theory.[8] If crime is a complex issue, as many criminologists believe, then explaining crime likely requires a complex theory with many concepts and propositions. Still, even among complex theories, parsimony is a desirable characteristic.

Testability

Testability is another important criterion by which to evaluate *scientific* theories. As noted previously, scientific theories can be tested scientifically or empirically. However, to call a theory unscientific is not necessarily to condemn it. People believe in many unscientific theories (e.g., intelligent beings visited Earth in ancient times) and those theories have consequences. To call a theory unscientific means only that the theory cannot claim what "good" scientific theories can claim—that the evidence of the senses makes it irrational to reject it. Yet, we should be skeptical about scientific observations because evidence from the senses might be wrong, as in the cases of hallucinations and optical illusions.

Another concern is whether a scientific methodology created for the physical sciences, such as physics and chemistry, is applicable to the social sciences, such as criminology. Many critical criminologists, especially postmodernist criminologists (described in Chapter 8) believe that it is not (see the discussion of problems with positivist theories in Chapter 3). Unlike in the physical sciences, argue these critical criminologists, there are no law-like regularities to discover in the social sciences. Thus, what science can offer should not be overestimated.

Scientific theories are tested through the processes of verification and falsification. *Verification* involves the observation and confirmation of a theoretical proposition's predicted relationship. For example, to verify the proposition that as poverty increases, crime increases, concomitant increases in poverty and crime must be observable and observed. *Falsification* involves disproving a proposition by the observation of disconfirming examples. Thus, given the aforementioned proposition, if it were observed that in some place at some time, poverty increased, while crime decreased, then the proposition and theory of which it is a part would have to be questioned. Finding disconfirming examples for a proposition does not necessarily condemn it, but it does suggest that the theory's explanatory power is limited. The limitation may be a function of the unique historical circumstances in which the theory was produced because most theories are products of their times. When evaluating theories, therefore, it is important to consider the historical context in which the theory emerged, which is a focus of this book.

For most social scientists, falsification is the more critical test of a theory. The principal reason for this is that theories can *never* be proven true, but they can be falsified. Theories can never be proven true because there is always the possibility that an observed relationship may be a function of some other, unconsidered factor. To illustrate, consider the very strong positive relationship between the sale of ice cream and the homicide rate: As the sale of ice cream increases, the homicide rate increases and vice versa. Does this mean that ice cream sales cause homicide? Of course not! What it means is that both the sale of ice cream and the homicide rate are related to a third factor that causes both of them to increase or decrease together. As one might guess, that third factor is the weather. As it gets hotter, both ice cream sales and homicides increase; when it gets cooler, both decrease. The relationship between the sale of ice cream and the homicide rate (and it is a real relationship) is called a *spurious relationship*. Because of the potential for spurious relationships, most social scientists consider falsification the hallmark of the scientific method.

Empirical Validity

Finally, compelling scientific theories are those theories that have demonstrated empirical validity. This means that a theory's propositions have been verified and have withstood attempts at falsification. Theories with empirical validity are more compelling than those without it. Throughout this book, numerous crime theories are presented and described, as is the research designed to test those theories. Some theories enjoy widespread empirical support, while other theories do not. Research, however, is an ever-evolving enterprise with the development of new methodologies, analytical tools, and approaches, so a theory may have received empirical support under older research standards, but fails to do so under current standards.

In addition, some research is more rigorously conducted than other research. Factors such as sample size, sample selection, and variable operationalization can all affect the quality of research findings. A sample is a subset of a larger group or population to which the researcher would like to generalize the study's findings. Variable operationalization has been discussed previously in this chapter.

In sum, when theory is evaluated, all that accurately can be said is that one theory is more or less compelling, believable, or convincing than another theory. What makes one theory more compelling, believable, or convincing than another theory is that the more compelling theory has greater explanatory power, has been adequately tested, and has more empirical validity, for example, has successfully withstood more attempts to falsify it, than has the less compelling theory. It is not accurate to say that a theory is true or false or right or wrong.

The Problem of Defining Crime

For many criminologists, an appropriate definition of crime remains an elusive goal. One problem is that many dangerous and harmful behaviors are not defined as crimes, while many less dangerous and less harmful behaviors are. Consider the different ways crime is defined, and the problems with defining crime.

Social Definitions of Crime

The broadest definitions of crime are social definitions. A typical social definition of crime is behavior that violates the norms of society — or, more simply, antisocial behavior. A *norm* is any standard or rule regarding what human beings should or should not think, say, or do under given circumstances. Because social definitions of crime are broad, they are less likely than narrower definitions to exclude behaviors that ought to be included. Nevertheless, there are several problems with social definitions of crime.

First, norms vary from group to group within a single society. There is no uniform definition of antisocial behavior. Take, for example, the acts involved in gambling, prostitution, abortion, and homosexual behavior. As current public debates indicate, there is much controversy in the United States over whether those acts should be crimes. Even with acts about which there seems to be a consensus, such as murder and rape, there is no agreement on what constitutes such acts. For example, if a patient dies from a disease contracted from a doctor who did not wash his or her hands before examining the patient, has the doctor committed murder? Or, if a man has sexual intercourse with an intoxicated woman who initially consents to the act but retracts her consent during the act, has the man committed rape? These examples illustrate the difficulty of determining what, in fact, constitutes antisocial behavior, let alone crime.

Second, norms are always subject to interpretation. Each norm's meaning has a history. Consider abortion, for example. For some people, abortion is the killing of a fetus or a human being. For other people, abortion is not killing, because, for them, human life begins at birth and not at conception. For the latter group, the abortion issue concerns women's freedom to control their own bodies. For the former group, abortion constitutes an injustice to the helpless.

Third, norms change from time to time and from place to place. For example, the consumption of alcohol was prohibited in the United States during the 1920s and early 1930s but is only regulated today. Until the passage of the Harrison Act in 1914, it was legal in the United States to use opiates such as opium, heroin, and morphine without a doctor's prescription. Such use is prohibited today. In some states, the use of marijuana is legal for medical or recreational purposes, but is illegal in other states. Casino gambling is allowed in some states but forbidden in other states. Prostitution is legal in a few counties in Nevada but illegal in the rest of the United States. Prior to the mid-1970s, a husband could rape his wife with impunity in all but a handful of states. Today, laws in every state prohibit a husband from raping or assaulting his wife.

A Legal Definition of Crime

In an attempt to avoid the problems with social definitions of crime, a legal definition of crime is commonly used in the United States. A typical legal definition of crime is this: an intentional violation of the criminal law or penal code, committed without defense or excuse and penalized by the state. The major advantage of a legal definition of crime, at least on the surface, is that it is narrower and less ambiguous than a social definition of crime. If a behavior violates the criminal law, then by definition it is a crime. However, although a legal definition eliminates some of the problems with social definitions of crime, a legal definition of crime has problems of its own.

First, some behaviors prohibited by the criminal law arguably should not be. This problem of "overcriminalization" arises primarily in the area of so-called victimless crimes. Lists of victimless crimes typically include gambling, prostitution involving consenting adults, homosexual acts between consenting adults, and the use of illegal drugs. Ultimately, whether those acts should or should not be prohibited by criminal law depends on whether they are truly victimless—an issue we will not debate here. Perhaps less controversial are some of the following illegal behaviors:

- In California, it is illegal to trip horses for entertainment, to possess bear gallbladders, or to peel an orange in your hotel room.
- In Colorado, it is illegal to throw shoes at weddings.
- In Connecticut, it is illegal to walk across the street on your hands.
- In Idaho, it is illegal for a man to give his sweetheart a box of candy weighing less than 50 pounds.
- In Michigan, it is illegal for a woman to cut her hair without her husband's permission.
- In North Dakota, it is illegal to serve beer and pretzels at the same time in any bar or restaurant.
- In Pennsylvania, it is illegal to sing in the bathtub.
- In Tennessee it is illegal to shoot any game other than whales from a moving automobile.[9]

A second problem with a legal definition of crime is that for some behaviors prohibited by criminal law, the law is not routinely enforced. "Nonenforcement" is common for many white-collar and government crimes. It is also common for blue laws, for example, those that require stores and other commercial establishments to be closed on Sundays. Many jurisdictions in the United States have blue laws, or they did have until recently. The principal problem with the nonenforcement of prohibitions is that it causes disrespect for the law. People come to believe that because criminal laws are not routinely enforced, there is no need to routinely obey them.

A third problem with a legal definition of crime is the problem of "undercriminalization." That is, some behaviors that arguably should be prohibited by criminal law are not. Have you ever said to yourself that there ought to be a law against whatever it is you are upset about? Of course, most of the daily frustrations that people claim ought to be crimes probably should not be. Some people argue, however, that some very harmful and destructive actions or inactions that are not criminal should be. Examples include the government allowing employers (generally through the nonenforcement of laws) to maintain unsafe working conditions that cause employee deaths and injuries, and corporations' intentional production of potentially hazardous products to maximize profits.[10]

In sum, competing definitions of crime exist and there are problems with all definitions. Consequently, students should be mindful of the way in which theorists define crime and the implications those definitions have for theory and research.

Why Is Theory Important, or Why Study Crime and Delinquency Theory?

Everything people do in life is based on theory. However, many people often are not conscious or aware of the theory that they are using. Nevertheless, whatever they do, they do for a reason. Similarly, everything that is done in criminal justice is based on theory, although most people are unaware of the theory on which those actions are based. Theory is studied, then, to explain and understand why people do what they do. People who are uninterested in theory are people who move blindly through life or, in the case of criminal justice, intervene in other people's lives with only vague notions about why they are doing what they do.

This book focuses on theories of crime and delinquency. These theories are studied in an attempt to understand why people commit criminal and delinquent acts. The ultimate goal of this endeavor is to improve the quality of life, the effort toward which, it is assumed, can be aided by the reduction of socially harmful behaviors, whether legally defined as criminal or not. Absent a great amount of luck, however, that goal will be accomplished only by means of a clear theoretical understanding of the problem.

Study Questions

1. What is theory?
2. What are the components of theory?
3. What are the philosophical assumptions on which all theories are based?
4. How are theories judged or evaluated in relation to each other?
5. Can a theory be proven true? If yes, how? If not, why not?
6. What are some problems with defining crime?
7. Why is theory important?

Notes

1. Much of the discussion in this chapter is from Kerlinger (1964) and Babbie (1992).
2. See for example Wilson and Herrnstein (1985:436).
3. Gouldner (1971); see also Einstadter and Henry (1995), whose work focuses on these assumptions.
4. Montague (1953); see also Brennan (1953); Chisholm (1966); Christian (1977); Honer and Hunt (1968); Mead (1959).
5. Ritzer (1975:7).
6. See Tittle (1995:28).
7. See Tittle (1995:35).
8. Reynolds (1971:134–135).
9. Loony Laws at www.loonylaws.com/ (accessed September 21, 2014). Some of these statutes may have been removed from a state's criminal code.
10. For additional examples and further discussion of this issue, see Bohm (1993); Barak (1991); Barak and Bohm (1989); Coleman (1998); Friedrichs (1996); Simon (2006).

2

Classical and Neoclassical Theory

Enlightenment Philosophy and Classical Theory
Beccaria and Deterrence Theory
Rational Choice Theory
A Critique of Classical Theory
Neoclassical Theory

Classical theory is a product of the philosophy of the Enlightenment, a period of social history roughly spanning the time of transition between the Protestant Reformation (1517) and the American and French Revolutions (1776 and 1789, respectively). The Enlightenment, or the "Age of Reason," was characterized by an intellectual challenge to the then-dominant theological worldview and theologically derived knowledge based on revelation and the authority of the Church.

During the "Middle Ages" or the "Dark Ages," the nearly thousand years between the fall of the western Roman Empire (476) and the Reformation, the Catholic Church was the primary cultural and social influence in the Western world. Catholic theology constituted the source of virtually all knowledge, as Carl Becker, a noted philosopher, describes:

> Existence was ... regarded by the medieval man as a cosmic drama, composed by the master dramatist according to a central theme and on a rational plan.... The duty of man was to accept the drama as written, since he could not alter it; his function, to play the role assigned. That he might play his role according to the divine text, subordinate authorities—church and state—deriving their just powers from the will of God, were instituted among men to dispose them to submission and to instruct them in their proper lines.[1]

Enlightenment Philosophy and Classical Theory

The challenge to the theologically based worldview and the authority of the Catholic Church came from Enlightenment thinkers who promoted a new, "scientific" worldview based on reason. For Enlightenment thinkers, who drew many of their ideas from the Greek or "classical" philosophers Socrates (469–399 B.C.), Plato (427–347 B.C.), and Aristotle (384–322 B.C.), reason, especially in those areas where personal observation was possible, was a legitimate and more democratic source of knowledge. *Reason*, for Enlightenment thinkers, referred to either the rationalism of Thomas Hobbes (1588–1679), René Descartes (1596–1650), Benedict de Spinoza (1632–1677), John Locke (1632–1704), Gottfried Wilhelm Leibniz (1646–1716), Francois-Marie Arouet de Voltaire (1694–1778), Charles de Secondat, the Baron de Montesquieu (1689–1755), Jean-Jacques Rousseau (1712–1778), and others, or the empiricism of Francis Bacon (1561–1626), Galileo Galilei (1564–1642), Johannes Kepler (1571–1630), and Isaac Newton (1642–1727), among others.[2]

Rationalism is based on *deductive logic*, which involves reasoning from the general to the particular or applying theory to a particular case. The scientist constructs a theory and then makes observations in an effort to support or refute the theory. Empiricism, on the other hand, is based on *inductive logic*, which involves reasoning from the particular to the general or moving from specific facts to theory. The scientist makes observations and then constructs a theory to explain the observations.[3] Modern scientific reasoning frequently combines deduction and induction.

As noted, the new, scientific worldview of the Enlightenment thinkers explicitly rejected the theological worldview, considering it a fraud or at least an illusion. Again, as Carl Becker explains:

> Renunciation of the traditional revelation was the very condition of being truly enlightened; for to be truly enlightened was to see the light in all its fullness, and the light in its fullness revealed two very simple and obvious facts ... the fact that the supposed revelation of God's purposes through Holy Writ and Holy Church was a fraud, or at best an illusion born of ignorance, perpetrated, or at least maintained, by the priests in order to accentuate the fears of mankind, and so hold it in subjection. The other ... that God had revealed his purpose to men in a far more simple and natural, a far less mysterious and recondite way, through his works. To be enlightened was to understand this double truth, that it was not in Holy Writ, but in the great book of nature, open for all mankind to read, that the laws of God had been

recorded. This is the new revelation, and thus at last we enter the secret door to knowledge.[4]

The Enlightenment thinkers assumed that human beings could understand
the world through science—the human capacity to observe and reason. Moreover, they believed that if the world and its functioning could be understood,
then it could also be changed. They rejected the belief that either the world or
the people in it were divinely ordained or determined.

Instead, they believed that people were *freewilled* and thus completely responsible for their actions. As the English common law scholar Sir Matthew Hale
(1609–1676) wrote in describing criminal intent (*mens rea*) and eligibility for
punishment: "'Man is naturally endowed with these two great faculties, understanding and liberty of will, and therefore is a subject' on whom criminal
sanctions are legitimately imposed, whenever he disobeys a law 'which in respect of these two great faculties he hath a capacity to obey.'"[5]

Human behavior also was considered to be motivated by a *hedonistic rationality*, where individuals weighed the potential pleasure of an action against
its possible pain. The concept of hedonistic rationality is associated with the
work of the English philosopher Jeremy Bentham (1748–1832), who described
his "felicity [or hedonic] calculus" in his *Introduction to the Principles of Morals
and Legislation* (1789). To determine the "amount" of pleasure and pain associated with an act, Bentham considered several factors such as the intensity
and the duration of the pleasure or pain.[6] This pseudo-mathematical model was
hardly a scientific analysis but, instead, was based on Bentham's personal evaluation of an act.[7] In any event, human beings committed crime, in this view,
because they rationally calculated that the crime would give them more pleasure than pain. Before the Enlightenment, crime was equated with sin and was
considered the work of demons or the Devil.[8]

Besides Bentham, other Enlightenment thinkers associated with the classical school of criminology were Cesare Bonesana, the Marchese de Beccaria
(1738–1794) of Italy, William Blackstone (1723–1780), John Howard
(1726–1790), and Samuel Romilly (1757–1818)—all of England—and Paul
Johann Anselm von Feuerbach (1775–1833) of Germany. These "classical criminologists" were primarily social reformers rather than social theorists.

All of these classical criminologists believed that in the realm of criminal
justice, social reform was necessary. Barbaric punishments were common both
before and during the Enlightenment. For example, in England during the eighteenth century, between about 100 and 200 offenses carried the death penalty.[9]

Consider the following account of the punishment of Robert-Francois
Damiens, who in 1757 stabbed, but did not kill, King Louis XV of France:

At seven o'clock in the morning of his execution day, Damiens was led to the torture chamber, where his legs were placed in "boots" that were squeezed gradually as wedges were inserted. A total of eight wedges were inserted, each at fifteen-minute intervals, until the attending physicians warned that an additional wedge could provoke an "accident" [Damiens' premature death]. Thereupon, Damiens was removed to the place where he would be executed.… The condemned man was placed on a scaffold, where a rope was tied to each arm and leg. Then, Damiens' hand was burned with a brazier containing burning sulphur, after which red-hot tongs were used to pinch his arms, thighs, and chest. Molten lead and boiling oil were poured onto his open wounds several times, and after each time the prisoner screamed in agony. Next, four huge horses were whipped by attendants as they pulled the ropes around Damiens' bleeding wounds for an hour. Only after some of the tendons were cut did two legs and one arm separate from Damiens' torso. He remained alive and breathing until the second arm was cut from his body. All parts of Damiens' body were hurled into a nearby fire for burning.[10]

The classicists, as Enlightenment thinkers, were concerned with protecting the rights of humankind from the corruption and excesses of the existing legal institutions.[11] Arbitrary and barbarous punishments were not the only problems. At the time, crime itself was poorly defined and extensive. Due process of law was either absent or ignored. For example, people could be arrested without warrants and be held in custody indefinitely without knowing why they were being held. Torture was routinely employed to extract confessions. Judgeships typically were sold to wealthy persons by the sovereign, and judges had almost total discretion.

Beccaria and Deterrence Theory

It was within that historical context that Beccaria wrote and published anonymously in 1764 his truly revolutionary work, *On Crimes and Punishments* (*Dei Delitti e delle Pene*). His book generally is acknowledged to have had "more practical effect than any other treatise ever written in the long campaign against barbarism in criminal law and procedure."[12] Historians of criminal law credit Beccaria's arguments with ending legal torture throughout Christendom.[13] At the time, however, Beccaria's treatise was not universally acclaimed. For example, in 1765, the Pope placed Beccaria's work on a list of banned books for its "extreme rationalism."[14] Nevertheless, in the book, Beccaria sets forth most of what we now call *classical criminological theory*.

According to Beccaria, the only justified rationale for laws and punishments is the principle of *utility*, that is, "the greatest happiness shared by the greatest number."[15] For Beccaria, "Laws are the conditions under which independent and isolated men united to form a society."[16] Criminal law should be based on positive sanction; that is, every member of society has a right to do anything that is not prohibited by law, without fearing anything but natural consequences. The source of law should be the legislature and not judges.

Beccaria believed that the basis of society, as well as the origin of punishments and the right to punish, is the *social contract*.[17] The social contract is an imaginary agreement entered into by persons who have sacrificed the minimum amount of their liberty necessary to prevent what the English philosopher Hobbes called "the war of all against all." With the demise of absolute monarchies based on the "divine right of kings" and the rise of constitutional monarchies, social contract theory was used during the Enlightenment to provide justification for the new political system.[18] In describing the social contract, Beccaria wrote:

> Weary of living in a continual state of war, and of enjoying a liberty rendered useless by the uncertainty of preserving it, they [people] sacrificed a part so that they might enjoy the rest of it in peace and safety. The sum of all these portions of liberty sacrificed by each for his own good constitutes the sovereignty of a nation, and their legitimate depository and administrator is the sovereign.[19]

However, Beccaria realized that establishing the social contract is not enough to prevent people from infringing on the remaining liberties of other people. Thus, Beccaria believed that punishment is necessary.

For Beccaria, the only legitimate purpose for punishment is deterrence, both special and general.[20] *Special* or *specific deterrence* is the prevention of particular individuals from committing crime again by punishing them, while *general deterrence* is the prevention of people in general or society at large from engaging in crime by punishing specific individuals and making examples of them. Beccaria summarized his position on punishment in the following way: "In order for punishment not to be, in every instance, an act of violence of one or of many against a private citizen, it must be essentially public, prompt, necessary, the least possible in the given circumstances, proportionate to the crime, dictated by the laws."[21]

It is important to emphasize that Beccaria promoted crime prevention over punishment. As Beccaria maintained, "It is better to prevent crimes than to punish them. This is the ultimate end of every good legislation [that is, to lead] men to the greatest possible happiness or the least possible unhappiness."[22] Interestingly, before Beccaria, the French Enlightenment philosopher Voltaire claimed that marriage was an effective deterrent to crime: "The more married men you have, the less crime there will be. Look at the frightful records of your registers of crime; you will find there a hundred bachelors hanged or wheeled for one father of a family.... The father of a family does not want to blush before his children. He fears to leave them a heritage of shame."[23] Beccaria did not include marriage as a way to prevent crime, but he did make six other recommendations:[24]

1. Encourage citizens to enter into the social contract.
2. Enact laws that are clear, simple, unbiased, and reflect the consensus of the entire population.
3. Impose punishments that are proportionate to the crime, prompt and certain, public, necessary, and dictated by the laws and not by judges' discretion.
4. Educate or enlighten the population. "Knowledge breeds evil in inverse ratio to its diffusion, and benefits in direct ratio." "The surest but most difficult way to prevent crimes is by perfecting education."
5. Eliminate corruption from the administration of justice.
6. Reward virtue. "The coin of honor is always inexhaustible and fruitful in the hands of the wise distributor."

In sum, Beccaria's main ideas are as follows: Human motivation is governed by a rational hedonism. A society based on a social contract is necessary to escape criminal violence and other predatory behavior. The state has the right to punish. Penalties should be legislated, with a scale of crimes and punishments. It is better to prevent crimes than to punish them.

Rational Choice Theory

A contemporary version of classical theory is *rational choice theory*, developed most fully by Derek Cornish (1939–) and Ronald Clarke (1941–).[25] In this theory, it is assumed that before many people commit crimes, they consider the risks and rewards. Economists have presented a more quantitative version of rational choice theory in their attempt to explain criminal behavior through a costs and benefits analysis.[26] The risks or costs and rewards or benefits may be either material (for example, money) or psychological (for instance, image or "street cred").

Cornish and Clarke's rational choice theory extends or modifies classical criminological theory in three ways. First, Cornish and Clarke do not believe that all people are rational all the time. They argue that people utilize a rationality that is limited, or "bounded" by incomplete information, time, and ability.[27] Second, they expand the concept of "risks" of crime to include not only official, state sanctions, but also informal sanctions (e.g., parental disapproval), shame, and other consequences such as the loss of a job. Finally, Cornish and Clarke argue that different people calculate the risks and rewards of crime differently. Drawing on other theoretical perspectives, they contend that the estimation of risks and rewards of crime is "influenced by such factors as the individual's level of self control, moral beliefs, strains, emotional state and association with delinquent peers."[28]

A Critique of Classical Theory

The classical school has been characterized as legal and administrative criminology,[29] denounced as "armchair criminology,"[30] and accused of being "constructed retrospectively by nineteenth-century criminal anthropologists who, hoping to become a 'school' in their own right, invented a forerunner with whom they might favorably compare themselves."[31]

The application of classical school tenets was supposed to make the criminal law fairer and easier to administer. To those ends, judicial discretion would be eliminated. Judges would only determine innocence or guilt. All offenders would be treated alike, and similar crimes would be treated similarly. Individual differences among offenders and unique or mitigating circumstances about the crime would be ignored. Mitigating circumstances or extenuating circumstances refer to features of a case that explain or particularly justify the defendant's behavior, even though they do not provide a defense to the crime. Examples of mitigating circumstances are youth, immaturity, or being under the influence of another person.

A problem with treating all offenders alike and similar crimes similarly is that all offenders are not alike and similar crimes are not always as similar as they might appear on the surface. Should first offenders be treated the same as habitual offenders? Should juveniles be treated the same as adults? Should the insane be treated the same as the sane? Should a crime of passion be treated the same as the intentional commission of a crime? The classical school's answer to all of those difficult questions would be a simple yes, because the school's focus is the harm caused by the criminal act and not the specific circumstances of the offender. For classical theorists, a murder at the hand of an insane offender creates the same harm as a murder at the hand of a sane offender and, therefore, they should be treated alike.

The theory of the classical school of criminology poses other problems as well. For example, classical theory assumes that there is a consensus in society, at least about the desirability of a social contract.[32] First, Bentham, who admired Beccaria's scholarship but differed from him on several fundamental points, rejected the idea of social contract as a basis of consensus in society, dismissing it as nothing more than a legal fiction.[33] Second, the logic of the social contract is questionable. For example, as much as it may be in everyone's interest to be protected from criminal violence, in a society in which the distribution of property is inequitable, it may not be in everyone's interest to have the present distribution of property protected. Why would a person without property agree to enter into a social contract to protect the existing distribution of property?

Classical theory also assumes that rational people will choose to enter into the social contract; thus, anyone who commits crime is pathological or irrational, that is, unable or unwilling to enter into a social contract.[34] Again, why would a person without property want to enter into a social contract to protect the existing distribution of property? Classical theory fails to consider that crime may be rational given the individual's social position.[35] On the other hand, classical theory, especially rational choice theory and economic models, has been criticized for overemphasizing the degree to which offenders rationally calculate the consequences of their actions.[36]

Placed in its historical context, classical theory turns out to be an ideological justification for the position of the then new and increasingly prosperous merchant or business class.[37] Beccaria's system of justice protected the newly propertied classes, while controlling all others, especially the old landed aristocracy who was in direct political competition with the new merchant or business class. Although Beccaria was born a member of the aristocracy as a marquis, he had no property and was a disaffected member of his class.[38] Other classical criminologists were members of the new merchant or business class or were in sympathy with them. Note that rational calculation of pains of punishment versus the pleasure of success makes more sense for property crime than for violent crime.

In addition, there were practical reasons (to the new merchant or business class) for making the laws more humane and reducing capital and corporal punishment. In the first place, under the system of barbarous punishments, judges and juries were frequently reluctant to convict, thus diminishing deterrence. By reducing the severity of punishments, judges and juries were more likely to convict, and, as a result, property was better protected. An added benefit of sending offenders to prison rather than killing or maiming them was that prisons indoctrinated work habits in prisoners (or so it was thought), preparing them for labor in the newly emerging industrial age. It was considered wasteful to destroy able-bodied workers.

Another problem with classical theory is the assumption that human beings are freewilled and completely responsible for their behavior. Among the first Enlightenment thinkers to counter those notions, and take what at the time was a very unpopular position, was the seventeenth-century philosopher Benedict de Spinoza. According to Spinoza, people often believe they are freewilled or choose freely, but this belief is a product of their ignorance of the causes that determine their actions or choices. Thus, as Spinoza concluded, "It is absurd to praise or blame people since they are and do what they must be and do. We should rather seek to understand the causes of their actions and states of mind."[39]

Besides, a belief in free will would seem to deny the contributions of all modern social sciences, as well as the success of the entire advertising industry. A major goal of the social sciences, after all, is to understand, predict, and control human behavior, and the sole purpose of the advertising industry is to create and maintain a market for commodities by manipulating human behavior.

Another problem is the apparent contradiction between the ideas of free will and social contract. If people cede a minimum amount of liberty as their share in the social contract, then they are no longer totally free but are minimally constrained by the state to which they ceded their liberty.

Beirne has argued that Beccaria has been misinterpreted and that he was "resolutely opposed to any notion of free will."[40] Beirne maintains that Beccaria believed that "human agents are no more than the products of their sensory reactions to external stimuli."[41] Bentham, too, rejected the idea that human beings had free will. In the opening sentence to *An Introduction to the Principles of Morals and Legislation* (1789), Bentham declared unambiguously that human behavior was determined by pleasure and pain:

> Nature has placed mankind under the governance of two sovereign masters, *pain* and *pleasure*. It is for them alone to point out what we ought to do, as well as to determine what we shall do. On the one hand the standard of right and wrong, on the other the chain of causes and effects, are fastened to their throne. They govern us in all we do, in all we say, in all we think: every effort we can make to throw off our subjection, will serve but to demonstrate and confirm it (emphasis in original).[42]

Neither Beccaria nor Bentham—the two pillars of classical criminological theory—apparently subscribed to the ontological assumption about free will.

Still another problem with classical theory is its belief in deterrence. In the first place, little scientific evidence supports the contention that people do not commit crimes because they are afraid of being punished.[43] A meta-analysis of forty empirical studies found that the effects of deterrence variables on crime/deviance are quite weak, and are weakened even more in the presence of other relevant variables.[44]

Second, even if punishment has some deterrent effect, research shows that punishment also has an "avoidance effect."[45] "Punishment avoidance" refers to escaping punishment after committing a crime or being aware of others who have escaped punishment after committing a crime. Stafford and Warr argue that "punishment avoidance may do more to encourage crime than punishment does to discourage it."[46] Several studies show that both direct and vicarious punishment avoidance increase offending or intentions to offend by decreasing perceptions of punishment risk.[47]

Third, even if deterrence exists (and this is not the place to delve into the methodological difficulties of demonstrating why people do *not* act in a given situation), then it probably is effective only for people who have been adequately socialized. How threatened are people whose lives are miserable beyond all hope? What about people ("outsiders") whose value systems are not likely to be changed? For those types of people, deterrence is unlikely to be effective.

Finally, classical theory, including its modern derivatives, has been criticized for being based on circular reasoning: The theory explains the phenomenon, and the phenomenon serves as evidence to support the theory (for example, people rationally choose to commit crimes and their crimes are evidence of their rational choices). The problem with a theory based on circular reasoning is that it cannot be falsified.[48] How is it possible to falsify the claim that criminal behavior was rational for the person who committed it?

Despite those problems, Beccaria's ideas, as previously noted, were very influential. France, for example, adopted many of Beccaria's principles in its Code of 1791, in particular, the principle of equal punishments for the same crimes. However, because classical theory ignored both individual differences among offenders and mitigating circumstances, applying the law in practice was difficult. Because of that difficulty, as well as new developments in the emerging behavioral sciences, modifications to classical theory and its application were introduced.

Neoclassical Theory

Several modifications of classical theory collectively are referred to as *neoclassical theory*.[49] The principal difference between the two theories has to do with classical theory's assumptions about free will. In the neoclassical revision, it was conceded that certain factors (for example, insanity) might inhibit the exercise of free will.[50]

Benjamin Rush (1745–1813), who is considered the founder of American psychiatry, was one of the first "psychiatrically inclined physicians" (at the time, they were called *mad-doctors*) to make the connection between what they called *moral insanity* and crime.[51] Other early psychiatrists to make the connection were Philippe Pinel (1745–1826) of France, James Cowles Prichard (1786–1848) of England, and Isaac Ray (1807–1881) of the United States.[52]

In making the insanity–crime connection, these early psychiatrists rejected the more than one-thousand-year-old tradition of equating crime with sin and provided the first secular and scientific theories of crime.[53] However, they did not attempt to explain all types of crime but rather focused on "recidivistic, often violent, apparently uncontrollable [crimes], committed by offenders who appeared incapable of remorse."[54] The concept of moral insanity would later become the basis for the psychiatric theory of psychopathy and the diagnosis of Antisocial Personality Disorder (both discussed in Chapter 5).[55]

The insanity–crime connection was formalized in legal procedure in 1843, when the M'Naghten Rule for determining legal insanity was formulated in England. The M'Naghten Rule was adopted in the United States shortly thereafter. With recognition of the connection between insanity and crime, the idea of premeditation was also introduced into legal proceedings as a measure of the degree of free will exercised,[56] and mitigating circumstances were considered legitimate grounds for an argument of diminished responsibility.[57]

Those modifications of classical theory, as embodied in the revised French Code of 1819, had two practical effects. First, they provided a reason for non-legal experts (such as mad-doctors) to testify in court as to the degree of diminished responsibility of an offender.[58] Second, offenders began to be sentenced to punishments that were considered rehabilitative.[59] The idea was that certain environments were more conducive than others to the exercise of rational choice.[60] However, consistent with the classical school's implicit ideology about the sanctity of preserving the distribution of private property, the modifications in the theory that were made conspicuously omitted consideration of economic pressure as a mitigating circumstance and a legal excuse for criminal responsibility.

In any event, the reason so much emphasis has been placed on the classical school of criminology and its neoclassical revisions is that together they are essentially the model on which criminal justice in the United States is based today. During the past forty years, at least in part because of dissatisfaction with the exercise of judicial discretion, determinate and mandatory sentences based on sentencing guidelines have all but replaced indeterminate sentences. In addition, a similar dissatisfaction with the discretion exercised by parole boards has led to the abolition of parole in the federal jurisdiction and in some states.

The revival of classical theory during the past forty years is also probably the result of a perceived failure on the part of criminologists to discover the causes of crime. In a renewed effort to deter crimes, judges currently are sentencing more offenders to prison for longer periods than at any other time in the history of the United States, and some states continue to use capital punishment. Ironically, one reason the theory of the classical school lost favor in the nineteenth century was the belief that punishment was not a particularly effective method of preventing or controlling crime.[61]

Study Questions

1. What is the cause of crime from the perspective of the classical school (including contemporary versions)?
2. How would classical theorists prevent crime?
3. What are problems with the theory of the classical school?
4. What changes or modifications to classical theory did the neoclassicists make? Why?

Notes

1. Becker (1932:7).
2. Zeitlin (1968:Chap. 1).
3. See Runes (1968); Babbie (1992).
4. Becker (1932:50–51).
5. Quoted in Stern (forthcoming:12).
6. http://www.iejs.com/Criminology/jeremy_benthams_hedonic_calculus.htm.
7. Curran and Renzetti (1994).
8. Some still hold this view today.
9. Vila and Morris (1997:8); Thompson (1975:22–23); Bedau (1982:7); Banner (2002:7).
10. From Jones (1987:26); also see Foucault (1977:3–6) for a somewhat different description of the same event.
11. Taylor et al. (1974:1).

12. Beccaria (1975:ix).
13. Beccaria (1975:ix).
14. Beirne (1991:782).
15. Beccaria (1975:8).
16. Beccaria (1975:11).
17. The English philosophers Hobbes and Locke wrote about the social contract in the seventeenth century, and the French philosopher Rousseau wrote about the social contract in a book published in 1762—two years before the publication of Beccaria's *On Crimes and Punishments.*
18. Levin (1973).
19. Beccaria (1975:11–12).
20. Beccaria (1975:42).
21. Beccaria (1975:99).
22. Beccaria (1975:93).
23. Cited in Horkheimer (1996:89). For a more recent discussion about marriage and its deterrent effect on crime, see Warr (2002:105).
24. Beccaria (1975:93–98).
25. Cornish and Clarke (1986).
26. See Curran and Renzetti (1994:20).
27. Cornish and Clarke (1986).
28. Cullen and Agnew (2006:410).
29. Vold (1958:23).
30. Curran and Renzetti (1994:22).
31. Rafter (2004:980).
32. See Taylor et al. (1974:3).
33. Sweet (n.d.).
34. Taylor et al. (1974:3); but see Vold and Bernard (1986:28–29) for a different view.
35. See Taylor et al. (1974:3).
36. Curran and Renzetti (1994:21); Tittle (1995:12).
37. Taylor et al. (1974:3).
38. Beccaria (1975).
39. Berofsky (1973:238).
40. Beirne (1991:807).
41. Beirne (1991:807).
42. Bentham (1996:11).
43. See Paternoster (1987); Finckenauer (1982).
44. Pratt, Cullen, Blevins, Daigle, and Madensen (2006).
45. Stafford and Warr (1993).
46. Stafford and Warr (1993:125).

47. See Paternoster and Piquero (1995); Piquero and Paternoster (1998); Piquero and Pogarsky (2002); Sitren and Applegate (2007).
48. Tittle (1995:10–11).
49. See Taylor et al. (1974:7).
50. Vold (1979:28).
51. Rafter (2004:983).
52. Rafter (2004).
53. Rafter (2004:985).
54. Rafter (2004:999).
55. Rafter (2004:1003).
56. Vold (1979:28).
57. Vold (1979:28).
58. Taylor et al. (1974:8).
59. Taylor et al. (1974:9).
60. Taylor et al. (1974:9).
61. See Vold and Bernard (1986:33).

3

Positivist Theories

Positive Philosophy
The Influence of Empirical or Experimental Science
Major Differences between Positivism and Classicism/Neoclassicism
A General Critique of Positivist Theories

The theories of the positivist school of criminology grew out of positive philosophy and the logic and methodology of empirical or experimental science. Positive philosophy was an explicit repudiation or reaction to the critical and "negative" philosophy of the Enlightenment thinkers, which according to positivists, questioned anything that was held to be an "objective truth," challenged the existing order, and promoted revolution.

Positive Philosophy

Positive philosophy emerged during a time of tremendous social change. The American (1775–1783) and French (1789–1799) revolutions, the consolidation of a powerful middle class, and the dawn of the Industrial Revolution all marked these social changes. Among the founders of the positivist school of thought and, according to some, the first modern sociologist was Claude Henri de Rouvroy, the Comte (Count) de Saint-Simon (1760–1825)—generally referred to as Saint-Simon. Saint-Simon, who fought with the French army during the American Revolution and supported the French Revolution, hated the anarchy that followed the French Revolution.[1]

Saint-Simon wanted to preserve the status quo, which, at the time for him, was the emerging middle-class society then in process of consolidating itself. He came to oppose radical reform, as manifested by the French Revolution, because he believed that society evolved and that each stage in the evolutionary development of society was necessary and perfect.

33

Perhaps more familiar than Saint-Simon is Isidore Marie Auguste Francois Xavier Comte (1798–1857), who is better known as Auguste Comte. Comte was Saint-Simon's secretary and protégé from 1817 until 1824, when they had a falling out. Apparently, Comte believed Saint-Simon was too much in a rush to apply his Christian-inspired socialistic ideas to contemporary politics without laying the proper intellectual foundations, while Saint-Simon faulted Comte for his opposition to Saint-Simon's socialistic ideas and his narrow focus on the scientific part of Saint-Simon's system. In any event, it was Comte who coined the term *positivism* in the 1820s.[2] Comte has also been credited with founding *sociology*—a concept he coined in 1839.[3]

During the period from 1817 to 1823, Comte and Saint-Simon worked on a manuscript entitled *Plan of the Scientific Operations Necessary for the Reorganization of Society* in which they suggested that politics should be referred to as *social physics* and should be studied in the manner of the physical or natural sciences. They also argued that human knowledge evolved through stages—the theocratic and the metaphysical—before reaching its final stage—the positive (or scientific). The positive stage is the final "perfect" stage in which truth is revealed through the scientific method. Comte acknowledged that the Enlightenment thinkers had contributed to the progression from the theocratic stage to the metaphysical stage by helping to break up the old feudal, theological order. However, he argued that Enlightenment philosophy obstructed further progress to the positive stage and, therefore, had outlived its usefulness.

Comte rejected the Enlightenment's notion of free will because he believed that people are subject to the natural laws, which positivists maintain are invariant, universally valid, discoverable only through reason, and superior to the laws of human beings or the state.[4] Furthermore, Comte did not embrace the French Revolution's credo of "liberty, equality, and brotherhood." He believed that the ideas of equality and of the sovereignty of the people were erroneous articles of faith and that they condemned superior people (like himself) to the will of the masses. Comte was no democrat (or socialist)! He believed that social order was not compatible with perpetual discussions about the foundations of society. The scientific elite, according to Comte, would determine what the natural laws are and would indicate to the lower classes how their lot in life may be slowly improved in accordance with those laws. He viewed social evils, such as crime, as products of ideas and manners—the glue that holds society together or the combustible material that breaks society apart—and not of basic economic and political institutions. As a result, he maintained that existing social institutions must not be altered or changed. He believed that people, especially the lower classes, should be submissive to authority and the natural laws and resign themselves to their lot in life—anything else would prove fatal to progression to the positive stage of society. In his *Système de poli-tique positive* (1851–1854), Comte unabashedly proclaimed himself Pope of the new positive religion.

In sum, positive philosophy was based on the idea that science had no other aim than the establishment of intellectual order, which, it was assumed, is the basis of every other order. The purpose of positive philosophy was to avert revolution and achieve the resignation of the masses to the conditions of the existing order. Politically, positive philosophy is extremely conservative.

The Influence of Empirical or Experimental Science

Publication of the first modern national crime statistics in France in 1827, together with official records of economic conditions, which became available in a few European countries in the 1600s, made it possible for positivists such as the French lawyer and statistician André-Michel Guerry (1802–1866), who, in 1829, was appointed to collect the moral statistics of Paris, and Belgian stat-istician Adolphe Quetelet (1796–1874) to empirically study the relationship between various economic conditions and crime.[5] In the late 1820s and early 1830s, both Guerry and Quetelet independently analyzed the annually pub-lished crime rates and discovered that the rates remained remarkably constant from year to year and that the contribution of various types of crimes to the overall crime rate varied little. From those findings, they concluded that crime must be a regular feature of social life; crime must be rooted in social arrange-ments; and, if those arrangements could be identified, crime could be elimi-nated. They also concluded that it was implausible that acts of free will could assume such a uniform character. According to Quetelet, "The possibility of es-tablishing moral statistics, and deducing instructive and useful consequences therefrom, depends entirely on this fundamental fact, that man's free choice disappears, and remains without sensible effect, when the observations are ex-tended over a great number of individuals."[6]

Guerry and Quetelet also used available statistics to examine the intuitively appealing proposition that poverty caused crime. Again, working independ-ently, they found that the relationship was more complex than they originally believed. For example, they found higher rates of property crimes, but lower rates of violent crimes, in the wealthiest regions of France. Guerry concluded that poverty itself was not the cause of property crime. Instead, he pointed to opportunity as the culprit, arguing that in wealthier areas there was more to steal. Quetelet, who analyzed data from Belgium and Holland in addition to

France, agreed with Guerry that opportunity was a cause of property crime. However, Quetelet also suggested that "relative poverty," where there is great inequality between poverty and wealth in the same area, also played a key role in both property and violent crimes. According to Quetelet, relative poverty incites people through jealousy to commit crimes. This is especially true where changing economic conditions cause the impoverishment of some people while others retain their wealth. Quetelet found less crime in poor areas than in wealthier areas as long as the people in the poor areas were still able to satisfy their basic needs. In short, Guerry and Quetelet were among the first social scientists (they were called *moral statisticians*) to use empirical analysis to show that crime was related to social arrangements. Guerry may also have produced the first crime map, when he along with his colleague, M. Balbi, published a statistical map showing the extent of education and crime in France.[7]

Also key to the development of positivism were new discoveries in biology. Especially important were findings that led to the identification of human beings with the rest of the animal world.[8] In the *Descent of Man* (1871), Charles Darwin (1809–1882) suggested that some people were "less highly evolved or developed than others"; some people "were nearer their ape-like ancestors than others in traits, abilities, and dispositions."[9]

At about the same time, experimentation with animals was becoming an increasingly accepted way of learning about human beings in physiology, medicine, psychology, and psychiatry.[10] Human beings were beginning to appear to science as one of many creatures, with no special connection to God.[11] Human beings were beginning to be understood, not as freewilled, self-determining creatures who could do anything that they wanted to do, but rather as beings whose action was determined by biological and cultural factors.[12]

Major Differences Between Positivism and Classicism/Neoclassicism

First, positivists assume that human behavior is determined and not a matter of free will.[13] Consequently, positivists focus on cause-and-effect relationships.

Causation is established when three to five conditions are met: (1) the presumed cause precedes the presumed effect in time, (2) the presumed cause and the presumed effect are empirically correlated with one another, and (3) the observed empirical correlation between the presumed cause and the presumed effect is not spurious—that is, the empirical relationship cannot be explained away as being due to the influence of some other factor or factors.[14] Two other conditions are also mentioned occasionally: (4) a credible story (theory) connecting the presumed cause with the presumed effect, and (5) the first four conditions are replicated in different contexts with different methodologies.[15] Even when all five conditions have been met, however, one cannot assert with certainty that a causal relationship exists; one may only conclude that a causal relationship probably exists.[16]

It is important to note that the ontological debate in philosophy over whether human beings are "freewilled" or "determined" is an ancient one. However, neither position seems to capture the way most people experience or interpret their behavior. To partially resolve the dilemma, many social scientists distinguish between a "hard" and a "soft" determinism. *Hard determinism* refers to an all-encompassing compulsion; human beings have no choices whatsoever when confronting situations. *Soft determinism*, a concept that has been attributed to the American philosopher William James (1842–1910) and has also been referred to as *conditional free will*,[17] allows for constrained choice. That is, in any circumstance human beings always have choices, however limited they may be. The most limited choice is to act or not to act. Generally, the more choices people have, the greater the "freedom" they experience. (This notion is what many social scientists mean by "freedom.") The number of choices people have is also an important indicator of social status: the more choices, the higher the status. Thus, rather than making a distinction between free will and determinism, the distinction made by most social scientists is between hard and soft determinism.

A second difference is that positivists assume that criminals are fundamentally different from noncriminals, either biologically, psychologically, sociologically, or in some combination of all three.[18] Positivists search for such differences through scientific inquiry.[19] When differences are found, classifications or categories, such as criminal and noncriminal, are created. Classical criminologists, on the other hand, assumed that there are no fundamental differences between people who commit crimes and those who do not. People who choose to commit crimes simply have the opportunity and calculate that the crimes will bring them more pleasure than not committing them or than the pain of getting caught and punished.

Third, positivists assume that social scientists, including criminologists, can be objective or value-neutral in their work.[20] Comte, for example, chided classical theorists about their attempts to comprehend and reason about reality without supporting their contentions with facts. (More will be said about this problem in the next section.)

Fourth, positivists frequently assume that crime is caused by multiple factors, for example, hormone imbalances, below-normal intelligence, inadequate socialization or self-control, and economic inequality.[21] Classical criminologists, as noted previously, assumed that crime is caused by individuals who freely choose to commit it (perhaps Beccaria and Bentham notwith-standing) after rationally calculating that the crime will provide them more pleasure than pain. (Neoclassical theorists conceded that some individuals might commit crimes because their free will and rational calculating ability are impaired.)

Fifth, positivists believe that society is based primarily on a consensus about moral values but not on a social contract, as classical theorists believed. Rather, for most positivists, social consensus is a product of either the French sociologist Emile Durkheim's (1858–1917) collective conscience (that is, the general sense of morality of the times) in more primitive or homogeneous societies or his interdependency of occupational roles (that is, the division of labor) in more advanced societies. (Both of those concepts are described in greater detail in Chapter 6.)[22]

A General Critique of Positivist Theories

Although there are problems peculiar to each positivist theory of crime causation, some of which will be described as the biological, psychological, and sociological theories are examined later in this book, problems generic to the theories as a group also have been identified. In this section, five of these general problems are presented. It is important to remember, as discussed in Chapter 1, that these problems do not necessarily condemn a theory. They only diminish the theory's explanatory power.

First is the problem of overprediction.[23] Positivist theories generally account for too much crime. At the same time, they do not explain exceptions well. For example, in a theory that suggests that crime is caused by poverty, the theory overpredicts because not all poor people commit crime. Also, the theory cannot explain adequately why many poor people do not commit crimes. Regarding the difficulty in explaining exceptions, positivist theories, especially many sociological theories, generally ignore individual differences. Large groups of people are presumed to respond similarly to the same biological, psychological, and especially sociological factors.

Second, positivist theories generally ignore the criminalization process. They take the legal definition of crime for granted. Ignored is the question why certain behaviors are defined as criminal whereas other, similar behaviors are not. The problem occurs because positivists generally separate the study of crime from a theory of the law and the state.[24]

Third is the problem with the consensual worldview, the belief in a normative consensus.[25] Most positivist theories assume that most people agree most of the time about moral values; that is, general agreement prevails about what is right and wrong and good and bad. The problem with such a view is that it ignores the issue of power, as well as the multitude of fundamental conflicts of value and interest in society. It also denies the existence of multiple and socially constructed realities and leads to a blind acceptance of the status quo.

A fourth problem is the belief in determinism, the idea that choice of action is not free but is determined by causes independent of will.[26] Positivists generally assume that human beings only adapt or react. A problem is that they also create. How else do you explain new social arrangements or new ways of thinking?[27]

Even if criminal behavior were determined, identifying the "cause" or "causes" of crime is a problem because establishing a lack of spuriousness (the absence of influential but unconsidered factors) may be impossible.[28] The belief in determinism allows the positivist to present an absolute situation uncomplicated by the ability to choose.[29] The belief makes rational planning and control logically possible, that is, with the help of the positivist.[30]

A fifth general problem with positivist theories is the belief in the ability of social scientists, including criminologists, to be objective or value-neutral in their work.[31] Assuming that an "objective reality" exists independent of their perception of it, positivists often fail to understand that what they know is a product of how they interpret what they observe. What is observed ultimately depends on an individual's cognitive apparatus, his or her past experiences, as well as the social context in which the observation is made. The problem is that social scientists, as well as all other human beings, are always biased. Human beings are biased by virtue of their being human. To deny this point is self-deception. Why do you suppose social scientists select a particular problem to study? For that matter, why do you suppose that social scientists choose their particular occupation? Perhaps it is because they have an interest in the subject matter. Many positivists fail to recognize that to describe and to evaluate such human action as criminal behavior is fundamentally a moral endeavor and, therefore, subject to bias. Those positivists who do recognize the problem of bias attempt to overcome it. Whether they ever can be successful is another matter.

Study Questions

1. What influence did Saint-Simon and Comte have on the development of positivist theory?
2. What influence did Guerry and Quetelet have on the development of positivist theory?
3. What influence did Darwin have on the development of positivist theory?

4. What are major differences between positivism and classicism/neoclassicism?
5. What are general problems with positivist theories?

Notes

1. Unless indicated otherwise, material in this section is from Comte (1974); Runes (1968); Saint-Simon (1964); and especially Zeitlin (1968).
2. Wilson (1973:532).
3. Vold and Bernard (1986:144).
4. See Runes (1968:206).
5. Unless indicated otherwise, the following description is from Vold and Bernard (1986:131–132); Taylor et al. (1974:37–38).
6. Quetelet on the Laws of the Social System (2000:271).
7. Guerry on the Statistics of Crime in France (2000:255).
8. Vold (1979:35).
9. Vold (1979:36).
10. Vold and Bernard (1986:36).
11. Vold and Bernard (1986:36).
12. Vold and Bernard (1986:36).
13. See Taylor et al. (1974:21–23, 31–32); Davis (1975).
14. See Babbie (1992:72).
15. Paternoster and Brame (2008:981).
16. Bernard et al. (2010:6).
17. See Fishbein (1990:30–31).
18. See Vold and Bernard (1986:45); Matza (1964:11–12).
19. See Taylor et al. (1974:11).
20. See Taylor et al. (1974:11, 19–21, 26); Davis (1975).
21. See Vold (1979:37, 47).
22. See Taylor et al. (1974:11–19, 31); Davis (1975); Durkheim (1933).
23. See Taylor et al. (1974:24–26); Matza (1964:21–22).
24. See Taylor et al. (1974:28); Matza (1964:5).
25. See Taylor et al. (1974:26–28, 31); Davis (1975).
26. See Taylor et al. (1974:29–32); Davis (1975).
27. See Taylor et al. (1974:54).
28. Robinson (1999).
29. Taylor et al. (1974:31–32).
30. Taylor et al. (1974:35).

31. See Taylor et al. (1974:11, 19–21, 26, 32); Gouldner (1971); Davis (1975). Rafter (1997:239–240) claims that psychiatrists used the concept of psychopathy to wrest control of criminology from psychologists who then dominated the field and with whom psychiatrists were in competition. Laub and Sampson (1991:1404) attribute the heated debates about criminological theory between Edwin Sutherland and Shelden and Eleanor Glueck to "their respective methodological and disciplinary biases." Daly and Chesney-Lind (1988:500) maintain that "a major feminist project today is to expose the distortions and assumptions of androcentric science [which reveals] that an ideology of objectivity can serve to mask men's gender loyalties as well as loyalties to other class or racial groups." Cullen, Gendreau, Jarjoura, and Wright (1997:387) argue that Herrnstein and Murray's showing that IQ is a powerful predictor of crime in their controversial book *The Bell Curve: Intelligence and Class Structure in American Life*, and their resultant crime control policies, are based on the authors' ideology, "not on intelligent science." For a recent study showing that criminological theorizing is driven by sociopolitical ideology, see Walsh and Ellis (1999).

4

Biological Theories

Physiognomy and Phrenology
Lombroso's Criminal Anthropology
Sheldon's Body Type Theories
Heredity Studies
Modern Biocriminology
A General Critique of Biological Theories

The claim recently was made that "the scientific study of crime actually began with biological theories, in the late 18th century," and that, "until the early 20th century, biological theories and criminology were virtually synonymous."[1] Biological theories of crime causation (biological positivism) are based on the belief that criminals are physiologically different from noncriminals. Early biological theories assumed that structure determines function.[2] In other words, criminals behave differently because structurally they are different.[3] Today's biocriminologists are more likely to assume that biochemistry determines function or, more precisely, the difference between criminals and noncriminals is the result of a complex interaction between biochemical and environmental factors (more about this later). To test biological theories, researchers try to demonstrate, through measurement and statistical analysis, that there are or are not significant structural or biochemical differences between criminals and noncriminals.[4]

Historically, the cause of crime from this perspective was biological inferiority. Biological inferiority in criminals was assumed to produce certain physical or genetic characteristics that distinguished criminals from noncriminals.[5] It is important to emphasize that the physical or genetic characteristics themselves did not cause crime, they were only the symptoms, or stigmata, of the more fundamental inferiority.[6] The concept of biological inferiority has lost favor among today's biocriminologists who generally prefer to emphasize the biological differences between criminals and noncriminals without adding the value judgment. In any event, several different methodologies have been employed to detect physical differences between criminals and noncriminals. They are physiognomy, phrenology, criminal anthropology, study of body types, heredity studies (including family trees, statistical comparisons, twin studies, and adoption studies) and, in the last twenty years or so, studies based on new scientific technologies that allow, for example, the examination of brain function and structure.

Physiognomy and Phrenology

Physiognomy is the judging of character or disposition from facial and other physical features. The Greek philosopher Aristotle is credited with writing the first systematic physiognomic treatise.[7] In his discussion of noses, for example, Aristotle wrote:

> [T]hose with thick bulbous ends belong to persons who are insensitive, swinish, and prone to acts of theft, fraud, and intemperance; sharp-tipped noses belong to the irascible, those easily provoked and liable to assaultive behavior and ruffianism; rounded, large obtuse noses are characteristic of the magnanimous; slender, eagle-like hooked noses belong to the noble; round-tipped noses to the hedonistic; noses with a very slight notch at the root belong to the impudent; open nostrils are a sign of passionate appetites, and in both men and women are frequently found in the sexually promiscuous.[8]

During the Middle Ages, a law specifying that when "two people were suspected of having committed the same crime, the uglier one should be regarded as more likely the guilty party" showed the influence of physiognomy during that period.[9] The "science" of physiognomy probably reached its peak in 1775, when the Swiss scholar and theologian Johann Kaspar Lavater (1741–1781) published a four-volume work on the subject called *Physiognomical Fragments*.[10] The book, according to Vold and Bernard, was well received in Europe at the time and was nearly as popular as Beccaria's *On Crimes and Punishments*.[11]

However, by the end of the eighteenth century, physiognomy had fallen into disrepute. As evidence, a British law declared, "all persons fayning to have knowledge of Phisiognomie or like Fantasticall Ymaginacions" are liable to "be stripped naked from the middle upwards and openly whipped until his body be bloudye."[12] Another British law held that "all persons pretending to have skill in physiognomy were deemed rogues and vagabonds and were liable to be publicly whipped or sent to the gaol until the following quarter sessions."[13] Today the "science" of physiognomy primarily is of historical interest, as the precursor of the better-developed phrenology.[14]

Phrenology (also called "cranioscopy," "craniology," or "zoonomy") is the estimation of character and intelligence based on an examination of the shape of the skull (or cranium).[15] Phrenology is associated with the work of Franz Joseph Gall (1758–1828) and his student and collaborator Johann Gaspar Spurzheim (1776–1832),[16] who are considered by some commentators as the fathers of criminology.[17]

The key propositions of phrenology are derived from Aristotle's belief that the brain is the organ of the mind:[18]

1. The exterior of the skull conforms to the interior and to the shape of the brain.
2. The "mind" consists of faculties or functions (for example, acquisitiveness, friendliness, hope, conscientiousness, and philoprogenitiveness— love of one's children).
3. These faculties are related to the shape of the brain and skull; hence, just as the brain is the "organ of the mind," these "bumps" are indicators of the "organs" of the special faculties.
4. The size of the special faculty organs determines the strength in which each faculty is manifested in each individual.
5. Each organ is considered as engaged, either independently in bringing forth its own product, or collectively with others in elaborating compound mental states.

Gall listed nearly twenty-six mental faculties; Spurzheim augmented Gall's list to increase the total to thirty-five.[19] Spurzheim divided the faculties into two major groups: feelings and intellectual faculties. He subdivided feelings into propensities (internal impulses inviting only to certain actions, such as combativeness, destructiveness, and secretiveness), and sentiments (impulses which prompt to emotion as well as to action, such as self-esteem, cautiousness, and benevolence). Intellectual faculties were subdivided into perceptive faculties (such as individuality, language, and order) and reflective faculties (such as comparison and causality).[20]

The propensities, sentiments, and intellectual faculties are presumed to be in equilibrium in the noncriminal, but in the criminal the propensities are dominant.[21] It is interesting to note that the propensities, sentiments, and intellectual faculties are analogous to Freud's later formulation of the id, ego, and superego. Whether Freud was familiar with the earlier formulation is not known.

Some phrenologists rejected the deterministic implications of the theory and believed that favorable social circumstances could allow an individual with an inferior skull shape to live a reputable life.[22] In any event, phrenology was very popular during the first half of the nineteenth century but eventually lost its appeal because of its determinism, which was assailed as being antireligious and anti-free will.[23] Also, the work of Charles Darwin—especially his *Origin of Species* (1859)—challenged phrenology's notion of a compartmentalized brain.[24] The popularity of Darwin's ideas helped shift the explanation of criminal behavior to evolutionary theories.

Lombroso's Criminal Anthropology

Criminal anthropology is the study of "criminal" human beings. It is associated with the work of an Italian army doctor, and later university professor, Cesare Lombroso (1835–1909). Lombroso, who is also known as the father of criminology,[25] first published his theory of a physical criminal type in 1876. Although he had autopsied nearly four hundred prisoners and had taken precise measurements of various bodily organs of approximately six thousand additional prisoners and three thousand soldiers, according to Lombroso, his theory emerged as a revelation following his autopsy of a reputed bandit by the name of Vilella.[26] As Lombroso explained:

> This was not merely an idea, but a revelation. At the sight of that skull, I seemed to see all of a sudden, lighted up as a vast plain under a flaming sky, the problem of the nature of the criminal—an atavistic being who reproduces in his person the ferocious instincts of primitive humanity and the inferior animals. Thus were explained anatomically the enormous jaws, high cheekbones, prominent superciliar arches, solitary lines in the palms, extreme size of the orbits, handle-shaped or sessile ears found in criminals, savages, and apes, insensitivity to pain, extremely acute sight, tattooing, excessive idleness, love of orgies, and the irresistible craving for evil for its own sake, the desire not only to extinguish life in the victim, but to mutilate the corpse, tear its flesh, and drink its blood.[27]

Lombroso's theory consisted of the following propositions:[28] First, criminals are, by birth, a distinct type; they are physically different from noncriminals. Second, those differences can be recognized by stigmata (signs) or anomalies like those listed in the previous quote. Third, criminals are distinguished from noncriminals if they have more than five stigmata. A person with three to five stigmata may exhibit criminal behavior, and criminality is unlikely in a person with less than three stigmata. Fourth, physical stigmata do not cause crime; they are only indicative of an individual who is predisposed to crime. Such a person is either an *atavist*—someone who exhibits the characteristics of a primitive human being or an evolutionary "throwback" to our ape-like ancestors—or a result of degeneration. According to Guglielmo Ferrero (1871–1942), one of Lombroso's young collaborators and son-in-law, resistance to regular and methodical work and impulsiveness are the principal characteristics of atavists.[29] Fifth, because of their personal natures, such persons cannot desist from crime unless they experience very favorable lives.

In subsequent editions of his book, Lombroso described other causes of crime besides atavism. Crimes were also caused by insanity, epilepsy, passion (a cause of political crimes), poor parenting or education ("habitual criminals"), predispositions activated by particular environmental conditions or opportunities ("criminaloids" or "occasional criminals"), and for reasons such as self-defense or the defense of family honor ("pseudocriminals").[30] In later editions of *The Criminal Man*, as well as in *Crime, Its Causes and Remedies* (originally published in 1911), Lombroso paid considerable attention to social causes of crime.

Lombroso is mostly remembered for his concept of the atavistic criminal, who, he estimated, comprised about 40 percent of all criminals.[31] Elsewhere, however, Lombroso estimated that the occasional criminal comprised about 75 percent of all criminals[32]—a curious mathematical discrepancy for someone who was known for his precise measurements. Critics argue that even if a criminal type exists—something about which many critics are dubious—they represent only a small percentage of all offenders and have received attention far out of proportion to their legitimate importance.[33]

Policy Implications

Late in life, Lombroso wrote an article in which he described the practical applications of his theory.[34] Lombroso maintained that the sole purpose of a nation's criminal code should be the defense of society, and, not surprisingly, the code should be based on knowledge of the criminal. To protect society, the courts should not consider extenuating circumstances, even insanity. Punishment should be guided by the offender's tendency. If the offender is a born criminal, he or she should be confined for life, even though the crime is relatively minor. Lombroso believed Italy's abolition of the death penalty in 1889 was a mistake. Harsh punishments should also be imposed on recidivists and offenders who enlist others in their crimes. Conversely, if the offender is an honest person impelled by some strong motive to commit a crime, he or she should be treated more leniently. Lombroso provided the example of individuals who espoused the ideas of class equality and the participation of laborers in profits. At one time, it was a crime to maintain those ideas, now (in the mid-1890s in Italy), observed Lombroso, those ideas are the basis of possible reforms.

Lombroso favored the compensation of crime victims, making the offender work to pay the victim if the offender lacked the money to pay the victim himself or herself. He also believed that the offender and not society should pay for the offender's imprisonment. He argued that reform should be directed at the occasional criminal because that category of offender was the only one for which much could be done. According to Lombroso, the occasional criminal only committed crimes when forced by circumstances. To reform occasional criminals, Lombroso advocated removing criminal opportunities by providing employment and keeping them away from the mischievous influence of alcohol by providing them with mental amusement. Most importantly, the tendency to crime, which appears in infancy, should not be allowed to continue in youth and become habitual.

Lombroso was disappointed that Italy's new criminal code was not based on his criminal anthropology. He noted that the only countries to adopt any of his ideas were the United States, England, Norway, and Switzerland. Each of those countries had attempted to restrict the consumption of alcohol. He was especially complimentary of the United States, which, according to Lombroso, had applied the scientific knowledge of criminal anthropology to criminal reform efforts. He cited the first bureau for degenerates and abnormal people established in Washington (presumably DC), but he had special praise for Zebulon Brockway (1827–1920), warden of the Elmira Reformatory in New York from 1876 to 1900, who supposedly based his reform strategies on Lombroso's ideas. Offenders received indeterminate sentences to the Elmira Reformatory and were not released until they were reformed, acquired a means of self-support, and had a place to work so they could earn a living. In 1893, it was claimed that 80 percent of Elmira inmates had been successfully reformed.[35]

Critique

Two main problems with Lombroso's criminal anthropology are apparent. First is the assumption that certain physical characteristics indicate biological inferiority. Unless independent evidence supports that assumption, other than the association of the physical characteristics with criminality, then the result is circular reasoning.[36] In other words, crime is caused by biological inferiority, which is itself indicated by the physical characteristics associated with criminality.

A second problem is the assumption that apes and other lower animals are savage and criminal. As Harvard paleontologist, evolutionary biologist, and historian of science Stephen Gould (1941–2002) remarked, "If some men look like apes, but apes be kind, then the argument fails."[37] In an effort to make the dubious connection, Lombroso had to engage in a tortured anthropomorphism. As Gould related:

> He [Lombroso] cites, for example, an ant driven by rage to kill and dismember an aphid; an adulterous stork who, with her lover, murdered her husband; a criminal association of beavers who ganged up to murder a solitary compatriot; a male ant, without access to female reproductives, who violated a (female) worker with atrophied sexual organs, causing her great pain and death; he even refers to the insect eating of certain plants as an "equivalent of crime."[38]

Despite those problems, Lombroso's theory was popular in the United States through the first decade of the twentieth century, until the publication in 1913 of Charles B. Goring's *The English Convict*. Goring (1870–1919) compared more than 2,300 prison inmates to a control group of "noncriminal" Englishmen.[39] He examined thirty-seven physical traits suggested by Lombroso to be associated with crime and found very little support for Lombroso's contention. What Goring did find, however, was that inmates were smaller in stature and less intelligent (by his own reckoning) than noncriminals. He extrapolated from these findings that criminals "are inherently inferior to law-abiding citizens."[40] This inferiority, he argued, was physical, intellectual, and moral.

Ferri and Garofalo

Two of Lombroso's students—Enrico Ferri (1856–1928) and Raffaele Garofalo (1852–1934)—together with Lombroso have been called the *Italian school of criminology*. Though they differed somewhat in their analyses of crime, they were all positivists and opposed the (supposed) free-will ontology of their fellow Italian Beccaria and the other classical thinkers. The subject of Ferri's doctoral dissertation was the problem of free will.[41]

Although Ferri emphasized biological causes of crime—he coined the term *born criminal*—he also believed that crime was the product of multiple factors, including physical factors (such as race, climate, and geography), anthropological factors (such as age, gender, and psychological attributes), and social factors (such as population density, religion, customs, organization of government, and economic conditions).[42] Consistent with his socialist beliefs, Ferri advocated the following crime prevention policies: free trade, abolition of monopolies, subsidized housing, public savings banks, better street lighting, birth control, freedom of marriage and divorce, state control of weapons manufacturing, foundling homes, and public recreation facilities.[43] Later in life he became a fascist and, in the 1920s, was invited by Mussolini to draft a new penal code for Italy.[44] His penal code, which reflected his positivist and so-cialist/fascist beliefs, was rejected for departing too much from classical legal thought.[45]

Garofalo, on the other hand, rejected Ferri's belief in environmental causes of crime as well as Lombroso's theory of atavism. Instead, Garofalo, adopting principles of Social Darwinism, believed that crime was a natural product of adaptation; criminals were physically unable to adapt to society. Therefore, argued Garofalo, most criminals were unfit to survive and should be elimi-nated from society through extermination in the case of criminals who com-mitted serious offenses or long-term imprisonment, life imprisonment, or overseas transportation for criminals who committed less serious offenses. For criminals who committed crimes under exceptional circumstances and who were not likely to repeat them, Garofalo advocated "enforced reparation."[46]

It should not be surprising that Garofalo's ideas, like those of Ferri, were popular during Mussolini's fascist regime in Italy. This underscores a poten-tial problem with positivist theories: They can easily be used to justify, on a scientific basis, ideas that promote racial purity, national power, and au-thoritarian leadership.[47]

Sheldon's Body Type Theories

Body type theories are an extension of Lombroso's criminal anthropology. William H. Sheldon (1898–1977), whose work in the 1940s was based on ear-lier work by psychiatrist Ernst Kretschmer (1888–1964) in the 1920s, is per-haps the best known of the body type theorists.[48] According to Sheldon, human beings can be divided into three basic body types, or somatotypes, which cor-respond to three basic temperaments: the endomorph, the mesomorph, and the ectomorph.[49] The *endomorph* is soft, fat, a comfortable person who loves luxury, and generally an extrovert.[50] *Mesomorphs* are athletically built, muscular, with a more active, assertive, and aggressive temperament.[51] *Ectomorphs* are tall, lean, delicate, fragile, and generally introverted and shy.[52]

Sheldon argued that everyone has elements of all three types but that one type usually predominates. In a study of two hundred Boston delinquents be-tween 1939 and 1949, Sheldon found that delinquents were more mesomor-phic than nondelinquents and that serious delinquents were more mesomorphic than less serious delinquents.[53] Subsequent studies by Sheldon Glueck (1896–1980) and his wife Eleanor Glueck (1898–1972)—Harvard Law School's famed criminologist team—in the 1950s and by Juan B. Cortes with Florence M. Gatti in the 1970s also found the association between mesomorphy and delinquency.[54] The studies by Cortes and Gatti, moreover, used more precise measurement techniques than those by either Sheldon or the Gluecks, who were criticized on this account.

Critique

The major criticism of the body type theories is that differences in behavior reflect the social selection process and not biological inferiority.[55] In other words, delinquents are more likely to be mesomorphic than nondelinquents because, for example, mesomorphs are more likely to be selected for gang membership. Additionally, the finding that delinquents are more likely than nondelinquents to be mesomorphic contradicts the general assumption that criminals (or delinquents) are biologically inferior, at least with regard to physique.

Policy Implications

If one assumes that crime is the product of biological inferiority, then the crime prevention implications are rather straightforward: isolate criminals, sterilize them, exterminate them, or employ some combination of the three. Sheldon's ambitions, however, were loftier than simply reducing crime. He wanted "to save aristocratic ectomorphic stock from being 'killed off' by urban conditions, competition from inferior stocks, and the leveling effects of democracy."[56]

Physiognomists, phrenologists, criminal anthropologists, and body type theorists were the first criminal profilers.

Heredity Studies

A variety of methods have been employed to test the proposition that criminals are genetically different from noncriminals or that criminality is inherited. As noted previously, they include family-tree studies, statistical-comparison studies, twins studies, and adoption studies.

Family-Tree Studies

Perhaps the earliest methodology was the use of family trees. This was the technique used by Richard L. Dugdale (1841–1883) and by Arthur H. Estabrook (1885–1973) in their studies of the Juke family (a pseudonym).[57] Dugdale's study was first published in 1875, and included 709 Juke family members: 540 of Juke blood and 169 related by marriage. Estabrook's study expanded Dugdale's study, was published in 1916, and included 2,820 Juke family members (including all of Dugdale's 709): 2,094 of Juke blood and 726 related by marriage. The Juke family presumably had 171 criminals—mostly thieves and prostitutes (140 identified by Dugdale and an additional 31 identified by Estabrook)—118 of Juke blood and 53 related by marriage. Also of concern to both Dugdale and Estabrook was that of the 709 Juke family members reported by Dugdale and the 2,820 Juke family members reported by Estabrook, 180 and 366 family members, respectively, were paupers who had either been in the poorhouse or received outdoor relief at a cost to the state of New York of about $1.3 million (between 1800 and 1875) for the 180 of Dugdale's Jukes and $2 million (between 1800 and 1915) for Estabrook's 366 Jukes.[58]

Even though only about six percent of the Jukes had criminal records (69 percent with Juke blood and 31 percent related by marriage) and approximately thirteen percent of them were paupers (82 percent with Juke blood and 18 percent related by marriage), proponents of the eugenics movement used the studies by Dugdale and Estabrook, and others studies like them, "to demonstrate scientifically that a large number of rural poor whites were 'genetic defectives.'"[59] (During the latter part of the nineteenth century and the early part of the twentieth century, the eugenics movement promoted the selective breeding of human beings to produce "desirable" genetic characteristics and the prevention of individuals with undesirable genetic characteristics from reproducing.)

A primary problem with the family tree method is that a finding that criminality appears in successive generations does not prove that criminality is inherited or is the product of a hereditary defect. For example, the use of a fork in eating has been a trait of many families for many generations, but that does not prove that the use of a fork is inherited. Ironically, Dugdale believed that the environment was primarily to blame for the Jukes' troubles. He wrote that the "environment tends to produce habits which may become hereditary." To improve public morality, Dugdale advocated public health and infant education. Dugdale understood that the family tree method could not adequately separate hereditary influences from environmental influences.[60]

Statistical-Comparison Studies

A second methodology used to test the proposition that crime is inherited or is the product of a hereditary defect is statistical comparison. Charles Goring—the same Charles Goring whose research undermined Lombroso's criminal anthropology—was perhaps the first social scientist to argue that if criminality exhibited the same degree of family resemblance as other physical traits, such as eye or hair color, then criminality, like those other traits, must be inherited.[61] In tests of his theory, Goring indeed found that associations between general criminality, as measured by imprisonment, and parental and fraternal resemblance for ordinary physical traits, as well as for inherited defects such as insanity, were remarkably similar.

Goring was not naive, however, and recognized that the associations that he found might be the result of environmental factors rather than, or in addition to, genetic factors. Thus, in separate analyses he attempted to determine the influence of environmental factors. A problem was that he considered only eight environmental factors. A more telling criticism of Goring's findings is that he limited his study to male offenders, although he notes that the ratio of brothers to sisters in prison is seventeen to one. If criminality is inherited in the same way that hair or eye color is, then one would expect it to affect females to relatively the same extent as it does males unless, of course, criminality is a sex-linked trait, which obviously it is not. In short, statistical comparisons cannot adequately separate hereditary influences from environmental influences.

Twins Studies

A third, more sophisticated method of testing the proposition that crime is inherited or is the result of a hereditary defect is the use of twin studies.[62] Heredity is assumed to be the same in identical twins because they are the product of a single egg. Heredity is assumed to be different in fraternal twins because they are the product of two eggs fertilized by two sperm. The logic of the method is that if there is greater similarity in behavior between identical twins than between fraternal twins, then the behavior must be due to heredity, since environments are much the same. Nearly a century of using this methodology reveals that identical twins are more likely to demonstrate concordance (where both twins have criminal records) than are fraternal twins, thus supporting the hereditary link.

A problem with the twin studies, however, is the potential confounding of genetic and environmental influences. Evidence indicates environments are more similar for identical than fraternal twins. For example, compared to fraternal twins, identical twins tend to be treated more alike by their parents and others, spend much more time together (and thus share the same environments more frequently), are more likely to have the same friends, share the same classroom, go out together more often, report greater closeness, and share a greater sense of mutual identity.[63] For nine months they also shared a critical environment inside the same mother.[64] All those factors are important environmental influences, and, when environmental influences are controlled, studies show that the difference in criminality between identical and fraternal twins is not significant.[65]

A more significant problem with the twin studies is the recent finding that identical twins are not identical; they do not have identical DNA. Researchers have discovered differences in the DNA sequence of identical twins. These differences are reflected in "copy number variations" or the number of copies of each gene.[66] Human beings normally carry two copies of most genes—one from the mother's chromosome and one from the father's chromosome. However, gene mutations (deletions, insertions, and duplications) can alter the number of genes on a chromosome. These copy number variations are common, occur in hundreds of places in the human genome, can increase or decrease a gene's activity level, and vary in number from one individual to another.[67]

Adoption Studies

A fourth method, and the most recent and sophisticated way of examining the inheritability of criminality, is the adoption study.[68] The first such study was conducted in the 1970s. In this method, the criminal records of adopted children (almost always boys) who were adopted at a relatively early age are compared with the criminal records of both their biological parents and their adoptive parents (almost always fathers). The rationale is that if the criminal records of adopted boys are more like those of their biological fathers than like those of their adoptive fathers, the criminality of the adopted boys can be assumed to be the result of heredity.

Findings of the adoption studies reveal that the percentage of adoptees who are criminal is greater when the biological father has a criminal record than when the adoptive father has one. However, there is also an interactive effect. In other words, a greater percentage of adoptees have criminal records when both fathers have criminal records than when only one of them does. Thus, like the twin studies, the adoption studies presumably demonstrate the influence of heredity but cannot adequately separate it from the influence of the environment. A problem with the adoption studies is the difficulty of interpreting the relative influences of heredity and environment, especially when the adoption does not take place shortly after birth or when, as is commonly the case, the adoption agency attempts to find an adoptive home that matches the biological home in family income and socioeconomic status.[69] Another confounding factor is the influence of the prenatal environment.[70]

In sum, an analysis of more than sixty years of research using studies of families, twins, and adoptees found that claims of a genetic link to criminality are based on very weak statistical evidence; indeed, the more methodologically sound the study, the weaker the relationship found.[71]

Modern Biocriminology

Modern biocriminologists explore how biological factors, in conjunction with environmental factors, lead to the development of certain traits that are linked to antisocial behavior.[72] Such behavior may or may not be defined by society as a crime. The contribution of biological factors to human behavior is a subject of interest across many disciplines including psychology, psychiatry, developmental biology, cognitive neuroscience, and behavioral ecology.[73] Modern criminologists, however, have been somewhat reluctant to embrace this body of knowledge, possibly because of its implicit connection to the early, and now discredited, work of Lombroso; its ties to the eugenics movement; and its use by the Nazis to justify the extermination of millions of people, mostly Jews, during the Holocaust.[74]

Nonetheless, within the past twenty years, significant progress has been made uncovering biological risk factors that predispose individuals to antisocial behavior.[75] Researchers have defined antisocial behavior in various ways, but definitions generally include a wide range of behaviors whose "main characteristic is a violation of the basic rights of others."[76] These behaviors include aggression, crime, violence, and delinquency, among others.[77]

It is essential to emphasize that just because a behavior is found to have a genetic link does not mean that the behavior is inevitable or unalterable. Predisposition does not mean predestination.[78] Advances in molecular genetics show that the environment regulates genetic activity through epigenetic factors, which are the biochemical markers that attach to genes and influence how they are expressed by either activating them or silencing them.[79] Epigenetic changes are regular and natural occurrences but also can be influenced by such factors as age, disease, and environment or lifestyle. This research suggests that even if there were a "crime gene" or genetic disposition for crime, and even if the entire human population had the gene or disposition, the gene or disposition would have to be activated by factors external to the gene before the gene or disposition could express itself. Genes are not self-activating.

Considerable research demonstrates the moderating effects of social factors on biological risks for antisocial behavior.[80] For example, a recent review of thirty-nine studies found that genetic and environmental factors interact to give rise to biological and social risk factors for antisocial and violent behaviors.[81] Specifically, genetic predispositions are more deleterious in the presence of adverse environments, such as those involving child maltreatment, poor family atmosphere, lower social class, and adult violence.[82]

The biological factors that have been linked to antisocial behavior include both heritable (capable of being passed on to the next generation through the genes) and nonheritable characteristics. Characteristics that have been shown to be at least somewhat heritable include brain structure and function, abnormal levels of certain hormones and neurotransmitters, and low arousal.[83] Those that are not genetic include obstetric factors (those pertaining to before and during childbirth), exposure to environmental toxins, and brain injury.[84]

Brain Disorders

At least some unprovoked violent criminal behavior is believed to be caused by tumors and other destructive or inflammatory processes of the limbic system.[85] Psychopaths (discussed in Chapter 5 on psychological theories) are also believed to suffer from limbic system disorders.[86] The *limbic system* is a structure surrounding the brain stem and is the source of feelings of pleasure and pain.[87] It also controls, in part, the life functions of heartbeat, breathing, and sleep, and is believed to moderate expressions of violence, such emotions as anger, rage, and fear, and sexual response.[88] Violent criminal behavior has also been linked to disorders in other parts of the brain.[89]

Advances in brain imaging technology have dramatically enhanced the ability of researchers to see the structure and functioning of the brain. For example, *positron emission tomography* (PET) allows researchers to see which parts of the brain are active during cognitive tasks, while *magnetic resonance imaging* (MRI) provides a detailed, three-dimensional picture of brain anatomy that can be "sliced" along any plane.[90]

Numerous brain imaging studies have found that violent felons show (1) reduced activity in the prefrontal cortex (located right beneath the forehead), which is responsible for executive functions, including mediating conflicting thoughts, making choices between right and wrong or good and bad, predicting future events, and governing social control, such as suppressing emotional or sexual urges; (2) over activity in the anterior cingulate gyrus (located in the midfrontal cortex), which is involved in self-regulation and control of thoughts, feelings, and behavior; and (3) abnormalities in the left temporal lobe (located on the left side of the brain just above the ear), which is involved with aggression, dark or violent thoughts, mild paranoia, mood and temper control, and emotional stability.[91]

The frontal and temporal regions of the brain are presumed to regulate the expression of aggression, so deficits in those areas may predispose a person to aggressive behavior,[92] especially in the presence of negative social influences.[93]

Evidence suggests that chronic violent offenders have much higher levels of brain disorder when compared to the general population.[94]

Hormone and Neurotransmitter Abnormalities

Abnormal levels of certain hormones and neurotransmitters also have been linked to antisocial behavior.[95] Hormones are signaling molecules released into the bloodstream by the endocrine system to regulate physiological function, behavior, and mood. Abnormal levels of the hormones testosterone and cortisol have been shown to be associated with antisocial behavior.

Testosterone is a sex hormone that has long been associated with aggressive behavior. Men have much more testosterone than women and that may be one of the reasons why men commit much more crime than women. Research suggests that testosterone may be related to social dominance, rather than aggression *per se*.[96]

Cortisol is released by the adrenal gland in response to physical and psychological stress. Unusually low levels of cortisol have been found in antisocial children, adolescents, and adults.[97] Individuals with low levels of cortisol may be less responsive to the threat of punishment.[98]

Neurotransmitters are chemicals in the brain that transmit messages from one neuron to another and are "crucial for most of the brain's functions, including mood, behavior, [and] emotion."[99] Although there are at least 75 different types of neurotransmitters,[100] three of them in particular—serotonin, dopamine, and norepinephrine—have been implicated in antisocial and impulsive behaviors. Serotonin is widely held to be a "braking system" for impulsive drives.[101] Abnormally low levels of serotonin have been linked to antisocial behaviors involving impulsivity, including substance abuse, suicidal impulses, and completed suicides.[102] On the other hand, high levels of dopamine have been associated with violence, aggression, gambling, and substance abuse.[103] Apparently, cocaine increases the level of dopamine, which activates the limbic system to produce pleasure.[104] Finally, elevated levels of norepinephrine also have been correlated with aggressive behavior.[105]

While level and activity of neurotransmitters is considered a heritable characteristic, neurotransmitters are highly sensitive to environmental manipulations.[106] Sociocultural factors such as socioeconomic status, stress, and nutrition have been found to influence the relationship between neurotransmitters and behavior.[107]

Low Arousal

According to biocriminologist Adrian Raine, the relationship between low arousal and antisocial and criminal behaviors has been found to be "the strongest psychophysiological finding" in modern bio-criminological research.[108] *Psychophysiology* refers to how a psychological state or process can be measured physiologically. For example, being nervous is a psychological state which often leads to "sweaty palms," a measurable physiological response. A large body of research suggests that low arousal, as indicated by a low resting heart rate, low skin conductance activity, or a disproportionate level of slow-wave EEG (electroencephalogram) patterns, is linked to antisocial or aggressive behavior.[109] Autonomic under-arousal has been shown to be at least partially heritable;[110] nonetheless, there is evidence that its effect on behavior is mediated by specific environmental conditions such as socioeconomic status.[111]

Low arousal may contribute to aggressive behavior in two ways. First, individuals with low arousal may be unusually fearless and, therefore, not fear punishment, or they may not fear the danger often involved in criminal behavior.[112] Second, low arousal may encourage antisocial stimulation-seeking behaviors, including violence, to elevate autonomic arousal to normal levels.[113]

Although a number of heritable characteristics have been linked to antisocial behavior, several nongenetic factors, such as obstetric factors, exposure to environmental toxins, and brain injury have been found to increase the likelihood of impulsive and sensation-seeking criminal behavior.[114]

Obstetric Problems

Compelling evidence links antisocial behavior to several obstetric factors, such as minor physical anomalies, prenatal nicotine and alcohol exposure, and birth complications.[115] Additional research has shown that complications during pregnancy or birth, such as anoxia (lack of oxygen) or preeclampsia (hypertension and fluid retention during pregnancy), may lead to brain damage which, in turn, may predispose a person to antisocial behavior and adult criminality.[116] A disruptive family environment has been found to enhance this link considerably.[117]

Exposure to Toxic Substances

Exposure to toxic substances is another factor that has been associated with antisocial behavior.[118] Most of this research has focused on exposure to lead, which has been linked to impaired intellectual development, hyperactivity, and impulsivity.[119] But other toxic substances linked to aggression and other forms of antisocial behavior include methyl mercury, polychlorinated biphenyls (PCBs), and tobacco.[120] The relationship between alcohol use and violence has been well documented.[121] Other substance-related factors associated with antisocial behavior are high-sugar diets, certain chemical, mineral, and vitamin deficiencies in the diet, diets high in carbohydrates, hypoglycemia (low blood sugar level), other drugs besides alcohol, certain allergies, ingestion of food dyes, exposure to radiation from fluorescent tubes and television sets, and all sorts of brain dysfunctions such as attention deficit/hyperactivity disorder.[122]

Brain Injury

Finally, brain injury resulting from head trauma or physical abuse has been associated with aggressive behavior.[123] As previously noted, damage to the frontal lobes, which are responsible for planning and the inhibition of impulsive behavior, in particular, is implicated in increased impulsive and aggressive behavior.[124] In addition, brain injury has been linked to the inability to understand the difference between right and wrong—a finding that could have a significant impact for defendants in criminal cases because the insanity defense is premised upon being able to understand the distinction between the two.[125]

A General Critique of Biological Theories

In the preceding sections, the different biological perspectives and the methodologies of each one have been described. Problems peculiar to a particular perspective or methodology have also been identified. In this section, some of the general problems with nearly all biological theories are presented.

One of the problems with biological theories of crime causation is that their crime prevention implications are so unsavory for many people. For most of the theories, besides those for which specific crime prevention implications already have been identified, the choice is to exterminate, isolate, or sterilize offenders. Despite their distastefulness for some, at one time or another, each of the penalties has been imposed. Regarding sterilization, between 1911 and 1930 in the United States, as part of the eugenics movement, at least sixty-four thousand people were legally sterilized for their "criminality, alcoholism, sodomy, bestiality, feeblemindedness, and tendency to commit rape."[126] Sterilization was used in the United States well into the 1970s in such states as Virginia, North Carolina, and California.[127] Today, chemical castration is available or mandated in at least nine states—California, Florida, Georgia, Iowa, Louisiana, Montana, Oregon, Texas, and Wisconsin.[128]

A second problem is that most of the biologically oriented research is methodologically poor.[129] For example, generalizations are made from small samples, subjects are not randomly selected or assigned, and there are either no control groups or inadequate ones. This is less true of more recent research, however.

Third, most of the subjects of this research are incarcerated at the time of study, which creates generalization problems.[130] Incarcerated offenders are not representative of all offenders (only those who have been caught, convicted, and imprisoned). Nor do prisoners include all people who have the biological trait in question, which makes it impossible to determine whether prisoners are overrepresented with regard to the trait. With only prisoners as subjects, it is impossible to determine whether any observed effect (such as criminality) is due to the trait in question or to the experiences of confinement.

Fourth, the biology of an individual only provides a behavioral potential, not a realization.[131] Many people possess the physical characteristics associated with criminality but do not engage in crime, and many people who lack the physical characteristics associated with criminality do commit crime. Besides, the overall behavioral uniformities that exist in every society, given genetic diversity, suggest the primary influence of the environment on behavior.[132]

Fifth, "no behavior is per se criminal."[133] The relationship between biology and crime involves the interaction of biology and environment within the context of legislatively proscribed behavior.[134] The problem is that biological positivists, especially early researchers, rarely question the criminalization process. That is, they rarely consider why some behaviors are defined as criminal, whereas other similar behaviors are not.

Finally, very little of the "crime problem" can be considered to be related primarily to biological factors.[135] Obviously, the dramatic decrease in the volume and severity of crime during the last two decades (according to government statistics) has not been accompanied by an equally dramatic shift in the biological composition of the population.[136] Nor, for that matter, can biological factors easily account for the great variation in crime rates across geographic areas (for example, cities, states, nations). People of different geographic areas are not that different biologically.

In sum, there probably are no positivist criminologists today who would argue that a biological or genetic imperative for crime exists. Nor, for that matter, are there many criminologists today, of any ideological persuasion, who would deny that biology has some influence on criminal behavior. Thus, the position held by most criminologists today is that criminal behavior is the product of a complex interaction between biology and environmental or social conditions.[137] What is inherited is not criminal behavior, but rather the way in which the person responds to the environment.[138] In short, biology or genetics provides an individual with a predisposition or a tendency to behave in a certain way.[139] Whether a person actualizes that predisposition or tendency and whether the subsequent behavior is defined as crime depend primarily on environmental or social conditions.

Study Questions

1. What is the cause of crime according to biological theories?
2. What is the perspective on which biological theories of crime causation are based?
3. What methodologies have been used to test the perspective on which biological theories of crime causation are based? (Describe them.)
4. What are some other, newer areas of biological research into crime causation?
5. How would biological positivists prevent crime?
6. What are general problems with biological theories of crime causation?
7. How do biological theories of crime causation compare to classical and neoclassical theories?

Notes

1. Rafter (2008:10, xi).
2. Vold (1979:51). Structure and function probably are reciprocally related to each other. That is, not only does structure determine function but function also determines structure.
3. See Vold and Bernard (1986:84).
4. Vold (1979:51).
5. See Vold and Bernard (1986:47).
6. Vold (1979:52).
7. "Musings on Physiognomy" (2000:5).
8. "Musings on Physiognomy" (2000:6).
9. Curran and Renzetti (1994:39).
10. Vold and Bernard (1986:48). The theory has also been attributed to the sixteenth-century physiognomist Giovanni Battista Della Porta (see Williams and McShane, 1994:32).
11. Vold and Bernard (1986:48).
12. "Musings on Physiognomy" (2000:7).
13. "Musings on Physiognomy" (2000:5).

14. Vold and Bernard (1986:48).
15. "Phrenology Epitomized" (2000:17).
16. Vold and Bernard (1986:48–49).
17. See Martin, Mutchnik, and Austin (1990:24).
18. Vold and Bernard (1986:48); "Phrenology Epitomized" (2000:17).
19. "Phrenology Epitomized" (2000:17).
20. "Phrenology Epitomized" (2000:18–24).
21. Vold and Bernard (1986:49).
22. Straton (2000:38).
23. Vold and Bernard (1986:49–50).
24. Rafter (2008:13).
25. See Williams and McShane (1994:33).
26. Taylor, Walton, and Young (1974:41).
27. Cited in Taylor et al. (1974:41).
28. See Vold and Bernard (1986:50–51); also see Lombroso (1968:xxii, xxiv, xxv).
29. Ferrero (2000:98).
30. Curran and Renzetti (1994:43); also see Lombroso (1968).
31. Lombroso (1968:xxx).
32. Lombroso (2000:79–80).
33. See Smith (2000:357).
34. Lombroso (2000).
35. Fitz Round (2000:236).
36. See Vold and Bernard (1986:57).
37. Gould (1981:125).
38. Gould (1981:125).
39. Goring (1913).
40. Akers and Sellers (2004:48).
41. Lanier and Henry (1998:93).
42. Lanier and Henry (1998:94–95); Lilly, Cullen, and Ball (1989:30); Vold and Bernard (1986:41).
43. Lilly et al. (1989:30); Vold and Bernard (1986:41).
44. Lilly et al. (1989:30–31).
45. Lilly et al. (1989:31).
46. Lanier and Henry (1998:96); Lilly et al. (1989:32–34); Vold and Bernard (1986:44).
47. Lilly et al. (1989:34–35); Vold and Bernard (1986:42).
48. Kretschmer was the first medical theorist "to distinguish personalities according to the type of mental disease toward which they might be predisposed" (Kahler 1967:202).
49. Sheldon (1949).

50. Sheldon (1949).
51. Sheldon (1949).
52. Sheldon (1949).
53. See Vold and Bernard (1986:60).
54. Glueck and Glueck (1956); Cortes (1972).
55. See Curran and Renzetti (1994:53); Vold and Bernard (1986:63).
56. Rafter (2008:168).
57. Dugdale (1877); Estabrook (1916).
58. Estabrook (1916:1–2).
59. Wray and Newitz (1997:2).
60. Fishbein (1990:44).
61. Goring (1913); also see Vold and Bernard (1986:52–55).
62. See Burt and Simons (2014); Wilson and Herrnstein (1985:90–95); Vold and Bernard (1986:87–90).
63. Burt and Simons (2014:232); Curran and Renzetti (1994:59); Fishbein (1990:44–45).
64. Morris (1998:324).
65. See for example Dalgard and Kringlen (1976); but also see Fishbein (1990:44) for a different view.
66. Bruder et al. (2008).
67. DNA Learning Center (n.d.); Lobo (2008).
68. See Burt and Simons (2014:238-241); Wilson and Herrnstein (1985:95–100); Vold and Bernard (1986:90–92).
69. See Burt and Simons (2014:238-241); Vold and Bernard (1986:92); Fishbein (1990:45–46).
70. Burt and Simons (2014:240).
71. Walters (1992). Also see Burt and Simons (2014).
72. Cullen and Agnew (2006); Raine (2002b).
73. Jones (2006).
74. Fishbein (2000); Raine (2002b); Rafter (2008:Chap. 8).
75. Baker, Bezdjian, and Raine (2006); Raine (2002b).
76. Scarpa and Raine (2003: 210).
77. Baker et al. (2006).
78. Jones (2006).
79. Burt and Simons (2014:244).
80. Baker et al. (2006); Cullen and Agnew (2006); Goldman and Fishbein (2000); Moffitt (1993); Raine (2002a); Raine (2002b); Scarpa and Raine (2003).
81. Raine (2002a).
82. Scarpa and Raine (2003); also see Walsh (2000).

83. Baker et al. (2006); Moffitt (1993), Rowe (2007); Scarpa and Raine (2003).
84. Elliott (2006); Robinson and Kelley (2000); Scarpa and Raine (2003).
85. See for example Fishbein (2000).
86. Shah and Roth (1974); Mark and Ervin (1970).
87. Fishbein (1990:38).
88. Fishbein (1990:37).
89. Raine, Buchsbaum, and LaCasse (1997).
90. Rowe (2007).
91. Raine (2002b:57).
92. Raine (2002b); Peskin, Gao, Glenn, Rudo-Hutt, Yang, and Raine (2014).
93. Raine (2002a).
94. Pallone and Hennessy (1998); Raine et al. (1997).
95. Goldman and Fishbein (2000); Raine (1993); Rowe (2007); Peskin, Gao, Glenn, Rudo-Hutt, Yang, and Raine (2014).
96. Archer (2006).
97. Peskin, Gao, Glenn, Rudo-Hutt, Yang, and Raine (2014).
98. Peskin, Gao, Glenn, Rudo-Hutt, Yang, and Raine (2014).
99. Goldman and Fishbein (2000:9−4).
100. Wortley (2011:68).
101. Coccaro, Kavoussi, and McNamee (2000).
102. Baker et al. (2006); Lane and Cherek (2000); Rowe (2007).
103. Baker et al. (2006); Goldman and Fishbein (2000).
104. Curran and Renzetti (1994:78); also see Fishbein (1990:47); Ellis and Walsh (1997:259)
105. Lane and Cherek (2000); Raine (1993).
106. Baker et al. (2006).
107. Baker et al. (2006).
108. Raine (2002b:50).
109. Baker et al. (2006); Ortiz and Raine (2004); Raine (2002b); Scarpa and Raine (2003).
110. Baker et al. (2006); Ortiz and Raine (2004); Raine (1993); Scarpa and Raine (2003).
111. Farrington (1997).
112. Raine (1993).
113. Baker et al. (2006); Eysenck (1997).
114. Cullen and Agnew (2006); Scarpa and Raine (2003).
115. Raine (2002a).
116. Raine (2002b).
117. Piquero and Tibbetts (1999); Raine (2002a); Raine, Brennan, and Mednick (1994).

118. Baker et al. (2006); Moffitt (1993).
119. Baker et al. (2006); Robinson and Kelley (2000).
120. Lanphear, Vorhees, and Bellinger (2005).
121. Baker et al. (2006).
122. Wakschlag, Pickett, Cook, Benowitz, and Leventhal (2002); Robinson and Kelley (2000); Walters (1992).
123. Baker et al. (2006); Elliott (2006); Robinson and Kelley (2000).
124. Baker et al. (2006).
125. Rowe (2007); Fradella (2007).
126. Burt and Simons (2014:229, n. 1); Lilly et al. (2007:29).
127. Burt and Simons (2014:229, n. 1); Lilly et al. (2007:30); Zucchino (2012).
128. Park (2012).
129. National Institute for Juvenile Justice and Delinquency Prevention (NI-JJDP) (1977:127); Walters and White (1989); Fishbein (1990:39–40).
130. See Taylor et al. (1974:44, 285, fn. 7); Walters and White (1989:478); Fishbein (1990:39).
131. NIJJDP (1977:110).
132. NIJJDP (1977:110).
133. NIJJDP (1977:111).
134. NIJJDP (1977:111); Fishbein (1990).
135. NIJJDP (1977:111).
136. NIJJDP (1977:111); Taylor et al. (1974:43).
137. See Burt and Simons (2014); Wilson and Herrnstein (1985:70); Fishbein (1990:41).
138. Fishbein (1990:42).
139. Fishbein (1990:42); Ellis and Walsh (1997:229–230).

5

Psychological Theories

In this chapter, psychological theories of crime causation (*psychological positivism*) are examined. Few distinctly psychological theories of crime causation exist. When crime is examined from a psychological perspective, it generally is explained using conventional psychological theories that were developed to explain other phenomena. The chapter begins with a description of the relationship between intelligence and criminality and proceeds to discussions of psychoanalytic theories, personality, and humanistic psychological theories. Learning or behavioral theories are reserved for the section on the modifications to Sutherland's differential association theory in Chapter 6.

Intelligence and Crime

Attempts to measure intelligence began in the late 1800s and are most closely associated with the work of French psychologist Alfred Binet (1857–1911).[1] Although Binet originally developed his intelligence test to identify students who needed extra help in school, other researchers and policy makers in the United States used the intelligence test to measure "innate" intelligence[2] and to promote several draconian social policies, such as eugenics.

The idea that crime is the product primarily of people with low intelligence was popular in the United States between 1914 and about 1930. It received some attention again during the mid-1970s and experienced a modest revival in the mid-1990s, beginning with the publication of Richard Herrnstein and Charles Murray's *The Bell Curve* in 1994. The belief requires only a slight shift in thinking from the idea that criminals are biologically inferior to the idea that they are intellectually inferior.

Goddard and Feeblemindedness Theory

One of the earliest promoters in the United States of the relationship between low IQ and crime was H. H. Goddard (1866–1957), himself a proponent of the eugenics movement. In 1914, he published *Feeblemindedness: Its Causes and Consequences*. In the book, Goddard argued that criminals are *feeble-minded*, an old-fashioned term that has been replaced by the more modern *mentally challenged* (of below-normal intelligence).

To test his proposition, Goddard first had to determine what IQ level constituted feeblemindedness, so he administered IQ tests to all inmates of the New Jersey Training School for the Feebleminded at Vineland where he worked. He discovered that none of the tested residents had a mental age over thirteen and therefore concluded that a mental age of twelve (which is equivalent to an IQ of 75) was the upper-threshold level of feeblemindedness.[3] At the time, Goddard believed that an IQ above 75 was normal. Today, however, 90 to 110 is considered the normal range for IQ.

In any event, armed with a standard for feeblemindedness, Goddard and many other psychologists began testing a variety of different populations, including prison and jail inmates. The proportion of subjects in those studies determined to be feebleminded varied greatly from a low of 28 percent to a high of 89 percent.[4] The studies of prisoners, however, revealed that 70 percent had IQs of 75 or less which, for Goddard, provided strong support for his proposition that criminals are feebleminded.[5]

A problem arose when the Army Psychological Corps adopted Goddard's standard as a criterion for fitness for military service. When intelligence tests were administered to draftees for World War I, it was discovered using Goddard's criterion that about one-third of them were feebleminded.[6] Whether that was an accurate indicator of the intelligence level of the population at the time (as represented by the draft army) must remain the object of conjecture. However, as a practical matter, the army was not about to eliminate nearly one-third of draftees because of low-level intelligence. Consequently, Goddard changed his conclusions. In 1927, he wrote:

> The war led to the measurement of intelligence of the drafted army with the result that such an enormous proportion was found to have an intelligence of 12 years and less that to call them all feeble minded was an absurdity of the highest degree.... We have already said that

we thought 12 was the limit, but we now know that most of the twelve, and even of the ten [IQ = 63] and nine [IQ = 56], are not defective.[7]

Sutherland's Review

In 1931, E. H. Sutherland reviewed approximately 350 studies on the relationship between intelligence and delinquency and criminality.[8] The studies reported the results of intelligence tests of about 175,000 criminals and delinquents. Sutherland concluded from the review that although intelligence may play a role in individual cases, given the selection that takes place in arrest, conviction, and imprisonment, the distribution of the intelligence scores of criminals and delinquents is very similar to the distribution of the intelligence scores of the general population.

Gordon and Hirschi and Hindelang's IQ Theory

For the next forty years or so, the issue regarding the relationship between intelligence and crime and delinquency appeared resolved. However, in the mid-1970s, two studies were published that resurrected the debate, one by Gordon in 1976 and the other by Hirschi and Hindelang in 1977.[9] These studies found that IQ was an important predictor of both official and self-reported delinquency, as important as social class or race.[10] Hirschi and Hindelang acknowledged the findings of Sutherland's earlier review, noting that a decreasing number of delinquents had been reported as feebleminded over the years but that the difference in intelligence between delinquents and nondelinquents had never disappeared and had stabilized at about 8 IQ points.[11] They failed to note, however, that the 8 point IQ difference generally was within the normal range. Hirschi and Hindelang surmised that the relationship between intelligence and delinquency is indirect; its effect is mediated by school performance.[12]

Race-IQ-Crime Theory

In the mid-to-late-1990s, a series of books was published claiming that intelligence or IQ was primarily the product of genetics, and that genetic differences in intelligence could, in large measure, explain racial differences in crime. Specifically, the theory is that genetic differences in intelligence are the principal reason why Blacks commit a disproportionately high percentage of violent crime and "all categories of felony except those requiring access to large amounts of money, such as stock fraud."[13] In addition to Herrnstein and Murray's *The Bell Curve*

(1994), other books in this genre include J. Philippe Rushton's *Race, Evolution, and Behavior* (1995), Michael Levin's *Why Race Matters* (1997), and Arthur Jensen's *The g Factor* (1998).[14] The following description of their theory could have been easily placed in Chapter 4 on biological theories, because it is unquestionably biological. However, because of the theory's focus on IQ as the key explanatory factor, the theory is more accurately called *evolutionary biopsychological*.

The theory proposes that intelligence, in large measure, determines people's ability to control or restrain their impulses, and that most "street crime" is caused by people unable to control their impulses.[15] Put differently, the theory posits a positive relationship between IQ and impulse control, and a negative relationship between impulse control and crime. The theorists cite a large body of evidence showing significant average differences in IQ scores across different races, with Asians, on average, having the highest IQs, Blacks, on average, having the lowest IQs, and Whites having IQs that, on average, fall between those of Asians and Blacks. The theorists go on to argue that these IQ differences are mostly, but not exclusively, genetic-evolutionary in origin.

Evolutionary biologists generally believe that modern humans evolved in Africa about 200,000 years ago, and that some Africans began migrating out of Africa about 110,000 years ago. The further north people migrated out of Africa, the more they encountered different climates and geographies that required different skills and lifestyles. The different climates also necessitated differences in skin pigmentation and other physical characteristics and, thus, different races—Whites and Asians—evolved. Asians and Whites presumably split about 40,000 years ago. Because intelligence increased the chances of survival in harsh winter climates, unknown to those in Africa, the migrants had to evolve greater intelligence and lifestyle changes—hence the greater average intelligence level of Asians and Whites compared to Blacks. In sum, the theory holds that climatic and geographical changes genetically altered human beings into different races distinguishable, in part, by average intelligence. Intelligence largely determines impulse-control ability, which, in turn, determines the likelihood of crime.

Policy Implications

A corollary of the theory is that less intelligent Blacks are less responsible for their crimes because they have less impulse control.[16] This assumption and the race-intelligence-crime theory from which it is derived have been used to justify a number of policies to reduce crimes by Blacks. For example, proponents argue that welfare, especially Aid to Families with Dependent Children, must be eliminated because it has made "reckless" Black behavior "cost-free." In addition, race-based penalties must be established if rewards for good behavior prove ineffective because people with less self-control (disproportionately Blacks) require harsher penalties to deter them from crime. Finally, because Blacks, on average, exercise less self-control than other races and, therefore, are more difficult to deter, they should receive swifter punishment and stricter limits on appeals.

Critique

In the race-intelligence-crime debate, questions remain about (1) what IQ tests really measure; (2) the degree to which intelligence is a heritable characteristic; and (3) the value of "race" as a reliable, biologically based method of human categorization. Regarding the first concern, Bartol contends, "IQ scores and the concept of intelligence should *not* be confused. The term *IQ* merely refers to a standardized score on a test. *Intelligence*, on the other hand, is a broad, all-encompassing ability that defies any straightforward or simple definition."[17] Evidence suggests that IQ test scores do predict school achievement, but that does not mean that IQ test scores measure intelligence.[18]

With respect to the second concern, a considerable body of evidence suggests that *intelligence* is a product of environment, experience, and background *in addition to* a yet-undetermined degree of innate or natural intelligence (genetics).[19] There is general agreement that some degree of intelligence is innate, but specific genes for intelligence have not been discovered.[20]

As for the third concern, most researchers argue that skin color is a poor basis upon which to differentiate humans into "races."[21] According to the American Anthropological Association, "differentiating species into biologically defined 'races' has proven meaningless and unscientific as a way of explaining variation."[22]

Findings from the Human Genome Project also call the race-intelligence-crime theory into serious question. The Human Genome Project is an international research project designed to determine the sequence of chemical base pairs of DNA and to map the physical and functional characteristics of the approximately thirty thousand genes of the human genome.[23] Results of this vast project do not support the notion that separate, classifiable "races" exist within modern humans: "While different genes for physical traits such as skin and hair color can be identified between individuals, no consistent patterns of genes across the human genome exist to distinguish one race from another. There is also no genetic basis for divisions of human ethnicity."[24] Recent research has found that human beings are 99 percent identical genetically.[25]

In short, results of the Human Genome Project and related research have provided evidence that the concept of race is biologically meaningless and useless.[26] This is not to say that race has no real *social* meaning, because it does, but most scientists agree that it does not have a meaningful *biological* basis.[27] Consequently, the policy implications of the theory that were listed earlier seem harsh, mean-spirited, and racist.

As for intelligence and crime, the conclusion cannot be drawn with any degree of confidence that delinquents, as a group, are less intelligent than non-delinquents.[28] Most adult criminals are not feebleminded.[29] Obviously, low-level intelligence cannot account for gender differences in crime. Since IQ scores do not increase with age, why do most criminal offenders stop committing crimes as they get older? Furthermore, low-level intelligence certainly cannot account for complex white-collar and political crimes.[30]

Psychoanalytic Theories

Psychoanalytic theories of crime causation are associated with the work of Sigmund Freud (1856–1939) and his followers.[31] Freud did not theorize much about criminal behavior *per se*, but a theory of crime causation can be inferred from his more general theory of human behavior and its disorders. Had he contemplated the issue, Freud probably would have argued that crime, like other disorders, was a symptom of more deep-seated problems. Considered here are four deep-seated problems of which crime might be considered symptomatic by Freud: (1) difficulties or problems during one of the psychosexual stages of development, (2) an inability to sublimate (or redirect) sexual and aggressive drives, (3) an inability to successfully resolve (as to settle a problem) the Oedipal (in men) or Electra (in women) complex, and (4) an unconscious desire for punishment.

Psychosexual Development Stage Theory

According to Freud, five normal, universal stages characterize human *psychosexual development*: (1) the oral stage, (2) the anal stage, (3) the phallic stage, (4) the latency stage, and (5) the genital stage. Crime has been considered by some psychoanalytic positivists as symptomatic of problems during four of the five stages. The problems are either a *fixation* (arrested development) at a particular stage or a *regression* (a return) to an earlier one.

The *oral stage* of psychosexual development (from birth to around one year old) is the period of breast-feeding, and alcoholism and drug addiction have been considered symptomatic of problems during this stage. Presumably alcohol and drugs satisfy the need for infantile oral pleasure.

The *anal stage* is the toilet-training period (from one through three years old), and embezzlement and armed robbery have been attributed to problems in this stage. The embezzler or robber unconsciously "holds on to" or "will not let go of" the symbol for excrement (the stolen goods).

Problems during the *phallic stage* (around three to six years of age), during which the child begins to understand the pleasure that can be had from his or her sexual organs, have been associated with an excessive interest in sex resulting, in extreme cases, in sexual assault, rape, or prostitution—the result of unresolved Oedipal or Electra conflicts (to be discussed shortly).[32] Unresolved Oedipal or Electra conflicts have also been used to explain sexual promiscuity, hostility toward male authority figures, and running away.[33]

No references could be found that associated any criminal behaviors with the *latency stage* (from about six years of age to puberty), during which the sex drive seems to disappear (it is repressed).

Finally, prostitution and homosexuality (which is not a crime, although in some states certain homosexual acts are) have been considered symptomatic of problems with sexual identity during the *genital stage*, which begins with the onset of puberty.

Sexual and Aggressive Drive Sublimation Theory

A second deep-seated problem of which crime has been considered symptomatic is the inability to sublimate sexual and aggressive drives. For Freud, all human beings are born with those two drives; they are the primary sources of human motivation.

Ideally, people are able to *sublimate* (redirect) sexual and aggressive drives either to legal nonsexual or nonaggressive outlets or to legal sexual and aggressive outlets. Examples of the former are reading and hobbies of various sorts; examples of the latter are marriage and contact sports.

If unsuccessful at sublimating the drives, they will be either acted out (perhaps as violent criminal behavior) or *repressed* (rendered unconscious). *Unconscious* refers to mental processes of which the person is unaware. If the drives are repressed, they may be acted out anytime in later life, again possibly as criminal behavior. The acting out of repressed sexual and aggressive drives might explain the supposedly inexplicable crime, as when the angelic, church-going, Eagle Scout kills, dismembers, and cannibalizes a victim.

Repressed sexual and aggressive drives, if not acted out, can lead to mental conflict that manifests itself in *anxiety* (distress or worry). To keep anxiety under control and to maintain psychic equilibrium, the ego employs a variety of *defense mechanisms*. Defense mechanisms safeguard the conscious mind against feelings and thoughts that are too difficult to tolerate.

Freud identified a variety of defense mechanisms. Among them are *perceptual vigilance* (seeing only what you want to see), *perceptual defense* (blocking out what you do not want to see), *repression* (forcing ideas out of your conscious mind), *rationalization* (intentionally misperceiving or redefining a situation), *introjection* (internalizing attributes of external objects or people and making them a part of your personality), and *projection* (attributing one's own repressed thoughts or emotions to someone else, e.g., projecting self-hatred onto victims).

Oedipal and Electra Complex Theory

A third deep-seated problem of which crime has been considered symptomatic is the inability to successfully resolve the Oedipal (in men) or Electra (in women) complex. This inability explains why an individual fails to develop a strong superego.

For Freud, the superego, together with the id and the ego, are the three parts of the mind. The *superego* is the conscience or source of morality and is mainly unconscious. Its functions include (1) approval or disapproval of the ego's actions, that is, judgment that an act is "right" or "wrong"; (2) critical self-observation; (3) self-punishment; and (4) self-love or self-esteem. The *id* is the energy system of the mind (*libido*); it is the source of the instinctive sexual and aggressive drives. The id resides in the unconscious and is governed by the *pleasure principle*; in other words, it only seeks pleasure. The id is controlled by the ego and superego. The *ego* is the part of the mind that mediates between the individual and reality. It is governed by the *reality principle*. Its prime function is the perception of reality and adaptation to it so as to maximize pleasure and minimize pain. The ego does not judge right from wrong or good from bad, which is the job of the superego.

Although concern here is with superego problems, it is important to note that criminality has also been attributed to a weak ego. An individual with a weak ego is characterized by "immaturity, poorly developed social skills, poor reality testing, gullibility and excessive dependence."[34] Such an individual may stumble into trouble because of a misreading of the external environment, temper tantrums, or following the lead of someone else.[35]

Returning to the *Oedipal* and *Electra* complexes, between the ages of three and six (during the phallic stage of psychosexual development), the child develops a monopoly feeling for the opposite-sexed parent. For Freud, this is a normal, universal process. At this age (during which the ego already has developed), the child realizes that the like-sexed parent will get mad if the other parent directs all of his or her attention to the child. The male child (we will return to the female child shortly) becomes afraid that his father will castrate him if this occurs. Because of a fear of castration, the little boy represses his desire for his mother and overreacts and identifies with his father. Presumably, the repressed desire for the mother manifests itself in little boys at this age frequently "hating" girls. In any event, the father (for males) is the symbol of the norms of society; he identifies symbolically right from wrong. If the process proceeds naturally, the little boy will develop normally, that is, develop a strong superego capable of controlling the id. However, if the father is cruel or if there is no father figure (note that a biological father is unnecessary), the little boy will not identify with the father and thus will not internalize the norms or authority of society. In other words, he will not develop a strong superego capable of controlling the id.

Needless to say, the process does not work in exactly the same way for little girls. Freud resolved the obvious difficulty by suggesting that females had "penis envy" and reacted to a fear of symbolic castration. Other than overreacting and identifying with the mother, who, for little girls, represents the norms of society, the rest of the process operates the same way.

Individuals who do not successfully resolve the Oedipal or Electra complex and thus do not develop a strong superego capable of controlling the id were called *psychopaths* by Freud. A lack of empathy and compassion for others, no subjective conscience, and no sense of right and wrong characterize psychopaths. Psychopathy and its connection to crime will be discussed at greater length in a later section.

Unconscious Desire for Punishment Theory

Finally, a fourth deep-seated problem of which crime has been considered symptomatic is an unconscious desire for punishment. In his essay "Criminality from a Sense of Guilt" (1915), Freud described the phenomenon.[36] He suggested that some people, with a strong or overdeveloped superego, commit crimes in order to be caught and punished—not for the crime for which they had been caught, but for something they had done in the past about which they felt guilty and for which they were not caught or punished. Obviously, this theory does not explain the large numbers of successful criminals.

Policy Implications

The principal policy implication of considering crime symptomatic of deep-seated problems is to provide psychotherapy or psychoanalysis. Psychoanalysis is a type of psychotherapy (other psychotherapies include cognitive therapy, behavioral therapy, cognitive behavioral therapy, and marital or family therapy), first developed by Freud, that among other things attempts to make patients conscious or aware of unconscious and deep-seated problems to resolve the symptoms associated with them. Methods used include a variety of projective tests (such as the interpretation of Rorschach inkblots, dream interpretation, and free association).

Another policy implication that derives logically from Freudian theory is to provide people with legal outlets to sublimate or redirect their sexual and aggressive drives.

Psychoanalysis and the psychoanalytic theory on which it is based are components of a medical model of crime causation that had, to varying degrees, informed criminal justice policy in the United States for a century between the mid-1870s and the mid-1970s. The general conception of this medical model is that criminals are biologically or, in this case, psychologically "sick" and in need of treatment.

A General Critique of Psychoanalytic Theories

First, although evidence indicates that at least some criminal offenders have psychological problems, the bulk of the research on the issue suggests that most criminals are not psychologically disturbed or, at least, no more disturbed than the rest of the population.[37] Few criminal offenders have major psychiatric disorders.[38]

Second, even if a person who commits a crime has a psychological disturbance that does not mean that the psychological disturbance causes the crime. Many people with psychological disturbances do not commit crimes, and many people without psychological disturbances do commit crimes.[39]

Third, there are problems with psychotherapy and the theory on which it is based. For example, psychoanalytic theory and psychoanalysis as an approach to rehabilitation generally focus on the individual offender and not on the individual offender in interaction with the environment in which the criminal behavior occurs.[40] Criminal behavior is considered a personal problem and not a social one. Yet, the personality may not play a significant role in the cause of criminal behavior.[41] The theory also suggests that the personality is set in early childhood and remains relatively stable over time. This may not be true and seems to preclude the possibility of personality change.

Psychotherapy rests on faith. Much of its theoretical structure is scientifically untestable. Unconscious processes, which play such a major role in psychoanalytic theories, can only be measured indirectly.

Psychoanalytic theories of crime have also been criticized for being based on circular reasoning. That is, criminal behavior is presumed to be caused by mental illness which, itself, is indicated by the criminal behavior.[42]

Another criticism of Freud's theory has to do with its generalizability. The theory is based on Freud's work with mostly upper-middle-class and upper-class female patients.[43] Some critics wonder whether the theory applies equally well to other types of people.

The behaviors that are treated in psychotherapy are not criminal; they are the deep-seated problems.[44] Criminal behavior is assumed to be symptomatic of the deep-seated problems. That assumption may not be true. Many people who do not engage in crime have deep-seated problems, and many people who do not have deep-seated problems do engage in crime.

Another problem is that psychoanalytic "talking therapies" require the client to have a reasonable level of verbal intelligence,[45] an ability that many criminal offenders lack. A related problem is that psychotherapy rests on the assumption that if people change their verbal behavior (through psychotherapy), they will change their actual behavior.[46] That assumption may not be true. What people say and do often are very different.

Most psychotherapies also require the client to be strongly motivated to sit through weekly (or more frequent) sessions for a year or longer.[47] Many criminal offenders do not have the necessary motivation to complete (or to engage in) the lengthy process. From a practical standpoint, even if criminal offenders were motivated to complete the lengthy process, the delivery of long-term psychotherapy, especially the one-on-one variety, is too expensive and inefficient to be used widely in correctional settings anyway.[48]

Perhaps the most telling problem is that people who receive psychiatric and psychoanalytical treatment generally are no more likely to be cured than people who do not receive such treatment.[49]

Many years ago, in reviewing the impact of psychiatry on corrections, Paul W. Tappan made an observation that is still relevant today:

> The focus upon mental pathology has resulted in a conception of criminals as sick people.... The prevalent idea of criminal illness is highly misleading. Criminals are not generally neurotic, psychotic, or psychopathic.... Worse, by merely attaching a general label to the offender, one may be led to assume quite erroneously that the problem has been solved thereby or that it is necessary only to provide some vague psychotherapy to resolve the difficulty.[50]

Personality Theories

Personality refers to "the complex set of emotional and behavioral attributes that tend to remain relatively constant as the individual moves from situation to situation."[51] Over the last hundred years, tests have been developed to measure personality characteristics like extroversion, shyness, timidity, friendliness, and so on. The Minnesota Multiphasic Personality Inventory (MMPI) is one of the most widely used personality tests. It includes a list of 567 statements that measure a number of traits including, but not limited to, psychopathic deviate, social introversion, depression, and paranoia. More recently, several other measures of personality have been developed including Costa, Jr. and McCrae's five-factor model,[52] Eysenck's PEN (Psychoticism, Extraversion, Neuroticism) model,[53] Tellegen's three-factor model,[54] and Cloninger's temperament and character model.[55] These tests differ from the MMPI by measuring personality more broadly, rather than focusing on "pathological" elements.[56]

Although many criminologists tend to dismiss the importance of personality, psychologists and some criminologists have identified personality traits that are linked to aggressive or criminal behavior.[57] In 1950, an extensive study of five hundred delinquents and five hundred nondelinquents by Sheldon and Eleanor Glueck found that delinquents were "more extroverted, vivacious, impulsive, and less self-controlled" than the nondelinquents; they were also "more hostile, resentful, defiant, suspicious, and destructive."[58]

More recently, Caspi and his colleagues examined the relationship between personality traits and delinquency in a sample of youth from New Zealand and the United States.[59] Their results show that youth who score high in "negative emotionality" and low in "constraint" are more likely to be involved in delinquency than those who score low in "negative emotionality" and high in "constraint."[60] Youth high on negative emotionality "have a low general threshold for the experience of negative emotions such as fear, anxiety, and anger, and tend to break down under stress."[61] Youth who score low on constraint tend to reject conventional norms, seek thrills, and act in an unconstrained and fearless manner.[62] Caspi and his colleagues surmise that negative emotionality and constraint are "a constellation of personality traits, not merely a single trait, that might be linked to criminal involvement."[63]

Miller and Lynam conducted a meta-analysis of nearly sixty studies that examined personality and antisocial behavior.[64] (A meta-analysis is a statistical technique that provides a systematic overview of quantitative research that has examined a particular question.) Their findings show that antisocial individuals tend to score fairly low on scales of "agreeableness" and "conscientiousness."[65] In other words, antisocial individuals are "hostile, self-centered, spiteful, jealous, and indifferent to others" (i.e., low in "agreeableness"). They also tend to "lack ambition, motivation, and perseverance, have difficulty controlling their impulses, and hold nontraditional and unconventional values and beliefs" (i.e., low in "conscientiousness").[66]

Wortley maintains that of all the personality traits linked to criminality impulsivity has been the subject of the most research and has yielded the most consistent positive findings. He also notes that an interaction between impulsivity and adverse situational factors, such as poor neighborhoods, increases the likelihood of delinquency.[67]

Theory of the Psychopath

One personality type that has received considerable attention from researchers and the popular media is the psychopath (also called *sociopath* and *antisocial personality*). Based on what psychiatrists know about the psychopathic personality, the popular image of the "psychopathic killer" or "violent sociopath" may be overstated. According to Lilienfeld and Arkowitz, psychopathy:

> consists of a specific set of personality traits and behaviors. Superficially charming, psychopaths tend to make a good first impression on others and often strike observers as remarkably normal. Yet they are self-centered, dishonest and undependable, and at times they engage in irresponsible behavior for no apparent reason other than the sheer fun of it. Largely devoid of guilt, empathy and love, they have casual and callous interpersonal and romantic relationships. Psychopaths routinely offer excuses for their reckless and often outrageous actions, placing blame on others instead. They rarely learn from their mistakes or benefit from negative feedback, and they have difficulty inhibiting their impulses.[68]

Although they are overrepresented in prisons—up to 25 percent of all inmates by some estimates[69]—psychopaths are as likely to be successful in the world of business and politics as to turn to crime.[70] Psychopaths are more likely to be male than female, and psychopathy is present in different cultures.[71] Despite the way they are often portrayed in the popular media, most psychopaths are not violent, and most violent people are not psychopaths.[72] Psychopaths are almost always rational and rarely have psychotic breaks with reality.

Psychiatrists disagree about whether psychopaths can benefit from treatment.[73] Some psychiatrists argue that psychopaths can be taught "basic prosocial life skills to help them avoid the needless troubles that their behaviors cause."[74] Other psychiatrists recommend that psychopaths should "be locked up until they reach middle age, or even that they be executed."[75]

Theory of the Criminal Personality

Samuel Yochelson (1906–1976) and Stanton Samenow (1941–) developed a theory of the criminal personality that, in many respects, is similar to the theory of the psychopath.[76] The criminal personality and the psychopath share many of the same characteristics. A notable difference between the two theories is that individuals with a criminal personality, according to Yochelson and Samenow, freely choose to commit their crimes, whereas the psychopath's behavior is presumed to be determined by psychological factors (most notably in Freud's view by an unresolved Oedipal or Electra complex). Another difference between the two theories is that fear (of embarrassment, injury, and death) is a key component of the criminal personality but not of the psychopath.

Theory of a Violence-Prone Personality

The notion of a "violence-prone personality" has received little support.[77] Rather, most researchers suggest that certain personality characteristics, in combination with environmental stimuli, can increase the likelihood that some people will engage in aggressive or criminal behavior.[78] That said, the mystery remains as to why some people satisfy their desire for thrills or their rejection of conventional norms through legal activity such as bungee jumping or getting a tattoo, while others engage in illegal activity such as assaulting a rival or cheating on their taxes.

Humanistic Psychological Theory

Humanistic psychological theory refers primarily to the work of Abraham Maslow, Seymour Halleck, and Philip Zimbardo. The theories of Maslow and Halleck are fundamentally psychoanalytic, but here they are called humanistic because they assume that human beings are basically good even though sometimes they are constrained by society to act badly. By contrast, the Freudian theories assume that human beings are inherently bad, motivated by sexual and aggressive drives. Zimbardo's theory is social-psychological, but it also assumes that human beings are basically good even though situational factors sometimes cause them to do evil.

Maslow's Needs Theory

Abraham Maslow (1908–1970) attempted to integrate insights from several neo-Freudians, including Alfred Adler (1870–1937), Erik Erikson (1902–1994), Karen Horney (1885–1952), and Erich Fromm (1900–1980), into a single theoretical framework. Maslow did not apply his theory to crime *per se*, but inferences are made from Maslow's work about what he would have said about the causes of crime had he addressed the subject.

Maslow postulated that human beings are motivated by a *need hierarchy* comprising five basic levels of needs.[79] The most basic of the needs are the *physiological needs* (food, water, and procreational sex). Next are the *safety needs* (security, stability, freedom from fear, anxiety, chaos, and so forth) followed, in order, by the *belongingness and love needs*, the *esteem needs* (self-esteem and the esteem of others), and, finally, the *need for self-actualization* (being what one can, being true to one's nature, and becoming everything that one is capable of becoming).

According to Maslow, during a given period a person's life is dominated by a particular need. It remains dominated by that need until the need has been relatively satisfied, at which time a new need emerges to dominate the person's life. From this view, crime may be understood as a means by which individuals satisfy their basic human needs. They choose crime because they cannot satisfy their needs legally or, for whatever reason, choose not to satisfy their needs legally.

Policy Implication

An obvious crime prevention implication of the theory is to help people satisfy their basic human needs in legitimate ways. In his presidential address to the Academy of Criminal Justice Sciences, Francis T. Cullen (1951–) argued that the relatively high crime rates in the United States, compared to other industrialized nations, are at least partly the result of inadequate social support.[80] *Social support* is the provision, both the perceived and the actual provision, of such diverse things as material aid, financial assistance, advice, guidance, emotional support, feedback, social reinforcement, and socializing.[81] Cullen notes that social support can occur at different social levels: "Micro-level support can be delivered by a confiding individual, such as a spouse or a best friend. But social support also can be viewed as a property of social networks and of communities and larger ecological units in which individuals are enmeshed."[82]

Cullen, sounding very much like a radical criminologist (he maintains that "notions of social support appear in diverse criminological writings"), concludes his address by criticizing "the excessive individualism in the United States, which too often degenerates into a politics justifying either the crass pursuit of rights or materialistic self-aggrandizement."[83] He notes that "in this context, there is a lack of attention to the public good, service to others, and an appreciation for our need for connectedness."[84] Thus, his address is "a call to revitalize our common bonds and to build a society supportive of all its citizens."[85] Maslow likely would agree.

Halleck's Oppression and Psychological Advantages of Crime Theories

Seymour L. Halleck (1929–) views crime as one among several different adaptations to the helplessness caused by oppression.[86] For Halleck, there are two general types of oppression, *objective* and *subjective*. Each has two subtypes. The subtypes of objective oppression are *social oppression* (for example, oppression resulting from racial discrimination) and the *oppression that occurs in two-person interactions* (for instance, a parent's unfair restriction of a child's activities). The subtypes of subjective oppression are *oppression from within* (guilt from the superego) and *projected or misunderstood oppression* (a person's feeling of being oppressed when, in fact, he or she is not).

For Halleck, the subjective emotional experience of either type of oppression is helplessness, which is adapted to by the individual in one of six different ways. Some people adapt to the feeling of helplessness by simply conforming, that is, accepting the oppression and feeling of helplessness; sometimes suffering in silence; accepting the rules of society. Other people adapt through activism, that is, active efforts to change the environment by following the rules. Halleck notes that a combination of conformity and activism is generally considered normal by society. Another adaptation is a different type of activism where the individual attempts to change the environment by legal attempts to change the rules of society. Mental illness, which involves an indirect effort to change the environment through the communication of suffering, is a fifth possible adaptation, and criminality is the sixth type. Criminality is the attempt to change the environment by illegally breaking the rules of society or by creating new but illegal rules.

Halleck suggests that the criminal adaptation is more likely when alternative adaptations are not possible or are blocked by other people. He also maintains that criminal behavior is sometimes chosen as an adaptation over other possible alternatives because it offers gratifications (psychological advantages) that could not be achieved otherwise.[87] Halleck lists fourteen psychological advantages of crime:[88]

1. The adaptational advantages of crime in changing one's environment are more desirable than illness or conformity.
2. Crime involves activity, and when man is engaged in motoric behavior, he feels less helpless.
3. However petty a criminal act may be, it carries with it a promise of change in a favorable direction.
4. During the planning and execution of a criminal act the offender is a free man. (He is immune from the oppressive dictates of others.)
5. Crime offers the possibility of excitement.
6. Crime calls for the individual to maximize his faculties and talents which might otherwise lie dormant.
7. Crime can relieve feelings of inner oppression and stress.
8. Crime increases external stresses which allow the individual to concentrate upon these threats to his equilibrium and temporarily allow him to abandon his chronic intrapsychic problems.
9. Once a person has convinced himself that the major pressures in his life come from without, there is less tendency to blame himself for his failures.
10. Adopting the criminal role provides an excellent rationalization for inadequacy.
11. Crime has a more esteemed social status than mental illness.
12. America has an ambivalent attitude toward crime. Although crime is regularly condemned, it is also glamorized.
13. Deviant behavior sometimes helps the criminal to form close and relatively nonoppressive relations with other criminals.
14. Crime can provide pleasure or gratify needs.

Policy Implications

Halleck's oppression theory suggests at least three crime prevention implications. First, sources of social oppression should be eliminated wherever possible. Second, alternative, legal ways of coping with oppression must be provided. Third, psychotherapy should be provided for subjective oppressions.

Critique

Besides some of the general criticisms of positivist theories and psychotherapy listed in the last section, a major problem with the theories of both Maslow and Halleck is that they do not go far enough; they are not radical. That is, they do not identify and analyze the sources of need deprivation (in Maslow's theory) and objective oppression (in Halleck's theory) and their more fundamental relationship to criminality, however defined.

Zimbardo's System-Situation-Person Theory

Philip Zimbardo (1933–) is perhaps best known for the Stanford Prison Experiment (SPE), which has informed his theory of crime and other "evil" behaviors.[89] In the experiment, "normal" (determined by a battery of tests) male Stanford University student volunteers were randomly assigned to be guards or prisoners in a simulated prison environment. In less than a week, the guards had become dominant and abusive toward the prisoners. The prisoners, in turn, became "mindlessly obedient to the guards' demands" and seemed "zombie-like." The prisoner role dominated all expressions of individual behavior as the prisoners became fixated on their present circumstances and adopted and accepted the guards' negative images of them. Half of the prisoners had to be released early from the experimental prison because of severe emotional and cognitive problems that did not last long but were intense at the time. Even Zimbardo and some of his other experimenter colleagues got caught up in the experimental conditions and did things they later regretted.

The primary lesson of the SPE for Zimbardo is that situational and systemic factors influence good people to do evil things, more so than individualistic or dispositional factors, such as genetic makeup, personality traits, character, or free will.[90] In defining the relationship between the person, situation, and system, Zimbardo writes:

> The Person is an actor on the stage of life whose behavioral freedom is informed by his or her makeup—genetic, biological, physical, and psychological. The Situation is the behavioral context that has the power, through its reward and normative functions, to give meaning and identity to the actor's roles and status. The System consists of the agents and agencies whose ideology, values, and power create situations and dictate the roles and expectations for approved behaviors of actors within its spheres of influence.[91]

Put somewhat differently, situational factors, such as the prison environment and its rules and roles, are the behavioral or social contexts that influence the human action of those under their control. For most people, situational factors are difficult to resist. Systemic factors, such as political and economic power structures and their rules and roles, create situational factors by providing institutional support, authority, and resources. The fundamental problem for Zimbardo, in short, is that "'bad systems' create 'bad situations' create 'bad apples' create 'bad behaviors,' even in good people."[92]

Another lesson of the SPE is that all people are capable of serious criminal behavior under the right situational circumstances. In other words, everyone can learn to be good or evil regardless of genetic inheritance, personality, or family legacy.

A third lesson is that by assuming a good versus evil dichotomy, that is, the idea that "criminals" are fundamentally different from "noncriminals," as is done in the U.S. legal system, for example, "good" people can deny their complicity in "creating, sustaining, perpetuating, or conceding to the conditions" that contribute to crime. Zimbardo cautions that this understanding does not excuse a person's criminal behavior or absolve him or her from responsibility; it only provides a better theory of criminal behavior and a guide to more productive ways of dealing with it.

Many of Zimbardo's ideas have their origins in the symbolic interactionism of George Herbert Mead and appear to have influenced some critical criminologists, such as Stuart Henry and Dragan Milovanovic (all are addressed in Chapter 8).

Policy Implication

According to Zimbardo, by understanding how social influence operates and how people become vulnerable to it, people can resist it instead of being manipulated by it. He advocates addressing criminal behavior using a public health model rather than a medical model of criminality.

Critique

Zimbardo's critics argue that there is "little scientific evidence indicating that situations are more important than dispositions for explaining behavior." They point out that a recent summary of more than twenty-five thousand studies shows that "personality and situations contribute almost equally to various outcomes, and many studies demonstrate the complex ways in which people react differently to similar situations." Critics maintain that "people vary in their propensity for antisocial behavior and that environments transact with personalities." They claim that "some people are more likely to turn out to be bad apples than others, and this is particularly evident in certain situations."[93]

Study Questions

1. What is the relationship between intelligence and criminality and delinquency?
2. In Freudian theory, what is crime? What are causes of crime in Freudian theory?
3. What has research discovered about the relationship between personality and criminality?

4. How would Maslow explain crime?
5. How would Halleck explain crime?
6. How would Zimbardo explain crime?
7. What are some crime prevention implications of psychological/psychoan-alytic theories?
8. What are some general problems with psychological/psychoanalytic theo-ries of crime causation?
9. How do psychological/psychoanalytic theories of crime causation compare with theories previously described in this book?

Notes

1. Curran and Renzetti (2001).
2. Curran and Renzetti (2001).
3. See Vold and Bernard (1986:72).
4. Vold and Bernard (1986:72).
5. See Vold and Bernard (1986:72); also see Gould (1981).
6. Vold (1979:83).
7. Quoted in Vold (1979:83).
8. Sutherland and Cressey (1974:152).
9. Gordon (1976); Hirschi and Hindelang (1977).
10. Gordon (1976); Hirschi and Hindelang (1977); also see Vold and Bernard (1986:77); Andrews and Bonta (1994:133). Note that the studies dealt with delinquency and not adult criminality.
11. Hirschi and Hindelang (1977); also see Vold and Bernard (1986:78).
12. Also see Wilson and Herrnstein (1985:171, Chap. 10); Denno (1985).
13. Levin (1997:291).
14. Also see Ellis and Walsh (1997). For a critique of *The Bell Curve* and by implication the other books, see Cullen, Gendreau, Jarjoura, and Wright (1997).
15. The following description is from Rushton (1995) and Levin (1997). The latter proposition is shared by social control theory described in Chapter 6.
16. See Levin (1997:324–327).
17. Bartol (1991:132).
18. Winfree and Abadinsky (2010).
19. Gould (1996).
20. Sternberg, Grigorenko, and Kidd (2005:52).
21. Sternberg et al. (2005:50).

22. See the AAA website at http://www.aaanet.org/issues/policy-advocacy/AAA-Statement-on-Race.cfm.

23. Patrinos (2004).

24. Human Genome Project Information at http://www.ornl.gov/sci/techresources/Human_Genome/elsi/minorities.shtml (accessed August 18, 2009).

25. Connor (2006).

26. Mountain and Risch (2004:S48).

27. Smedley and Smedley (2005).

28. Vold (1979:97); however, see Andrews and Bonta (1994:133) for a different view.

29. Vold (1979:97).

30. See Vold (1979:97); Cullen et al. (1997:391).

31. Unless indicated otherwise, material in this section is from Freud (1953); Hutchins (1952); Andrews and Bonta (1994); Woodworth and Sheehan (1964); Hall (1954). Theorists who have applied psychoanalytic theory to the explanation of crime and delinquency are Aichorn (1935); Healy and Bronner (1926, 1936); Alexander and Healy (1935); Abrahamsen (1944, 1960); Friedlander (1947); Redl and Wineman (1951, 1952).

32. Einstadter and Henry (1995:110).

33. Martin, Mutchnick, and Austin (1990:79).

34. Andrews and Bonta (1994:74).

35. Andrews and Bonta (1994:74).

36. Also see Martin et al. (1990:78–79).

37. See Curran and Renzetti (1994:128).

38. Andrews and Bonta (1994:210).

39. Curran and Renzetti (1994:110).

40. See Jeffery (1977:132, 138).

41. Vold and Bernard (1986:128); but see Andrews and Bonta (1994:63) for the opposite view.

42. Einstadter and Henry (1995:116–117); Curran and Renzetti (1994:128); Vold and Bernard (1986:116).

43. Martin et al. (1990:84).

44. See Jeffery (1977:138–139).

45. Andrews and Bonta (1994:195).

46. See Jeffery (1977:138).

47. Andrews and Bonta (1994:195).

48. Andrews and Bonta (1994:195).

49. Vold and Bernard (1986:117).

50. Tappan (1951:11).

51. Bernard, Snipes, and Gerould (2010).

52. McCrae and Costa (1990).
53. Eysenck (1977).
54. Tellegen (1985).
55. Cloninger, Svrakic, and Przybeck (1993).
56. Bernard et al. (2010:73).
57. Cullen and Agnew (2006).
58. Glueck and Glueck (1950:275).
59. Caspi et al. (1994).
60. Caspi et al. (1994).
61. Caspi et al. (1994:169).
62. Caspi et al. (1994).
63. Caspi et al. (1994:167).
64. Miller and Lynam (2001).
65. Miller and Lynam (2001).
66. Miller and Lynam (2001).
67. Wortley (2011:99–100).
68. Lilienfeld and Arkowitz (2007–2008:80).
69. Lilienfeld and Arkowitz (2007–2008).
70. Winfree and Abadinsky (2010).
71. Lilienfeld and Arkowitz (2007–2008).
72. Lilienfeld and Arkowitz (2007–2008).
73. Bernard et al. (2010).
74. Bernard et al. (2010:75). See also Hare (1999).
75. Bernard et al. (2010:75).
76. See Yochelson and Samenow (1976).
77. Walters (2000:186).
78. Walters (2000).
79. Maslow (1970, originally published in 1954).
80. Cullen (1994).
81. Cullen (1994:530).
82. Cullen (1994:530–531); also see Chamlin and Cochran (1997) and De-Fronzo (1997).
83. Cullen (1994:551).
84. Cullen (1994:551–552).
85. Cullen (1994:552). Cullen and Wright (1997) have recently combined social support theory and general strain theory (see Chapter 6).
86. Halleck (1967).
87. See Katz (1988) for a similar view.
88. Halleck (1967:76–80).
89. Zimbardo (2008); also see Warr (2002:64–65).

90. This also was the lesson of psychologist Stanley Milgram's famous experiment of obedience to authority. See Milgram (1974).
91. Zimbardo (2008:445–446).
92. Zimbardo (2008:445).
93. Donnellan, Fraley, and Krueger (2007).

6

Macrosociological Theories

The Contributions of Durkheim
The Theory of the Chicago School or Social Disorganization Theory
Situational Crime Prevention and Routine Activity Theories
Functionalism
Anomie and Strain Theories

In Chapters 6 and 7, sociological theories of crime are examined. Unlike biological or psychological theories that, for the most part, explore factors related to crime that are *internal* to the individual, sociological theories of crime look for correlates of crime that are *external* to the individuals involved. Examples of possible external causes of crime include neighborhood organization, poverty, poor parenting, and delinquent peers. The material in this chapter focuses on macrosociological theories, which examine how the organization or structure of a society can generate an environment conducive to crime.

The Contributions of Durkheim

Many of the sociological theories of crime (*sociological positivism*) have their roots in the work of the French sociologist Emile Durkheim (1858–1917).[1] Like Saint-Simon and Comte before him, Durkheim's theory emerged during a period of profound social change in France. French society was still recovering from the Revolution of 1789, Napoleon's defeat at Waterloo, and defeats in the Franco-Prussian War.[2] In addition, the Industrial Revolution was sweeping across Europe.[3] According to one commentator, "[i]n terms of immediacy and massiveness of impact to human thought and values, it is impossible to find revolutions of comparable magnitude anywhere in human history."[4]

Rejecting the idea that social phenomena, such as crime, can be explained solely by the biology or psychology of individuals, Durkheim argued instead that society is not the direct reflection of the characteristics of its individual members. Rather, society is a unique reality; it is more than a simple aggregate of individuals.[5] For Durkheim, social laws and institutions are "social facts" that dominate individuals by limiting their choices, and all that people can do is to submit to them. The coercion may be formal as, for example, by means of law, or informal as, for example, by means of peer pressure.[6] Like Comte before him, Durkheim maintained that, with the aid of positive science, all that people can expect is to discover the direction or course of social laws so that they can adapt to them with the least amount of pain.

In *The Division of Labor in Society* (1893), Durkheim describes how modernization changes the way in which society regulates the behavior of its members. *Modernization* refers to the transition from a rural, agrarian society (or what Durkheim called a *mechanical society*) into a more industrialized society (or *organic society*). Durkheim believed that occupational specialization (that is, the *division of labor*), which was becoming more commonplace at the time, limited people's ability to choose, and forced them to live in a world characterized by a "forced division of labor." Consequently, people were often forced into roles in which their natural abilities were generally not used.[7] Furthermore, Durkheim argued that modernization weakens the collective conscience. The *collective conscience* refers to the general sense of morality of the times or the shared beliefs and attitudes that unify a society.[8] A consequence of both the division of labor and a weakening of the collective conscience for Durkheim is what he called *anomie*.

For Durkheim, *anomie* is the breakdown of social norms or the dissociation of the individual from the collective conscience and is expressed in two interrelated ways: *lack of regulation* and *lack of integration*.[9] In the former, the collective conscience is unable to regulate human desires; in the latter, "individualism" is promoted to such a degree that people become so selfish or egoistic that they no longer care about the welfare of other human beings. Durkheim argued that anomie is the cause of many social ills including crime. However, Durkheim did not test his theory of anomie on crime. In his work *Suicide* (1897), he examined how anomie can lead to higher rates of suicide. He assumed that because crime and suicide are "social ills," anomie would have a similar effect on both phenomena.[10]

For Durkheim, crime, too, is a social fact.[11] It is a normal aspect of society, because it is found in all societies. Nevertheless, different types of societies should experience greater or lesser degrees of crime. Not only did Durkheim believe that crime is a normal aspect of society, he also believed that crime is functional for society.[12] For example, crime marks the boundaries of morality.[13] In other words, people would not know what acceptable behavior was if it were not for crime. Crime also functions to promote social solidarity by uniting law-abiding people against crime. In a sense, the punishment of criminals is the payoff to citizens who obey the law.[14] According to Durkheim, the social solidarity function of crime is so important that crime would have to be created if it did not already exist. Additionally, crime is functional because it provides a means of achieving necessary social change through, for example, civil disobedience and, under certain circumstances, directly contributes to social change, as, for example, in the repeal of prohibition.[15]

Policy Implications

To reduce crime, Durkheim advocated the development of a spontaneous division of labor in which unmerited social inequities would not exist.[16] To help achieve this goal, Durkheim promoted the formation of occupational associations and the abolition of inheritance.[17]

As noted, many of the major sociological theories of crime (actually theories of delinquency) come directly from Durkheim's ideas. Among them are anomie or strain theory, differential opportunity theory, theories of culture conflict, cultural transmission and cultural deviance, social disorganization theory, functionalist theory, control theories, and social reaction theories.

The Theory of the Chicago School or Social Disorganization Theory

In the 1920s, members of the Department of Sociology at the University of Chicago engaged in an effort to identify environmental factors associated with crime. Specifically, they attempted to uncover the relationship between a neighborhood's crime rate and the characteristics of the neighborhood. It was the first large-scale study of crime in the United States and was to serve as the basis for many future investigations into the causes of crime and delinquency.

The research of the Chicago School was based on a model taken from ecology; as a result, that school is sometimes called the Chicago School of Human Ecology.[18] *Ecology* is a branch of biology in which the interrelationship of plants and animals is studied in its natural environment.[19] In biology, this interrelationship is referred to as *symbiosis*. Robert Park (1864–1944) was the first of the Chicago theorists to propose this *organic* or *biological analogy*, that is, the similarity between the organization of plant and animal life in nature and the organization of human beings in societies.[20]

At the time, Chicago was the second largest city in the United States, with a population of more than two million people. Its population had doubled every ten years between 1860 and 1910 as the result of industrialization and massive immigration.[21] Park and his colleague, Ernest Burgess (1886–1966), described the growth of American cities like Chicago in ecological terms. Although recognizing that natural and historical factors could influence their growth, Park and Burgess nonetheless argued that cities tend to grow radially from their center in concentric circles through a process of invasion, dominance, and succession.[22] That is, a cultural or ethnic group invades a territory occupied by another group and dominates that new territory until it is displaced or succeeded by another group, and the cycle repeats itself. As for the concentric circles, from the core to the periphery, zone 1 is the central business district or, in Chicago, the "Loop"; zone 2 is the transitional area, usually the slums; zone 3 is the area where the homes of blue-collar workers are located; zone 4 is a residential area of nicer single-family houses and expensive apartments; and zone 5 is the suburbs.[23]

This model of human ecology was used by other Chicago theorists, most notably Clifford R. Shaw (1896–1957) and Henry D. McKay (1899–1980) in their studies of juvenile delinquency in Chicago.[24] Shaw assumed that delinquents were basically normal human beings and that their delinquent behavior was caused by environmental factors peculiar to specific neighborhoods. To test his theory, Shaw examined police and court records to find neighborhoods with the most delinquents. He then analyzed the characteristics of those neighborhoods. To aid them in their investigation, Shaw, together with McKay, created three types of maps: (1) *spot maps* that located the residences of the youth in police and court records, (2) *rate maps* that showed the percentage of the total juvenile population in 140-square-mile areas that had police or court records, and (3) *zone maps* that showed the rates of male juvenile delinquency within the concentric zones of the city.

An analysis of the maps showed that zone 2 consistently had the highest rates of delinquency in the city despite almost complete turnovers in the ethnic composition of the population living in that zone. Thus, for example, in 1884, approximately 90 percent of the population in zone 2 was Irish, German, Scandinavian, Scottish, or English, and the children of those groups had the highest rates of delinquency in Chicago. By 1930, 85 percent of zone 2 was Italian, Polish, Slavic, or Czech—almost a complete turnover, and the children of those groups had the highest rates of delinquency in Chicago. Furthermore, when the ethnic groups moved out of zone 2, the high delinquency rates did not follow them. In short, something about zone 2 produced high delinquency rates regardless of the ethnic composition of the population that lived there.

Shaw also discovered that even in the worst neighborhoods in zone 2, only about 20 percent of the youths had police or court records. Therefore, he began to assemble extensive "life histories" of individual delinquents to discover what environmental factors affected their behavior. From the life histories,[25] he confirmed that most of the delinquents were not much different from nondelinquents with regard to personality traits, physical condition, and intelligence. He did find that the areas of high delinquency were "socially disorganized." For the Chicago theorists, *social disorganization* is the condition in which (1) the usual controls over delinquents are largely absent, (2) delinquent behavior is often approved of by parents and neighbors, (3) many opportunities are available for delinquent behavior, and (4) little encouragement, training, or opportunity exists for legitimate employment.[26]

Shaw also discovered that delinquent activities began as play activities at an early age, that older boys taught these activities to younger boys, that the normal methods of official social control could not stop this process, and that it was only later in a delinquent career that a boy identified himself with the criminal world.[27] In sum, Shaw and his colleagues, using multiple levels of analysis, concluded that delinquency was the product of a *detachment from conventional groups*—a term nearly synonymous with Durkheim's concept of *lack of integration*—caused by social disorganization in certain areas of the city. As noted earlier, the theory is sometimes referred to as *social disorganization theory*.

Policy Implications: The Chicago Area Project

Because Shaw believed that juvenile delinquency was caused by social disorganization, he did not think that individual treatment of delinquents would be effective in reducing the problem.[28] So, in 1932, Shaw and his colleagues established the Chicago Area Project (CAP), which was designed to prevent delinquency through the organization and empowerment of neighborhood residents.[29] Twenty-two neighborhood centers, staffed and controlled by local residents, were established in six areas of Chicago. The centers had two principal functions. One was to coordinate community resources such as schools, churches, labor unions, and industries to solve community problems, and the other was to sponsor activity programs such as scouts, summer camps, and sports leagues to develop a positive interest by individuals in their own welfare and to unite citizens to solve their own problems.

For a quarter of a century, the CAP served neighborhoods of Chicago and only ceased operation in 1957 following Shaw's death.[30] Early evaluations of the project suggested that it had a negligible effect on delinquency.[31] However, CAP has since been resurrected and is still operating today. Newer research shows that CAP reduces recidivism.[32]

The Re-Emergence of Social Disorganization Theory

By the 1960s, Shaw and McKay's work had lost its appeal, but by the mid-1980s it enjoyed a re-emergence.[33] Their work fit in nicely with an examination of the "macro-level," or ecological correlates of crime that became popular in the early 1980s.[34] Macro-level analyses explore the effect of factors such as poverty rates, neighborhood characteristics, population density, and family disruption on rates of crime in a geographical unit like a city or region. "Micro-level" analyses, on the other hand, focus on how individual factors like personality or peer group contribute to an individual's criminality.

In 1989, Sampson and Groves published a test of social disorganization theory that has become a classic in criminology.[35] Using data from the British Crime Survey, the researchers measured social disorganization by asking questions that, when combined, indicated "whether community members were willing to supervise rowdy teenagers, had friends locally, and participated in neighborhood voluntary organizations."[36] Their findings "established that communities characterized by sparse friendship networks, unsupervised teenage peer groups, and low organizational participation had disproportionately high rates of crime and delinquency."[37] A replication of this study published in 2003 suggests that Sampson and Groves' results are consistent over time. Lowenkamp and his colleagues found that "certain structural characteristics of communities affect the ability of residents to impose social control mechanisms over their members, and that the loss of such control mechanisms affects rates of crime."[38]

Since its re-emergence, research based on the work of Shaw and McKay has received broad support. In 2005, Pratt and Cullen conducted a meta-analysis of more than two hundred empirical studies looking at the effects of several variables measuring "concentrated disadvantage," including "measures of racial heterogeneity, income-based estimates of socioeconomic status, and indicators of residential mobility."[39] They found that "[a]cross all studies, social disorganization and resource/economic deprivation theories receive strong empirical support."[40]

Sampson's Theory of Collective Efficacy

In an extension of social disorganization theory, Robert Sampson (1956–) and his colleagues argued in a series of articles that crime is higher in some urban areas because of residents' inability to exercise "collective efficacy."[41] *Col-*

lective efficacy combines indicators of "a particular kind of social structure (cohesion, with an emphasis on working trust and mutual support) with the culturally tinged dimension of *shared expectations* for social control."[42] In effect, Sampson and his colleagues argue that collective efficacy mediates the negative effects of concentrated poverty, residential mobility, and a lack of residential social ties on violence, victimization, and disorder.[43]

The results of their research suggest that collective efficacy is associated with lower rates of violence, even when structural characteristics such as poverty and population density, as well as several individual level characteristics such as race and socioeconomic status, are controlled. Collective efficacy also appears to have an independent effect on violence.[44] This work is significant because it identifies the mechanisms *through which* community disorganization can lead to higher crime rates. Namely, residents in neighborhoods lacking collective efficacy do not have the cohesiveness to act in an effective way to solve community problems.[45]

Several studies conducted internationally also have suggested that measures of social disorganization are related to both violent victimization and official measures of property crime.[46] For example, collective efficacy was found to minimize the rate of residential burglary in Tianjin, China.[47] Similarly, in an analysis of 2,500 neighborhoods in the Netherlands, Van Wilsem and his colleagues found that "the chance of becoming the victim of a crime is higher not only in disadvantaged neighborhoods, but also in neighborhoods that are undergoing strong socioeconomic improvement."[48] The finding that crime is higher in *improving* neighborhoods is consistent with Shaw and McKay's original contention that rapid residential turnover diminishes residents' ability to exercise collective social control. Apparently, this is the case even if those moving into the area are more affluent residents, which occurs in neighborhoods going through gentrification.

Critique

One of the problems with the theory of the Chicago School is the presumed relationship among social disorganization, detachment from conventional groups, and delinquency. The relationship may be a spurious one. In other words, other factors may contribute to social disorganization, detachment from conventional groups, and delinquency that make them appear to be related to each other when, in fact, they are not (remember the relationship between the sale of ice cream and the homicide rate?).

In this regard, one must ask, Why do cities develop in the way that they do? Why do delinquency areas emerge in certain areas of the city? Are delinquency areas inherent in the growth of cities? Most cities do not grow randomly. Their growth is predicated on the values and decisions of political and economic elites. The early Chicago neighborhoods, for example, were planned with great deliberation.

One of the factors that contributes to the decline of city neighborhoods is the decades-old practice of *redlining* where banks refuse to lend money for home improvements in an area because of the race or ethnicity of the inhabitants.[49] What usually occurs in redlined areas (a practice, incidentally, that still occurs today despite its illegality) is that neighborhood and property values decline dramatically until they reach a point where land speculators and developers, usually in conjunction with political leaders, buy the land for urban renewal or gentrification and make fortunes in the process. In short, political and economic elites may cause social disorganization, detachment from conventional groups, and delinquency, perhaps not intentionally, by the conscious decisions that they make.[50]

The Chicago theorists did not challenge the destructive practices of Chicago's political and economic elite; thus, they merely addressed the symptoms of the problem rather than its causes.[51] In so doing, the Chicago theorists revealed their own timidity (perhaps they were co-opted or "bought off"), antiurban bias, and romanticism—yearning for a return to village life and the social controls of communal living.[52]

From an entirely different vantage point, the Chicago theorists can be criticized for suggesting that certain inner-city neighborhoods were socially disorganized in the first place. Sutherland, who is discussed in Chapter 7 in the section on learning theories, recognized this problem when he substituted in his own theory the concept of "differential social organization" for the Chicago School's social disorganization. To call a particular area socially disorganized is to impose one's own values of what constitutes social organization (usually the values of the dominant culture) and to fail to appreciate that an area may be organized differently based on a different set of values, especially the values of the people who live in the area.[53] In short, critics suggest that the Chicago theorists observed diversity in social organization but, in light of their own biases (e.g., Park, Shaw, and McKay grew up in rural America), interpreted what they saw as social disorganization.[54]

Another related problem was the organic or biological analogy used by the Chicago theorists to describe the development of society.[55] Human society, as noted, is regulated by cultural and legal forces that only superficially resemble the forces that govern the survival of the fittest in nature. In their apparent naivete, the Chicago theorists neglected to consider the effects of political struggle on social change.[56]

Overprediction is another problem. The Chicago theorists could never explain adequately why only a relatively small percentage of youths in the delinquency areas actually became delinquent. Even within areas that were considered socially disorganized, there were groups, such as Asians or European Jews, whose children did not have high rates of delinquency.[57] If social disorganization and detachment from conventional groups were such powerful causes of delinquency, then why were not more youths affected by their influence? Social disorganization theory also does not explain especially bizarre delinquent behaviors (such as those thought to be evidence of mental illness) very well.[58]

The overprediction problem might be related to another one: the use of official police and court records to measure delinquency in a given area.[59] Perhaps the official records did not capture the true extent of delinquency in an area because many of the youths who engaged in delinquent activities escaped detection or official processing. On the other hand, neighborhoods in zone 2 may have evidenced the most delinquency because the official statistics do not capture much delinquency in middle- and upper-class neighborhoods.

The theory of the Chicago School has also been criticized for being based on circular reasoning.[60] That is, social disorganization is the cause of delinquency, and delinquency is an indicator of social disorganization.

Finally, there is the ecological fallacy and the problem with the utility of the theory. The *ecological fallacy* refers to the explanation of one level of analysis based on the examination of a different level of analysis (for instance, the explanation of individual behavior based on a study of group rates).[61] The Chicago theorists based their analysis on group rates and so, for example, they found that neighborhoods in zone 2 had the highest rates of delinquency. The problem is that the theory does not allow the prediction, with any degree of certainty, of who among those youths living in zone 2 is likely to become delinquent.[62] The theory's usefulness, therefore, is diminished.

Situational Crime Prevention and Routine Activity Theories

While the Chicago School examined the criminogenic characteristics of neighborhoods, two derivatives of that theory—*situational crime prevention theory* (sometimes called *opportunity theory*) and *routine activity theory*—focus on how *opportunities* to commit crime are presented by the physical environment and the everyday actions of individuals. In other words, attention is shifted from offender motivation to the presence of opportunities to commit crime, and what can be done to limit those opportunities.[63] Both perspectives borrow heavily from classical theory by assuming a rational, moti-vated offender.[64]

Situational Crime Prevention Theory

Situational crime prevention theory is most closely associated with the work of Ronald Clarke (1941–), who was discussed in Chapter 2 in connection with rational choice theory. Clarke argues that reducing crime is contingent on two fac-tors: reducing the physical opportunities needed to commit crime and increas-ing the risks of being caught.[65] Physical opportunities include unattended valuables, unlocked doors, and distracted pedestrians. One can "get caught" by a police of-ficer, or by any observer who is likely to take action against the offender, such as homeowners, doormen, parking lot attendants, and security officers.[66]

Clarke's opportunity theory was influenced by architect Oscar Newman's (1935–2004) *Defensible Space: Crime Prevention Through Urban Design.*[67] In his book, Newman extended the theory of the Chicago School to a consideration of the actual physical form of the urban environment and how that form affects crime. For example, he reports that poorly designed buildings and surround-ings of low- and middle-income housing projects have crime rates much higher than better-designed projects that have similar types of residents and densities.

Policy Implications

Defensible space is a model for residential environments designed to inhibit criminality through a range of mechanisms that include "real and symbolic barriers, strongly defined areas of influence, and improved opportunities for surveillance." The goal, like that of the Chicago Area Project before it, is to re-duce crime by bringing the environment under the control of its residents. The idea of increasing surveillance, incidentally, is the basis for the popular neighborhood watch programs.[68]

In January 1995, Henry G. Cisneros, then Secretary of Housing and Urban Development (HUD), published a widely distributed essay lauding the merits of defensible space. Cisneros recognized that defensible space is not a "cure-all" for the problems of crime and delinquency in inner-city neighborhoods and admitted that structural changes are necessary to affect the crime problem as a whole. Nevertheless, he believed that "the practical successes of defensible space initiatives [and] the fact that they can be implemented quickly and re-quire very little public funding ... make defensible space an approach well worth our consideration."[69]

According to both Cisneros and Newman, the most promising applications of the defensible space concept are to neighborhoods that are deteriorating but continue to "retain residents and other stakeholders who still have hope that traumatic decline can be prevented."[70] They are less optimistic about devastated areas of older cities where a sense of community has all but disappeared.

Critique

Despite Cisneros's optimism about the utility of defensible space, Wilson and Herrnstein warn that although "there are physical changes that may reduce the rates of some kinds of crime ... [t]he role played in this reduction by such factors ... remains unclear."[71]

Routine Activity Theory

Another derivative of the theory of the Chicago School is the routine activity theory of Lawrence E. Cohen (1945–) and Marcus Felson (1947–). Cohen and Felson's "routine activity approach" to criminality extends human ecology analysis to the explanation of crime and victimization rates over time.[72]

For Cohen and Felson, structural changes in the routine activities of everyday life affect crimes against both persons and property. Structural changes in routine activities influence those crimes through their effect on any one of three factors: (1) "motivated offenders" (for example, teenage boys, unemployed people, drug addicts), (2) "suitable targets" (such as unlocked homes or cars), and (3) "the absence of capable guardians against a violation" (for instance, the absence of police officers, homeowners, security systems).[73] Cohen and Felson maintain that all three of the factors are necessary for the successful completion of crimes.[74]

It is important to emphasize that Cohen and Felson do not attempt to explain criminal motivation but, instead, assume that all people will commit crime unless they are prevented from doing so. Criminal activities are viewed, by Cohen and Felson, as routine activities. They conclude that crime is so rooted in the legitimate opportunity structure of our society and in the freedom and prosperity that many people enjoy, that to reduce crime will require substantial modifications in our everyday way of life.[75]

Policy Implications

The crime prevention implications of routine activity theory focus on potential crime victims who must change their lifestyles so they are no longer such easy targets for criminal offenders. Much of the emphasis is on securing the immediate environment through creating defensible space, target hardening, and increasing the presence of capable guardians. Also implied in the theory, though de-emphasized by its authors, is increasing legitimate opportunities—a principal crime prevention implication of anomie theories (which are discussed later in this chapter).

Critique

Routine activity theory has been criticized for its assumption that all people will commit crime unless they are prevented from doing so—an assumption that this theory shares with social control theories (which are discussed in Chapter 7). Some criminologists take issue with the theory's assumption that criminal motivation is rooted in human nature.[76]

Another problem with routine activity theory is that it fails to explain its key concept—routine activities. In other words, the theory does not specify which routine activities, or which type of such activities, affect crimes.[77] Do all routine activities affect crimes? Do all routine activities influence the number of motivated offenders, the availability of suitable targets, or the degree of guardianship? Probably not. In addition, the theory does not specify how the three key concepts interact to affect crime. It treats them as equally important, which they probably are not. The theory, as formulated, has also been criticized for being applicable only to "ordinary" predatory crime.[78]

A problem with the crime prevention implications of routine activity theory or, specifically, with its focus on securing the immediate environment, is that such a strategy is likely only to displace the criminal activity of motivated offenders to less secure environments.[79] This is a problem with Newman's defensible space concept as well. Thus, taken to its logical conclusion, the theory creates a siege mentality in which people who can afford it secure themselves against crime, leaving those people who cannot afford it to fare for themselves as best they can. It also creates the justification for an Orwellian society in which surveillance of the population is pervasive and privacy is a rare commodity.

Finally, routine activity theory has been criticized for coming close to blaming the victim. In suggesting that a solution to the crime problem depends on potential victims changing their routine activities, the theory implies that the routine activities of women, for example, are what causes rape and sexual assault—an implication that many people, particularly feminist critics, find offensive.[80]

Functionalism

Talcott Parsons (1902–1979), a Harvard sociologist, is credited with the introduction of functional theory, or structural-functional theory, in the United States in 1937.[81] At the time, the United States and other western industrial societies were in the midst of the worst depression ever experienced and on the verge of World War II.[82] Many observers believed that free enterprise had failed and that capitalism was doomed to either socialism on the left or fascism on the right.[83]

Within this context, Parsons and his colleagues at Harvard engaged in an effort to produce a theory of society that would aid in the preservation of the free enterprise system (capitalism) and, of course, their privileged way of life. The result was functionalist theory, and its basic premise is as follows: The world is a system of interrelated parts, and each part makes a necessary contribution to the viability of the system (a *systems model* of society).[84] Crime, in this view, is a necessary part of the system (an idea borrowed from Durkheim).

To illustrate this theory as it is applies to crime, consider the explanation of the latent functions of female prostitution by Kingsley Davis (1908–1997), a student of Parsons and a former president of the American Sociological Association. Functions are presumed to be either manifest (intended) or latent (unintended and often unrecognized).[85] In describing its latent functions, Davis identifies the ways that female prostitution contributes to the viability of the social system—a not so obvious relationship that can only be revealed by the well-trained and astute social scientist.[86]

Davis points out that female prostitution functions to satisfy sexual desires with little psychic or financial investment.[87] It requires neither emotional involvement nor the expense associated with dating and marriage. More importantly, female prostitution helps preserve the institution of the family and the aura of the "good" girl by relieving wives and girlfriends of the chore of satisfying their husbands' and boyfriends' "perverse" sexual desires. It also allows a small number of women to service a multitude of lusting single men in society, including the less desirable among them. Finally, female prostitution is functional even for prostitutes themselves because in few other occupations can they earn as much. Similar functionalist arguments have been made for the urban political machine and even for poverty.[88]

Nearly one hundred years before Parsons, Karl Marx anticipated the functionalist argument. In a passage dripping with irony, Marx wrote:

> The criminal produces not only crimes, but also criminal law, and with this also the professor who gives lectures on criminal law, and in addition to this the inevitable compendium in which this same professor throws his lectures onto the general market as "commodities." ... The criminal moreover produces the whole of the police and of criminal justice, constables, judges, hangmen, juries, etc.; and all these different lines of business, which form equally many categories of the

social division of labor, develop different capacities of the human spirit, create new needs and new ways of satisfying them. Torture alone has given rise to the most ingenious mechanical inventions, and employed many honorable craftsmen in the production of its instruments.... Crime takes a part of the superfluous population off the labor market and thus reduces competition among the laborers—up to a certain point preventing wages from falling below the minimum— the struggle against crime absorbs another part of this population. Thus the criminal comes in as one of those natural "counterweights" which bring about a correct balance and open up a whole perspective of "useful" occupations.

The effects of the criminal on the development of productive power can be shown in detail. Would locks ever have reached their present degree of excellence had there been no thieves? Would the making of banknotes have reached its present perfection had there been no forgers? ... Crime, through its constantly new methods of attack on property, constantly calls into being new methods of defense, and so is as productive as strikes for the invention of machines. And if one leaves the sphere of private crime, would the world market ever have come into being but for national crime?[89]

Policy Implication

Because functionalist theorists view crime as an integral part of society, necessary for its existence, they do not want to prevent crime. They only want to contain it within acceptable boundaries so that it does not destroy society.[90]

Critique

One of the more obvious problems with functionalist theory is that it fails to ask the question, Functional for whom? Who is the system? Failure to entertain this question inhibits the exploration of just how a particular phenomenon, such as crime, affects different groups within society.[91] This problem stems from a second one: the erroneous assumption that there is a consensus in society about moral values. The theory ignores social conflict.[92] A third problem is the inherent class bias of the theory. It promotes the "system" and social stability, regardless of how oppressive the system might be, over alternative social arrangements and social change.[93] A fourth and related problem is that the conception of social order in functionalist theory is based on elite definitions and not the definitions of the average citizen.[94] Thus, a fifth problem is that the "system" is viewed as greater or more important than the individuals that constitute it.[95] Functionalist theory, in short, is an elitist and politically conservative ideology.[96]

Other problems with functionalist theory are that it presents a view of society that often bears little resemblance to the society most people experience, its empirical work is based largely on secondary sources, it ignores the criminalization process (that is, how the established power structure creates crime), and it is untestable.[97] Regarding testability, how could one possibly falsify a functionalist proposition?

Anomie and Strain Theories

Like functionalists, anomie theorists use a systems model to describe society. However, unlike functionalists, anomie theorists do not believe that all phenomena in society are functional. They believe that some phenomena are dysfunctional, that there are contradictions in society.[98]

Merton's Anomie Theory

In an article published in 1938, one year after Parsons introduced functionalist theory in the United States, Robert K. Merton (1910–2003), who was mentored by Talcott Parsons at Harvard,[99] observed that a major contradiction existed in the United States between cultural goals and the social structure. Adopting but also reformulating Durkheim's concept, he called the contradiction *anomie*. Specifically, Merton argued that in the United States the cultural goal of achieving wealth is deemed possible for all citizens even though the social structure limits the legitimate institutionalized means available for obtaining the goal. For Merton, legitimate institutionalized means are the Protestant work ethic (that is, hard work, education, and deferred gratification); illegitimate means are force and fraud.[100] Because the social structure effectively limits the availability of legitimate institutionalized means, a strain is placed on people. Some theorists have referred to Merton's anomie theory as *strain theory*.[101] However, Merton rejected the label "strain theory" because of its psychological connotations.[102] Merton believed that anomie could affect people in all social classes, but he acknowledged that it would most likely affect members of the lower class.[103]

Merton believed that individuals adapt to the problem of anomie in one of several different ways: (1) conformity, (2) innovation, (3) ritualism, (4) retreatism, or (5) rebellion.[104] According to Merton, most people adapt by conforming; they "play the game."[105] Conformers pursue the cultural goal of wealth only through legitimate institutional means. Innovation is the adaptation at the root of most crime. After rejecting legitimate institutional means, innovators pursue the cultural goal of wealth through illegitimate means. Ritualism is the adaptation of the individual who "takes no chances," usually a member of the lower middle class. Ritualists do not actively pursue the cultural goal of wealth (they are willing to settle for less, oftentimes hoping that their children will succeed where they have not) but follow the legitimate institutional means anyway. Retreatists include alcoholics, drug addicts, psychotics, and other outcasts of society. Retreatists "drop out"; they do not pursue the cultural goal of wealth, so they do not employ legitimate institutional means. When their behavior is defined as criminal, retreatists are also a source of crime. Last is the adaptation of rebellion. Rebels reject both the cultural goal of wealth and the legitimate institutional means of achieving it and substitute both different goals and different means. Rebellion can be another source of crime.

In summary, Merton believed that a source of some, but not all, crime and delinquency was anomie,[106] a disjunction or contradiction between the cultural goal of achieving wealth and the social structure's ability to provide legitimate institutional means of achieving the goal.

Cohen's Anomie Theory of Gang Delinquency

Beginning in the mid-1950s, renewed concern developed over the problem of juvenile gangs. Albert K. Cohen (1918–), a student of both Merton and Sutherland, adapted Merton's anomie theory in his attempt to explain gang delinquency.[107] In his book *Delinquent Boys: The Culture of the Gang*, Cohen argued that delinquent acts were generally engaged in by gangs rather than individually and that, unlike adult criminality which is usually utilitarian (serves a useful purpose), gang delinquency was mostly nonutilitarian, malicious, and negativistic.[108] Two other important characteristics of the delinquent gang's subculture were "short-run hedonism" ("there is little interest in long-run goals") and "group autonomy" ("intolerance of restraint except from the informal pressures within the group itself").[109] In attempting to explain gang delinquency, Cohen surmised that it was to gain status among peers or the result of status frustration.[110] Thus, Cohen substituted the goal of status among peers for Merton's goal of achieving wealth.[111]

For Cohen, anomie is experienced by juveniles who are unable to achieve status among peers by socially acceptable means (or "middle-class measuring rods"), such as family name and position in the community or academic or athletic achievement.[112] In response, either they can conform to middle-class values, generated primarily through the public school, and resign themselves to their subordinate position among their peers, or they can rebel (psychologists call it "reaction-formation") and establish their own value structures by turning middle-class values on their head.[113] These new value structures frequently promote the nonutilitarian, malicious, and negativistic behaviors described by Cohen. Juveniles who rebel in this way tend to find each other and to form groups or gangs to validate and reinforce their new values.[114] Like Merton, Cohen believed that anomie can affect juveniles of any social class but that it disproportionately affects juveniles from the lower class.[115]

Cloward and Ohlin's Differential Opportunity Theory

In their book *Delinquency and Opportunity: A Theory of Delinquent Gangs* (1960), Richard Cloward (1926–2001), another student of Merton's, and Lloyd Ohlin (1918–2008) extended Merton's and Cohen's formulations of anomie theory by suggesting that not all gang delinquents adapt to anomie in the same way. They have differential opportunities, both legitimate and illegitimate.

Cloward and Ohlin argue that the type of adaptation made by juvenile gang members depends on the *illegitimate opportunity structure* available to them.[116] They identified three delinquent subcultures or gang types: the criminal, the violent, and the retreatist.[117] According to Cloward and Ohlin, if illegitimate opportunity is available to them, most delinquents will form criminal gangs to make money. However, if neither illegitimate nor legitimate opportunities to make money are available, delinquents often become frustrated and dissatisfied and form violent gangs to vent their anger. Delinquents who adapt in this way probably were the nonutilitarian, malicious, and negativistic ones discussed by Cohen. Finally, some delinquents, for whatever reason, are unable to adapt by joining either criminal or violent gangs. They fail at both criminal and legal activities. These "double failures" retreat from society, as in Merton's retreatist adaptation, and become alcoholics and drug addicts.

Policy Implications

The crime prevention implications of anomie theory are straightforward: reduce aspirations, increase legitimate opportunities, or do both.[118] Increasing legitimate opportunities, already a cornerstone of the Black civil rights movement, struck a responsive chord as the 1960s began. Reducing aspirations, however, received little attention because to attempt it would be tantamount to rejecting the "American dream," a principal source of motivation in a capitalist society.

Attorney General Robert F. Kennedy was so impressed with Cloward and Ohlin's book that he asked Ohlin to help shape a new federal policy on juvenile delinquency.[119] Ohlin's work on that policy became a part of the Juvenile Delinquency Prevention and Control Act of 1961.[120] The legislation included a comprehensive action program, based on Cloward and Ohlin's ideas, to provide employment opportunities and work training, in combination with community organization and improved social services, to disadvantaged youths and their families.[121] The program was modeled after another effort begun by Cloward and Ohlin in the late 1950s in New York City called Mobilization for Youth.[122]

Later the new, national program was expanded to include all members of the lower class, and when Lyndon Johnson assumed the presidency after John F. Kennedy's assassination, the program became the foundation of Johnson's War on Poverty.[123] During the 1960s, billions of dollars were spent to implement the program and to extend legitimate opportunities to the disadvantaged. Some of the best-known products of the program were the Peace Corps, the Jobs Corps, the Comprehensive Employee Training Act (CETA), and Project Head Start.[124] However, the most tangible result of the effort was a tremendous backlash to what political conservatives argued was an ill-conceived effort to expand the welfare bureaucracy.[125] When Richard Nixon assumed the presidency, the program was discontinued because it had failed to achieve its goals.[126]

The failure of the program does not necessarily invalidate anomie theory or its crime prevention implications because, in actuality, the program was never given a fair opportunity to succeed. It encountered massive resistance from the beginning.[127] However, based on the discouraging results of many other subsequent educational and vocational training programs for delinquent youths, the program may have failed anyway even under the best of circumstances.[128]

Nanette J. Davis's assessment of the "opportunity programs" is even harsher. She argues that (1) morally, they functioned to promote negative stereotypes that blamed the victim; (2) economically, they functioned to funnel the poor into dead-end jobs that maintained "the underclass as a marginal labor force, to the advantage of employers"; and (3) politically, they maintained the status quo by controlling social unrest.[129] What the opportunity programs did not do was grant political power or provide financial resources.[130]

Anomie vs. Strain Theory

Several theorists contend that Merton's original theory, along with Cohen's and Cloward and Ohlin's extensions, describes two distinct concepts: strain and anomie.[131] They argue that, on the one hand, *strain* refers to "feelings and emotions that an individual experiences: feelings of stress or frustration or anxiety or depression or anger."[132] On the other hand, they maintain that *anomie* refers to "the characteristics of a society: a situation in which the social structure fails to provide legitimate means to achieve what the culture values."[133] Put differently, "strain" occurs at the individual (or micro) level and can be used to explain individual crime, while "anomie" occurs at the societal level and can be used to understand crime rates at the macro level. As already noted, Merton apparently rejected the "strain" interpretation, and whether Cohen, or Cloward and Ohlin intended to develop two distinct concepts is debatable.[134] Nevertheless, contemporary versions of anomie theory clearly reflect either the micro view or the macro view.

Agnew's General Strain Theory

Strain at the individual level has been most fully developed by Robert Agnew (1953–) in his *General Strain Theory* (GST).[135] Agnew argues that people may not be as goal directed or as conscious of their goals as Merton suggests.[136] According to Agnew, instead of pursuing specific goals, such as monetary success or the American dream, most people are more interested in being treated fairly and justly in whatever activities they pursue.[137] Thus, some people may conclude that based on their own, limited efforts, and compared especially to other people they know, a more limited outcome (for example, a "comfortable" standard of living) may be entirely fair and just.[138]

By integrating learning theory propositions and recasting anomie theory in social-psychological terms, Agnew also identifies additional sources of strain. Strain, he argues, is the result of negative relationships with others: "relationships in which others are not treating the individual as he or she would like to be treated."[139] Types of strain include (1) loss of positively valued stimuli (e.g., breaking up with your girlfriend or boyfriend), (2) experiencing negative or noxious stimuli (e.g., being punished by your parents or fired from your job), and (3) failing to achieve highly valued goals (e.g., dropping out of school due to financial hardship).[140] These strains then generate negative emotions like anger, disappointment, depression, fear, and frustration.[141] Consequently, individuals may engage in various behaviors in an attempt to "alleviate those negative emotions and/or strains associated with them,"[142] and some of those behaviors may be deviant or criminal.[143]

According to Agnew, not all people who are faced with strain will engage in crime. Many people will cope with strain lawfully. However, some people, asserts Agnew, "lack the ability to cope with strains in a legal manner [due to their] individual traits, such as intelligence, social and problem-solving skills, and personality traits."[144] Agnew also believes that some individuals choose crime because they view the costs of crime as low, relative to a legal coping mechanism. In some neighborhoods he writes, youth may receive praise for engaging in school-yard fights and be shunned for "ratting-out" a bully. In short, for Agnew, individuals with ineffective coping mechanisms or for whom crime is praiseworthy are likely to engage in crime as a result of strain.

Agnew's contention that negative relationships and strain are associated with crime has received empirical support from several studies.[145] As Moon and his colleagues observe, "[t]he significant number of studies with diverse populations and research designs that have examined the relationship between strain and delinquency have generally produced results that support GST."[146] In a recent examination of GST in a sample of middle-school students from South Korea, Moon and his colleagues found that several strains were significantly and positively related to one or more types of offending (status, property, and violent).[147] On the other hand, research exploring Agnew's second contention, dealing with why some people respond to strain through crime and others do not, has received inconsistent support.[148]

Messner and Rosenfeld's Institutional Anomie Theory

At the macro or societal level, Steven F. Messner (1951–) and Richard Rosenfeld's (1948–) institutional anomie theory of crime (IAT) is the leading contemporary version of anomie theory.[149] Like Merton, they argue that higher crime rates in the United States are the result of the American dream, which they define as "a commitment to the goal of material success, to be pursued by everyone in society, under conditions of open, individual competition."[150] They explain that:

> The American Dream contributes to high levels of crime in two important ways, one direct and the other indirect. It has a direct effect on crime through the creation of an anomic normative order, that is, an environment in which social norms are unable to exert a strong regulatory force on the members of society. It has an indirect effect on crime by contributing to an institutional balance of power that inhibits the development of strong mechanisms of external social control. The criminogenic tendencies of the American Dream are thus due in part to the distinctive content of the cultural values and beliefs that comprise it and in part to the institutional consequences of these values and beliefs.[151]

In other words, in addition to the strong societal push to achieve material success (direct influence), all other components of American society, such as the family, the church, and the political system, are subservient to economic institutions (indirect influence). For example, "family routines are dominated by the schedules, rewards, and penalties of the labor market."[152] Similarly, students generally seek an education so they can get a good job, not because they value an education *per se*.[153] Consequently, these noneconomic institutions are less able to "effectively socialize or train individuals and to effectively sanction deviant behavior."[154] In terms of policy, Messner and Rosenfeld, sounding very much like critical and radical criminologists (see Chapter 8), propose that a greater emphasis should be placed on mutual support and collective obligations in American Society, and that the push for individual rights and privileges should be de-emphasized.[155]

Attempts to test institutional anomie theory have yielded mixed results.[156] A recent study by Baumer and Gustafson examined whether geographic differences in instrumental crime (i.e., robberies, burglaries, larcenies, and auto thefts) are the result of "the interaction between the degree of commitment among citizens to pursue monetary success goals and the degree of weak commitment among citizens to pursue monetary success goals via legitimate means."[157] The researchers also examined the moderating effects of limited legitimate opportunities, limited educational opportunities, and participation in noneconomic social institutions (e.g., church, community programs). Their results are consistent with the predictions of IAT. They found that a high level of commitment to monetary success combined with weak commitments to legitimate means significantly increases instrumental crime. Further, this relationship is diminished when there is a high rate of participation in noneconomic social institutions.[158]

On the other hand, using data from the World Values Survey, Jenson did not find support for several of the IAT components.[159] For example, he could not substantiate characterizations of the United States as an overly materialistic nation that deemphasizes noneconomic values.

Critique

A criticism of the anomie theories of Merton, Cohen, and Cloward and Ohlin is that they have a middle-class bias.[160] In other words, the theories assume that members of the lower class really want to be middle class and that crime and delinquency among lower-class individuals are reactions to their failure to achieve middle-class goals. Walter B. Miller was one of those critics, and his theory of a unique lower-class culture is discussed in Chapter 7.

The theories of Merton, Cohen, and Cloward and Ohlin have also been criticized for their reliance on official statistics, which focused their attention on lower-class crime and delinquency and caused them to ignore white-collar and government crimes.[161] This need not be the case, however. First, Merton maintained that anomie could affect people in all social classes. Second, Merton's theory could be applied to white-collar crimes by emphasizing the elasticity of the American dream.[162] That is, when has a person achieved great material wealth? Even wealthy people could experience anomie because they have not realized their own expectations about achieving wealth. The recently exposed Ponzi schemes of Bernard Madoff and others are an apt example.

Merton's theory has been accused of the problem of overprediction. That is, if anomie is caused by the inability to achieve the American dream and is as widespread as Merton implies, then there ought to be much more crime than actually occurs.[163] Merton failed to mention that many potential innovators conform because they lack the opportunity, intelligence, or skills to commit crimes.[164] Potential innovators may also conform if their anomie is eased by social supports, an important intervening factor neglected by Merton.[165] (See the section on humanistic psychological theory in Chapter 5, for a description of the concept of social supports.)

A related criticism is that anomie theories ignore individual differences in the understanding of criminal behavior.[166] For example, Merton is charged with assuming that pursuit of the American dream "is a cultural imperative that cuts across class strata, groups, and interests."[167] As such, the theory does not adequately explain gender differences in crime, for example. Merton's theory has also been accused of failing to explain why people choose particular crimes to commit, or why people commit violent and other senseless acts.[168]

Research has also failed to uncover major discrepancies between the aspirations and expectations of delinquents—a necessary component in the production of anomie. Delinquents appear to be low on both.[169] However, this problem may stem from another problem, especially in Cloward and Ohlin's version of the theory. The problem is the lack of clarity of such key concepts as aspirations, opportunity, and delinquent subculture.[170] Another related criticism is that the existence of the specific delinquent subcultures or gang types postulated by Cloward and Ohlin is not supported by research.[171] Critics argue that delinquent gang members seldom specialize in particular delinquent activities. Critics also point out that delinquencies are seldom committed by gangs, but instead are committed by a few companions, usually one or two.[172]

Merton's version of the theory has been accused of simplifying and treating as abstractions enormously complex phenomena such as culture and social structure.[173] One may wonder, for example, how prevalent among the public is the "American dream," as defined by Merton (or, for that matter, Messner and Rosenfeld).[174] Other anomie theorists emphasize other cultural goals besides the "American dream," a point apparently recognized by Merton,[175] and some anomie theorists distinguish between short-term and long-term goals. Kornhauser suggests that anomie may be a product of frustration in achieving either universal human needs, such as those described by Maslow, or socially induced needs, such as Merton's "American dream."[176] Kornhauser also argues that Merton's distinction between goals and means is arbitrary and misleading. For example, honesty, truth, or even the accumulation of great material wealth can be both a means and a goal.[177]

Merton can also be criticized for failing to address the political and economic sources of cultural goals and the social structure that promotes anomie in the first place. Nanette J. Davis, for example, faults Merton for failing to recognize that the myth that "everyone can make it if he [or she] tries" probably is only a "rhetorical device that has the political utility for keeping the 'masses' in their place."[178] In short, Merton can be criticized for not being radical enough in his analysis.

Each of the theories ignores the criminalization process. That is, they fail to consider why or how some harmful and destructive behaviors are defined as criminal, while similar harmful and destructive behaviors are not. Anomie theories also fail to consider the effect that social control has on delinquency[179]—a major emphasis of labeling theory (to be discussed in Chapter 8).

Merton and Cohen stressed the anomie of "failure." What about the anomie of "success" (an event Durkheim anticipated) as experienced, for example, by the overnight superstar who is unable to cope with his or her newfound fame?[180] Each of the theories is based on circular reasoning. In other words, anomie is the cause of crime and delinquency, and crime and delinquency are indicators of anomie. Finally, the theories fail to explain why most delinquents, in gangs or otherwise, reform or abstain from criminality when they become adults, especially when social conditions remain relatively the same.[181]

Study Questions

The Contributions of Durkheim
1. What is the cause of crime for Durkheim?
2. How would Durkheim prevent crime?
3. What is Durkheim's major contribution to crime (actually, delinquency causation) theory?

4. How does Durkheim's theory of crime compare with theories described in previous chapters?

The Theory of the Chicago School or Social Disorganization Theory

5. How would the Chicago theorists explain crime?
6. How would the Chicago theorists prevent crime?
7. What are problems with the theory of the Chicago School?
8. What are two derivatives of the theory of the Chicago School? (Describe them.)
9. What are the policy implications of the two derivatives of the theory of the Chicago School?
10. What are problems with the two derivatives of the theory of the Chicago School?
11. How does the theory of the Chicago School and its derivatives compare with theories previously described in this book?

Functionalism

12. How do functionalists explain crime?
13. What are the policy implications of functionalist theory?
14. What are problems with functionalist theory?
15. How does functionalist theory compare with theories described previously in this book?

Anomie and Strain Theories

16. How would Merton explain crime?
17. How would Cohen explain gang delinquency?
18. What contribution did Cloward and Ohlin make to anomie theory?
19. In what ways have contemporary authors updated Merton's anomie theory?
20. How would anomie theorists prevent crime?
21. What are the problems with anomie theories?
22. How do anomie theories compare with theories described previously in this book?

Notes

1. However, unlike positivists in general, Taylor, Walton, and Young (1974:87) argue that Durkheim rejected the idea that society is based on a value consensus. Instead, they maintain that, for Durkheim, society, at least under a forced division of labor, is characterized by conflict over moral values.

2. Martin, Mutchnick, and Austin (1990:48).
3. See Vold and Bernard (1986:144).
4. Nisbet (1965:20).
5. Durkheim (1964:103).
6. Durkheim (1964:10, 13); also see Taylor et al. (1974:69).
7. Durkheim (1933:375); also see Taylor et al. (1974:75).
8. Durkheim (1933:79); also see Taylor et al. (1974:77).
9. See Taylor et al. (1974:77, 85, 87).
10. Bernard, Snipes, and Gerould (2010).
11. Durkheim (1964:67); also see Taylor et al. (1974:78). Beirne and Messer-schmidt (2000:94) observe that, "for Durkheim ... social phenomena (such as law and crime) have an objective existence of their own and exist quite independently of the individuals who experience them."
12. See Durkheim (1964:70).
13. Taylor et al. (1974:79).
14. See Vold and Bernard (1986:147–148).
15. Durkheim (1964:71); also see Taylor et al. (1974:80). Although Durkheim identifies functions of crime and argues that it is a normal aspect of society, he did not want to be known as an apologist for it. He noted that even though crime is a social fact, we must still abhor it (Durkheim, 1964:72, fn. 13).
16. Durkheim (1933:377).
17. Durkheim (1933:278–279, 378); also see Taylor et al. (1974:77–78, 87–88). Taylor et al. maintain that Durkheim, unlike Comte, was a radical in his politics and approach to social order.
18. Vold and Bernard (1986:160).
19. See Vold and Bernard (1986:160).
20. See Vold and Bernard (1986:161); Davis (1975:46).
21. Vold and Bernard (1986:161).
22. Park, Burgess, and McKenzie (1928).
23. See Vold and Bernard (1986:163–164).
24. Much of the material in this section is from Shaw (1929); Shaw and McKay (1931, 1942); and, especially, Vold and Bernard (1986:165–171).
25. See Shaw (1930, 1931, 1938).
26. See Vold and Bernard (1986:171). In a test of social disorganization theory, Sampson and Groves (1989), following the original conceptualization of Shaw and McKay, employed the following five indicators of social disorganization: (1) residents of low economic status, (2) many different ethnic groups, (3) a high frequency of residential turnover, (4) dysfunctional families, and (5) urbanization.

27. See Vold and Bernard (1986:171–172). Shaw and his colleagues believed that delinquency was culturally transmitted (hence, this part of the theory is sometimes referred to as *cultural transmission theory*; see Williams and McShane (1994:55). Kornhauser (1978:62) claims that within Shaw and McKay's theory is a distinct social control theory of delinquency that has been "blurred" by their "merging it with a cultural deviance [theory] in which they emphasized the 'cultural transmission' of delinquency by the delinquent gang." Social control theory is examined in the next chapter.
28. Vold and Bernard (1986:180).
29. See Vold and Bernard (1986:180–181).
30. Vold and Bernard (1986:181).
31. Vold and Bernard (1986:181).
32. National Institute for Juvenile Justice and Delinquency Prevention (1977:28); Schlossman, Zellman, and Shavelson (1984:46).
33. Cullen and Agnew (2006).
34. Pratt and Cullen (2005).
35. Lowenkamp, Cullen, and Pratt (2003).
36. Cullen and Agnew (2006:90).
37. Sampson and Groves (1989:799).
38. Lowenkamp et al. (2003:366).
39. Pratt and Cullen (2005:392).
40. Pratt and Cullen (2005:373).
41. Sampson (2006:152); see also Sampson, Raudenbush, and Earls (1997); Morenoff, Sampson, and Raudenbush (2001).
42. Sampson (2006:152).
43. Sampson (2006).
44. Sampson (2006).
45. Cullen and Agnew (2006).
46. See Van Wilsem, Wittebrood, and De Graaf (2006); Wong (2007); Zhang, Messner, and Liu (2007).
47. Zhang et al. (2007).
48. Van Wilsem et al. (2006).
49. See, for example, Wilson (1987).
50. See Vold and Bernard (1986:181–182); Einstadter and Henry (1995:142).
51. See Curran and Renzetti (1994:141–142); Vold and Bernard (1986:181–182); Einstadter and Henry (1995:142).
52. See Mills (1942).
53. See Suttles (1968).
54. See Matza (1969:48).

55. See Vold and Bernard (1986:174–175); Davis (1975:41–51); Katz (1988).
56. See Davis (1975:49).
57. See Einstadter and Henry (1995:134).
58. Tittle (1995:2).
59. See Curran and Renzetti (1994:142); Vold and Bernard (1986:173–174); Einstadter and Henry (1995:140–141).
60. See Taylor et al. (1974:125); Einstadter and Henry (1995:140).
61. Babbie (1992:96); Andrews and Bonta (1994:12–16).
62. See Wilson and Herrnstein (1985:290); Vold and Bernard (1986:176).
63. Cullen and Agnew (2006).
64. Bernard et al. (2010).
65. Clarke (1980).
66. Clarke (1980).
67. Clark (1992); Newman (1976, originally published in 1972). Also see Jeffery (1977) and Brantingham and Brantingham (1984) for extensions of Newman's theory.
68. See Williams and McShane (1994:61).
69. Cisneros (1995:3).
70. Cisneros (1995:23).
71. Wilson and Herrnstein (1985:309).
72. Cohen and Felson (1979). For other extensions of ecological theory, see Brantingham and Brantingham (1984); Bursik (1984); Stark (1987); Vila (1994).
73. Cohen and Felson (1979).
74. Cohen and Felson (1979).
75. Cohen and Felson (1979).
76. An extended discussion of this problem can be found in the section on social control theories presented in the next chapter.
77. Tittle (1995:14).
78. Tittle (1995:15).
79. See Einstadter and Henry (1995:70).
80. See Einstadter and Henry (1995:71).
81. See Davis (1975:65).
82. Davis (1975:65–66).
83. Davis (1975:66).
84. See Davis (1975:74, 92); also see Gouldner (1971).
85. Davis (1975:80–81, 92).
86. See Davis (1975:82).
87. Davis (1971); also see Davis (1975:81–82).
88. See Davis (1975:82–85).

89. Cited in Taylor et al. (1974:210–211).
90. See Durkheim (1964:66); also see Davis (1975:71–72, 88–89).
91. See Davis (1975:91).
92. See Davis, (1975:68, 92).
93. See Davis (1975:67).
94. See Davis (1975:67, 90).
95. See Davis (1975:72–73).
96. See Davis (1975:67).
97. See Davis (1975:68, 81, 90–92).
98. See Davis (1975:96).
99. Martin et al. (1990:212).
100. Vold and Bernard (1986:186–187).
101. See Hirschi (1969); Kornhauser (1978); Vold and Bernard (1986).
102. See Cullen and Messner (2007).
103. Vold and Bernard (1986:187).
104. Merton (1938).
105. But see Taylor et al. (1974:98) for another view.
106. Vold and Bernard (1986:193).
107. Cohen's theory of gang delinquency, as well as Cloward and Ohlin's theory of differential opportunity (to be discussed shortly), has been considered a subcultural theory rather than, or in addition to, an anomie theory (see Williams and McShane, 1994:105). Cohen was the first criminologist to apply the concept of subculture to the study of delinquency (Beirne and Messerschmidt, 2000:147).
108. Cohen (1955:25); also see Vold and Bernard (1986:194).
109. Cohen (1955:30–31).
110. Cohen (1955:65–66, 136); also see Vold and Bernard (1986:194).
111. Actually, for Cohen, status frustration was a problem only for working-class juveniles. For middle-class juveniles, on the other hand, delinquency was primarily a way of coping with a basic anxiety in the area of sex role identification (Cohen, 1955:164–169).
112. Cohen (1955:84–93).
113. Cohen (1955:28, 112–119, 133); also see Vold and Bernard (1986:195).
114. Cohen (1955:134–135); also see Vold and Bernard (1986:195).
115. Cohen (1955:37); also see Vold and Bernard (1986:195).
116. Cloward and Ohlin (1960:148).
117. Cloward and Ohlin (1960:Chap. 7); also see Vold and Bernard (1986:197).
118. See Taylor et al. (1974:94); Schur (1969:230–232).
119. Vold and Bernard (1986:201).
120. Vold and Bernard (1986:201).

121. Vold and Bernard (1986:201).
122. Curran and Renzetti (1994:169).
123. Curran and Renzetti (1994:169); Vold and Bernard (1986:201).
124. Williams and McShane (1994:121).
125. Vold and Bernard (1986:201–202).
126. Vold and Bernard (1986:201).
127. Curran and Renzetti (1994:169); Vold and Bernard (1986:201).
128. See Wilson and Herrnstein (1985:335) on vocational training programs; also see Vold (1979:223).
129. Davis (1975:118).
130. Davis (1975:118).
131. See Cullen (1984); Cullen and Agnew (2006); Siegel (2010); Bernard et al. (2010).
132. Bernard et al. (2010:164).
133. Bernard et al. (2010:164).
134. Bernard et al. (2010).
135. Agnew (1992).
136. Agnew (1992).
137. Agnew (1992).
138. Agnew (1992).
139. Agnew (1992:50).
140. Agnew (1992:50).
141. Bernard et al. (2010:165).
142. Botchkovar, Tittle, Antonaccio (2009:134).
143. Agnew (1992); See also Cullen and Agnew (2006).
144. Agnew (2006:208).
145. Baron (2004); Agnew (2006); Aseltine, Gore, and Gordon (2000); Mazerolle and Maahs (2000).
146. Moon, Morash, McCluskey and Hwang (2009:184).
147. Moon et al. (2009).
148. Cullen and Agnew (2006).
149. Cullen and Agnew (2006).
150. Rosenfeld and Messner (2006:192).
151. Rosenfeld and Messner (2006:198–199).
152. Rosenfeld and Messner (2006:197).
153. Bernard et al. (2010).
154. Cullen and Agnew (2006:163).
155. Bernard et al. (2010:169).
156. Messner and Rosenfeld (2006).
157. Baumer and Gustafson (2007).

158. Baumer and Gustafson (2007:651).

159. Jensen (2002).

160. See Vold (1979:223).

161. See Curran and Renzetti (1994:152, 164); Vold (1979:226); Taylor et al. (1974:106–107).

162. See, for example, Friedrichs (1996:232).

163. See Taylor et al. (1974:107); Kornhauser (1978:148).

164. Tittle (1995:5).

165. Cullen and Wright (1997).

166. See Andrews and Bonta (1994:95–96).

167. Davis (1975:102).

168. Lanier and Henry (1998:234); Tittle (1995:2).

169. Martin et al. (1990:284–285); Kornhauser (1978:180).

170. Martin et al. (1990:286–288).

171. Martin et al. (1990:288); Kornhauser (1978:159–160).

172. See Kornhauser (1978:243).

173. See Davis (1975:104).

174. Taylor et al. (1974:104–105); Kornhauser (1978:163, 166).

175. Williams and McShane (1994:91). For example, Messner and Rosenfeld (2001) emphasize the American cultural goal of consumption. In later writings, Merton argued that "cultural success goal" could be substituted for money with the same results.

176. Kornhauser (1978:139).

177. Kornhauser (1978:162).

178. Davis (1975:102); also see Kornhauser (1978:164).

179. See Taylor et al. (1974:108).

180. See Davis (1975:105).

181. See Matza (1964).

7

Microsociological Theories

In Chapter 6 macrosociological theories of crime were reviewed, emphasizing how the organization or structure of a society can generate an environment conducive to crime. In this chapter, the analysis shifts to microsociological theories, which examine how various social institutions (e.g., the family, the school, and religion) and processes (e.g., socialization) can encourage or inhibit criminal behavior.

Learning Theories

Tarde's Imitation Theory

Gabriel Tarde (1843–1904) was one of the first theorists to believe that crime was something learned by normal people as they adapted to other people and the conditions of their environment. His theory was a product of his experience as a French lawyer and magistrate and was described in his book *Penal Philosophy*, published in 1890.[1] Because he did not believe that criminals were unique, either physically or psychologically, Tarde completely rejected Lombroso's conception of the born criminal. "Perhaps one is born vicious," he wrote, "but it is quite certain that one becomes a criminal."[2]

For Tarde, becoming a criminal is a learning process, and learning is a social phenomenon. Reflecting the state of knowledge about the learning process in his day, Tarde viewed all social phenomena as the product of imitation. Through *imitation* or *modeling*, a person can learn new responses, such as criminal behavior, by observing others, without performing any overt act or receiving direct reinforcement or reward.[3] Although Tarde did not discuss it, behavior can also be learned by imitating symbolic models where verbal or written instructions are presented. Written instructions include such things as technical manuals; pictorial models include movies, television, and other audiovisual means. In short, for Tarde, criminal behavior is learned by observing and imitating the criminal behavior of other people, something Tarde believed was more likely in urban areas.[4]

Sutherland's Differential Association Theory

The first twentieth-century criminologist to forcefully argue that criminal behavior was learned was Edwin H. Sutherland (1883–1950). His *theory of differential association* developed over thirteen years, between 1934 and 1947,[5] and, together with its more recent modifications, remains one of the most influential theories of crime causation today. The theory explains crime both at the macro level (differences in crime rates among groups) and at the micro level (differences in individual criminal behavior)—though the former has been largely ignored.[6] In addition, the theory can be used to explain *white-collar crime* (a term Sutherland coined) as well as street crime.[7] In his text, Sutherland lists the nine propositions of his theory with accompanying commentary:[8]

1. Criminal behavior is learned. Negatively, this means that criminal behavior is not inherited, as such; also, the person who is not already trained in crime does not invent criminal behavior, just as a person does not make mechanical inventions unless he has had training in mechanics.
2. Criminal behavior is learned in interaction with other persons in a process of communication. This communication is verbal in many respects but also includes the "communication of gestures."
3. The principal part of the learning of criminal behavior occurs within intimate personal groups. Negatively, this means that the impersonal agencies of communication, such as movies and newspapers, play a relatively unimportant part in the genesis of criminal behavior.
4. When criminal behavior is learned, the learning includes (a) techniques of committing the crime, which are sometimes very complicated, sometimes very simple; (b) the specific direction of motives, drives, rationalizations, and attitudes.
5. The specific direction of motives and drives is learned from definitions of the legal codes as favorable and unfavorable. In some societies an individual is surrounded by persons who invariably define the legal codes as rules to be observed, while in others he or she is surrounded by persons whose definitions are favorable to the violation of the legal codes. In our

American society these definitions are almost always mixed, with the consequence that we have culture conflict in relation to the legal codes.

6. A person becomes delinquent because of an excess of definitions favorable to violation of law over definitions unfavorable to violation of law. This is the principle of *differential association*. It refers to both criminal and anticriminal associations and has to do with counteracting forces. When persons become criminal, they do so because of contacts with criminal patterns and also because of isolation from anticriminal patterns. Any person inevitably assimilates the surrounding culture unless other patterns are in conflict; a southerner does not pronounce "r" because other southerners do not pronounce "r." Negatively, this proposition of differential association means that associations which are neutral so far as crime is concerned have little or no effect on the genesis of criminal behavior. Much of the experience of a person is neutral in this sense, for example, learning to brush one's teeth. This behavior has no negative or positive effect on criminal behavior except as it may be related to associations which are concerned with the legal codes. This neutral behavior is important especially as an occupier of the time of a child so that he or she is not in contact with criminal behavior during the time he or she is so engaged in the neutral behavior.

7. Differential associations may vary in frequency, duration, priority, and intensity. This means that associations with criminal behavior and also associations with anticriminal behavior vary in those respects. "Frequency" and "duration" as modalities of associations are obvious and need no explanation. "Priority" is assumed to be important in the sense that lawful behavior developed in early childhood may persist throughout life, and also that delinquent behavior developed in early childhood may persist throughout life. This tendency, however, has not been adequately demonstrated, and priority seems to be important principally through its selective influence. "Intensity" is not precisely defined, but it has to do with such things as the prestige of the source of a criminal or anticriminal pattern and with emotional reactions related to the associations. In a precise description of the criminal behavior of a person, these modalities would be related in quantitative form and a mathematical ratio would be reached. A formula in this sense has not been developed, and the development of such a formula would be extremely difficult.

8. The process of learning criminal behavior by association with criminal and anticriminal patterns involves all of the mechanisms that are involved in any other learning. Negatively, this means that the learning of criminal behavior is not restricted to the process of imitation. A person who is seduced, for instance, learns criminal behavior by association, but this process would not ordinarily be described as imitation.

9. While criminal behavior is an expression of general needs and values, it is not explained by those general needs and values, since noncriminal behavior is an expression of the same needs and values. Thieves generally steal in order to secure money, but likewise honest laborers work in order to secure money. The attempts by many scholars to explain criminal behavior by general drives and values, such as the happiness principle, striving for social status, the money motive, or frustration, have been, and must continue to be, futile, since they explain lawful behavior as completely as they explain criminal behavior. They are similar to respiration, which is necessary for any behavior, but which does not differentiate criminal from noncriminal behavior.

Modifying a premise from the theory of the Chicago School, Sutherland maintained that differential associations would not produce criminality if it were not for *differential social organization*.[9] In other words, the degree to which communities promote or inhibit criminal associations varies with the way or the degree to which they are organized (that is, the extent of culture conflict).[10]

Critique of Sutherland's Theory

Sutherland's theory has been criticized on several grounds, and some of those criticisms provide the groundwork for more contemporary conceptualizations of his work. First, Sutherland's differential association theory does not explain why individuals have the associations they have, or why the number of definitions favorable or unfavorable to the violation of the law varies from one social context to another.[11] Reference to differential social organization still begs the question of why or how society is differentially organized.

A second criticism of differential association theory is that it is untestable.[12] For example, Curran and Renzetti ask, "How can 'an excess of definitions favorable to law violation' be measured or observed?"[13] Even if such definitions could be measured and observed, one critic wonders where an excess of definitions favorable to law violation could be found.[14] As the Chicago theorists Shaw and McKay noted, even in the worst neighborhoods, most residents are law-abiding and subscribe to conventional values. Even residents who do commit crimes generally endorse conventional values much of the time.

A common way that researchers have tried to overcome the criticism of untestability is by examining the influence of delinquent peers on offending. Presumably, the more delinquent peers with whom one associates, the more likely he or she is to be exposed to definitions favorable to law violation. Consequently, by examining the number and importance of delinquent peers, researchers can gauge the extent to which someone is exposed to definitions that are supportive of law violation. As would be predicted by Sutherland's theory, research has found that association with delinquent peers is strongly associated with delinquent behavior.[15] In fact, after their extensive review of research in this area, Akers and Jensen conclude that "[o]ther than one's own prior deviant behavior, the best single predictor of the onset, continuance, or desistance of crime and delinquency is differential association with conforming and law-violating peers."[16] This finding remains robust regardless of the type of delinquency under investigation.

A third criticism of Sutherland's theory involves the question of whether differential associations cause crime or are a result of crime.[17] Current research suggests that the effect of associating with delinquent peers on delinquency is reciprocal. In other words, association with delinquent peers is related to delinquency, and youth who engage in delinquency are likely to associate with delinquent peers.[18]

Some critics question whether differential associations cause crime at all. If differential associations are so important, then how is the criminal behavior of the recluse Ted Kaczynski—the so-called Unabomber—explained?[19] For that matter, why do most correctional officers and probation and parole officers not violate the law? After all, they are exposed to definitions favorable to law violation during much of their workdays. Perhaps the answer is that different people respond differently to procriminal definitions, something Sutherland's theory ignored.[20]

Sutherland has also been criticized for underemphasizing the importance of the media in crime causation.[21] Sutherland maintained that "the impersonal agencies of communication, such as movies and newspapers, play a relatively unimportant part." Sutherland formulated his theory long before the ubiquity of blockbuster action films, violent video games, cable television, and YouTube, so the fact that he downplayed the influence of the media on delinquency, to some extent, can be understood. The research on media violence and aggression, moreover, has failed to show that exposure to media violence causes violent criminal behavior.[22]

Finally, Sutherland's theory has been criticized for failing to "present a good description of definitions favorable or unfavorable to crime."[23] Although some theorists argue that those who engage in crime reject mainstream values entirely,[24] as suggested previously, it is generally held that most law violators ascribe to mainstream values, disapprove of crime in general, and condone some criminal acts only in specific situations.[25] This was the belief of Gresham Sykes (1922–2010) and David Matza (1930–), who, in 1957, published an influential study entitled "Techniques of Neutralization: A Theory of Delinquency," where they address this weakness in Sutherland's work.[26] Their goal in the study was to provide what they believed was a missing piece in Sutherland's differential association theory, that is, "the specific content of what is learned—as opposed to the process by which it is learned."[27]

Sykes and Matza's Neutralization Theory

According to Sykes and Matza, "Much delinquency is based on what is essentially an unrecognized extension of defenses to crimes, in the form of justifications [or rationalizations] for deviance that are seen as valid by the delinquent but not by the legal system or society at large."[28] Sykes and Matza described five techniques of neutralization: (1) *denial of responsibility* ("I didn't mean to do it" or "I'm sick"), (2) *denial of injury* ("Nobody got hurt"), (3) *denial of victim* ("They had it coming to them" or "We weren't hurting anyone"), (4) *condemnation of the condemners* ("Everybody does it"), and (5) *appeal to higher loyalties* ("I only did it for the gang").[29] For Sykes and Matza, it is by learning those defenses that the juvenile is able to neutralize or deflect the internal guilt and the disapproval of others.

Most delinquents, according to Sykes and Matza, believe in the dominant value system of society. Indeed, if asked, most delinquents would readily admit that their delinquent activities are wrong. Consequently, to engage in crime, delinquents must be able to justify their delinquent behavior and thus reduce the guilt they would feel otherwise.[30]

Critique of Neutralization Theory

Note that Sykes and Matza's *neutralizations* are very similar to Freud's *defense mechanisms*, which were discussed in Chapter 5. Sykes and Matza's neutralizations, however, are made prior to a delinquent act—to free an individual of guilt to commit it—while Freud's defense mechanisms are generally employed after a delinquent act to reduce guilt (and anxiety) caused by it. Some research suggests that neutralizations occur both before and after delinquent acts—supporting both Freud and Sykes and Matza.[31] However, a recent review of the research on neutralization theory found little evidence supporting Sykes and Matza's claim that neutralizations are employed before the commission of an illegal act.[32]

Another problem with Sykes and Matza's neutralization theory involves the degree to which juvenile offenders, and people generally, are committed to conventional values and norms. If they are not committed—a presumption of many social control theories—neutralization is unnecessary.[33] Matza later (in 1964) conceded that few people (juveniles or adults) are *always* committed to conventional values and norms, but, instead, that most people typically *drift* between law-abiding and law-violating behaviors. Whether or not they commit crime depends largely on opportunity. Neutralization theory has also been criticized for failing to explain how neutralizations originate or who invented them.[34]

In their recent review of the research on neutralization theory, Maruna and Copes conclude that results are mixed, and supportive results are often weak.[35] Interestingly, they observe that neutralization theory may not be a theory that explains the "why" of criminal causation, but, instead, is a theory that only provides an understanding of the cognitive methods that allow an otherwise law-abiding individual to continue to break the law. In other words, for Maruna and Copes, Sykes and Matza's neutralization theory is useful in explaining how crime is maintained or continued, but not how it originates.[36]

New Developments in Learning Theory

Given the time period during which Sutherland's theory of differential association was produced (1934–1947), he can be forgiven for having a rather simplistic conception of the learning process.[37] However, over the ensuing years, modifications and additions have been made to Sutherland's theory as new developments in learning theory have emerged. For example, Daniel Glaser (1918–) modified Sutherland's theory by introducing *role theory* and by arguing that criminal behavior could be learned by identifying with criminal roles and not just by associating with criminals.[38] Thus, a person could imitate the behavior of a drug dealer without actually having met one. Glaser obviously believed that the media had a greater influence on the learning of criminal behavior than Sutherland believed they had.

Robert L. Burgess (1931–) and Ronald L. Akers (1939–), as well as C. Ray Jeffery (1921–2007), adapted the principles of operant conditioning and behavior modification, developed by psychologist B.F. Skinner (1904–1990), and the principles of modeling, as developed by Albert Bandura (1925–), to the explanation of criminal behavior. The first three theorists integrated psychological concepts with sociological ones. Burgess and Akers call their reformulation of Sutherland's theory *differential association–reinforcement theory*, and in a later elaboration, Akers calls it *social learning theory*.[39] Jeffery calls his interpretation the *theory of differential reinforcement*.[40] More recent applications of modern behavioral psychology to an understanding of criminality are found in the works of James Q. Wilson (1931–2012) and Richard Herrnstein (1930–1994), Akers, and D. A. Andrews (1941–) and James Bonta (1949–).[41]

Akers and Jensen maintain that social learning theory has received considerable empirical support.[42] They relate that social learning theory "has been tested in relation to a wider range of forms of deviance, in a wider range of settings and samples, in more different languages, and by more different people, has survived more 'crucial tests' against other theories and is more strongly and consistently supported by empirical data than any other social psychological explanation of crime and deviance."[43] Reaching a different conclusion, Sampson claims that "the data show the results on imitation and reinforcement are either weak or inconsistent"—a conclusion Sampson contends that Akers admits.[44] In any event, in the following discussion, the more general term *learning theory* is used to describe this approach.

Learning theory explains criminal behavior and its prevention with the concepts of positive reinforcement, negative reinforcement, extinction, punishment, and modeling or imitation.[45] In learning theory, crime is committed because it is positively reinforced, negatively reinforced, or imitated. The imitation or modeling of criminal behavior has already been described in the earlier discussion of Tarde. Here the focus is on the other concepts.

Positive reinforcement is the presentation of a stimulus that increases or maintains a response. The stimulus, or *reward*, can be either material, such as money, or psychological, such as pleasure.[46] People steal (a response), for example, because of the rewards—for example, the objects or money—that they receive. They use drugs (at least at first) because of the rewards—for example, the pleasure—that the drugs give them.

Negative reinforcement is the removal or reduction of a stimulus whose removal or reduction increases or maintains a response. The stimulus in negative reinforcement is referred to as an *aversive stimulus*. Aversive stimuli, for most people, include pain and fear. A person who is negatively reinforced to steal may be stealing to remove or reduce the aversive stimuli of the fear and pain of poverty. Drug addicts are negatively reinforced to continue to use drugs because using them removes or reduces the aversive stimulus of the pain of drug withdrawal.

In short, both positive and negative reinforcement explain why a behavior, such as crime, is maintained or increases. Both types of reinforcement can simultaneously affect the same behavior. In other words, people may commit crime, in this view, both because they are rewarded for it and because it removes aversive stimuli.

Policy Implications of Learning Theory

According to learning theory, criminal behavior is reduced through extinction or punishment. It is important to emphasize that learning theory does not promise that crime or any other behavior necessarily can be eliminated by these means, only that it can be reduced. *Extinction*—which Akers and Andrews and Bonta call "negative punishment"[47]—is a procedure in which behavior that previously was positively reinforced is no longer reinforced. In other words, the rewards have been removed. Thus, if burglars were to continually come up empty in their quests (that is, not to receive rewards for their efforts), they would most likely no longer continue to burglarize. Similarly, if drug users no longer received rewards such as pleasure from their use of drugs, they would most likely no longer use them (assuming, of course, that they were not addicted and using the drugs for negative reinforcement).

Punishment—which Akers calls "positive punishment"[48]—is the presentation of an aversive stimulus to reduce a response. It is the principal method used in the United States and other countries to prevent crime or, at least, to reduce it. Most countries use imprisonment as a punishment for crimes. However, a problem is that prisons are also "schools of crime." That is, besides their aversive properties, prisons often provide an environment in which criminal behavior is learned, in which case imprisonment becomes counterproductive.

As a tool of criminal justice in the United States, punishment is not used effectively in other ways as well. That is, it is not used according to learning theory principles.[49] For example, for punishment to be effective, escape must be prevented. Escape is a natural reaction to the presentation of an aversive stimulus such as imprisonment. In the United States, the chances of an offender's escaping punishment (by escaping apprehension in the first place) are great. Also, if apprehended, many offenders, especially first-time offenders, are placed on probation, which probably does not always function as an aversive stimulus.[50]

According to learning theory principles, for punishment to be effective it also must be applied consistently and immediately. Consistent application of punishment is rare because most criminal offenders are not caught. As for immediacy, the process of criminal justice in the United States generally precludes punishment immediately after a criminal act has been committed. The criminal justice process, even when it is working efficiently, is a slow and methodical one.

In addition, extended periods of punishment should be avoided or the effectiveness of the punishment will be reduced. The United States currently imprisons more of its offenders for longer periods than any other country in the world, though in many cases inmates actually serve only a fraction of their original sentences. A related issue is that punishment is far less effective when the intensity with which the aversive stimulus is presented is increased gradually rather than when the stimulus is introduced at full intensity. Prolonged imprisonment is a gradual process of punishment that lacks the full intensity and immediacy of corporal punishment, for example.

To be effective, punishment also must be combined with extinction. That is, the rewards that maintain the behavior must be removed. In the United States, after imprisonment, offenders generally return to the environment in which their crimes were originally committed and rewarded. Additionally, for punishment to be effective, it must be combined with the positive reinforcement of alternative, prosocial behaviors and the availability of prosocial models as well.[51] Rarely does this happen.

Finally, according to learning theorists, positive reinforcement is a much more effective and preferred method of manipulating behavior than is punishment, because positive reinforcement does not suffer the disadvantages associated with punishment. Criminal justice decision makers often overlook that point. Among the disadvantages of punishment are that it causes generalization and negative self-concepts. Offenders frequently come to view themselves as bad instead of viewing only their behaviors as bad. Generalizing the evil people do to their personhood severely hampers efforts at rehabilitation. As noted previously, punishment also causes withdrawal or escape. By punishing offenders, the chances of their avoiding detection and capture the next time they commit criminal acts are increased. Finally, punishment causes aggression.[52] The punishing of offenders, particularly nonviolent ones, may inadvertently be producing violent offenders. For these reasons, then, the ineffectiveness of punishment in the United States should not be surprising because the way punishment is administered in this country violates most of the principles of learning theory.[53]

Critique of Learning Theory

Besides obstacles to applying punishment effectively, another problem with learning theory as applied to crime is the problem of overprediction. The theory accounts for too much crime and delinquency and has a hard time explaining exceptions.[54] Regarding the former, if criminality is so rewarding for the poor, for example, why do not more poor people commit it? Perhaps it is because they lack the opportunity, skill, or knowledge to commit it. Regarding exceptions, how can two brothers who have been raised in the same environment (and are exposed to the same rewards) turn out so differently, with one becoming a gangster and the other one becoming a priest? For that matter, why do people who have been rewarded for law-abiding behavior, such as successful businesspeople or government officials, still commit crimes?[55] Or why do people continue to commit crimes even though it has caused them much pain and agony?[56]

Learning theory, at least as it is used to explain crime, is based on circular reasoning.[57] By definition, a *reinforcing stimulus* is one that maintains or increases the probability of a behavior. Thus, it is impossible to determine in advance of observing a subsequent behavior whether any particular stimulus is or is not reinforcing.

Another fundamental problem is that if all criminal behavior is learned, and none is invented, then how does criminal behavior begin? What is the source of new types of crime?[58]

Learning theory also ignores the criminalization process. It fails to consider why the normal learned behaviors of some groups are criminalized, whereas the normal learned behaviors of other groups are not.[59] For example, why is marijuana consumption illegal, whereas cigarette or alcohol consumption is not? Learning theory ignores the effect that political and economic power has on the definition of criminal behavior.[60]

Finally, learning/ reinforcement theories, until recently, ignored the social structural influences on the determination of rewards and aversive stimuli.[61] That is, few stimuli are inherently rewarding or aversive, and what is rewarding in any society at any point in time may not be rewarding, or may even be aversive, in another context or under a different circumstance. In short, what generally gives stimuli rewarding or aversive properties is socially determined.[62]

Subcultural Theories

As noted earlier in this chapter, learning theories can be used to explain crime at both the micro and the macro levels. Learning theories at the macro level often claim that certain groups in the United States have learned values that are conducive to crime or that approve of or justify crime in certain circumstances, and that such values explain the higher rates of crime in these groups.[63] For example, some theorists suggest that a "subculture of violence" exists in the Southern United States and in some inner-city neighborhoods. A *subculture* refers to a subgroup within a dominant group or culture that has defined its own norms and values, which are often inconsistent or in conflict with those of the larger group. Subcultures emerge when a group of people in similar circumstances find themselves cut off from or denied access to mainstream society. Theorists in this tradition include Albert Cohen, Richard Cloward, and Lloyd Ohlin—all of whom were discussed in Chapter 6 under anomie theories—and Walter B. Miller, Marvin Wolfgang, Franco Ferracuti, and Elijah Anderson.

Miller's Theory of Lower-Class Culture

Walter B. Miller (1920–2004) argued that the lower class has "a long-established, distinctively patterned tradition with an integrity of its own."[64] Delinquent gangs, in Miller's view, are natural products of the values, or what he called the "focal concerns," of lower-class culture: trouble (the ability to handle it), toughness (physical and emotional strength), smartness (street savvy), excitement (ways that an otherwise drab existence is enlivened), fate (the belief that life outcomes are a matter of luck or chance), and autonomy (being independent of authority figures such as parents, teachers, or the police).

For Miller, delinquency is "normal" behavior of lower-class youths simply defined as delinquent by the middle and upper classes. In short, Miller believed that members of the lower class no more want to be middle class than members of the middle class want to be lower class.[65]

Critique of Miller's Theory

Perhaps the major problem with "cultural deviance" theories, such as Miller's, is explaining lower-class nondelinquency. Miller accomplishes the feat, and in doing so substantially alters his theory, by attributing lower-class delinquency to individuals or groups who deviate from lower-class culture or who are part of lower-class cultural subtypes.[66] If this were the case, however, then how can lower-class delinquency, or perhaps more accurately, lower-class behavior defined as delinquent by the middle and upper classes, be a product of lower-class culture?

Another major problem with Miller's theory is that no evidence, besides his own, supports it. Every other study, besides Miller's, shows that, "at the very least, overwhelming numbers of the poor give allegiance to the values and principles of the dominant American culture."[67] Additionally, there is no "evidence whatever that the poor perceive their way of life as good and preferable to that of other ways of life."[68] Besides, even if lower-class culture were characterized by Miller's focal concerns, those focal concerns are not necessarily related to delinquency.[69]

Wolfgang and Ferracuti's Subculture of Violence Theory

Marvin Wolfgang (1924–1998) and Franco Ferracuti (1927–), in their 1967 book *The Subculture of Violence: Towards an Integrated Theory in Criminology*, examined criminal homicides in Philadelphia and found that they were not distributed evenly across the city, but were concentrated in African-American neighborhoods.[70] They concluded that the high homicide rates were the result of a subculture of violence that defines "violence as a more appropriate, or even required, response to a wide variety of provocations and insults."[71]

Although they did not explain how the subculture originates, they did provide seven propositions summarizing their theory: (1) No subculture can be totally different from or totally in conflict with the society of which it is a part; (2) To establish the existence of a subculture of violence does not require that the actors sharing in these basic value elements should express violence in all situations; (3) The potential to resort or willingness to resort to violence in a variety of situations emphasizes the penetrating and diffusive character of this cultural theme; (4) The subcultural ethos of violence may be shared by all ages in a subsociety, but this ethos is most prominent in a limited age group, ranging from late adolescence to middle age; (5) The counter-norm is nonviolence; (6) The development of favorable attitudes toward and the use of violence in a subculture usually involve learned behavior and a process of differential learning, association, or identification; and (7) The use of violence in a subculture is not necessarily viewed as illicit conduct, and the users therefore do not have to deal with feelings of guilt about their aggression.[72]

Critique of Wolfgang and Ferracuti's Theory

Research examining Wolfgang and Ferracuti's subculture of violence theory has yielded largely unsupportive results.[73] Two lines of research characterize this tradition: one that seeks to explain the higher rate of violence in the Southern United States, and one that examines the presence of the subculture of violence among African Americans in urban areas. Research on the regional differences in violence has been plagued with methodological problems and yields little to no support for the subcultural thesis.[74] A more recent, nationwide study of the thesis found that "southern White males from rural areas are more approving of violence only under certain conditions, some of which may be construed as defensive in nature."[75] Likewise, little empirical evidence exists to support a subculture of violence among African-American males. One study, based on data from a national random sample, concluded that "white males express significantly more violent beliefs in defensive or retaliatory situations than blacks and that there is no significant difference between white and black males in beliefs in violence in offensive situations."[76]

Anderson's Code of the Street

In his 1999 book, *Code of the Street: Decency, Violence, and the Moral Life of the Inner City*, Elijah Anderson (1943–) described a contemporary version of a subculture of violence that persists in urban, largely African-American neighborhoods.[77] Although the subculture of violence is rejected by most inner-city inhabitants, it "places all young African-American men under much pressure to respond to certain situations, such as shows of disrespect, with violence."[78] Unlike the work of Wolfgang and Ferracuti, however, Anderson examined how structural disadvantage, cultural explanations, and racial discrimination combine to explain the high rate of violence among African-American youth.[79] For example, the loss of job opportunities in the inner city has deprived young African-American males of traditional, legitimately employed, male role models. Consequently, those young African-American males often turn to violence and an array of illegal activities.

Unlike earlier versions of subcultural theories, Anderson's work has received some empirical support.[80] For example, a recent study examined the influence of male role models and concentrated urban disadvantage on Black juvenile arrests for violence across several U.S. cities.[81] The results suggest that "older African-American men play an important role in the urban context, offering social control in the urban environment that detracts youth from the lure of the street code."[82] Similarly, in their study of more than seven hundred African-American adolescents, Stewart and Simons found that "neighborhood structural characteristics, living in a street family, and discrimination significantly predicted adopting the street code."[83]

Social Control Theories

Social control theories address the problems of crime and delinquency from an entirely different perspective than do the preceding theories. The seminal question for social control theorists is not why people commit crime and delinquency but rather why they do not. Why do people conform? In other words, social control theorists expect people to commit crime and delinquency unless they are prevented from doing so. They will commit crime, that is, unless they are properly socialized.[84]

Like many of the other sociological theories of crime causation that have been examined, social control theories, as previously noted, have their origins in the work of Durkheim. Not until the 1950s, however, did social control theories begin to emerge to challenge other, more dominant theories, such as anomie and differential association. Among the early social control theorists were Albert J. Reiss, Jr. (1922–2006), Jackson Toby (1925–), F. Ivan Nye (1918–2014), and Walter C. Reckless (1899–1988).[85] However, despite the important contributions of those early theorists, modern social control theory in its most detailed elaboration is attributed to the work of Travis Hirschi (1935–). Hirschi's 1969 book, *Causes of Delinquency*, has had a tremendous influence on current criminological thinking.[86]

Hirschi's Social Control Theory

As did proponents of earlier social control theories, Hirschi argues that delinquency should be expected if a juvenile is not properly socialized. For Hirschi, proper socialization involves the establishment of a strong moral bond between the juvenile and society. This *bond to society* consists of (1) *attachment* to others, (2) *commitment* to conventional lines of action, (3) *involvement* in conventional activities, and (4) *belief* in the moral order and law. Thus, delinquent behavior is likely to occur if there is (1) inadequate attachment, particularly to parents and school; (2) inadequate commitment, particularly to educational and occupational success; (3) inadequate involvement in such conventional activities as scouting and sports leagues; and (4) inadequate belief, particularly in the legitimacy and morality of the law. For Hirschi, although all four elements of the bond to society are important (the importance of involvement was not supported by his data, however), the most important and most basic element of the bond is attachment to others.

A unique feature of Hirschi's theory (his is a theory of delinquency and not of adult criminality) is that the data on which the theory is based come from self-report surveys rather than from official police or court records or victimization surveys. The self-report surveys, among other things, asked subjects whether they had committed crimes and other offenses.

Gottfredson and Hirschi's General Theory of Crime

In their 1990 book, *A General Theory of Crime*, Michael Gottfredson (1951–) and Travis Hirschi argue that the primary cause of a variety of deviant behaviors, including many different kinds of crime and delinquency, is ineffective child rearing, which produces people with low self-control.[87] The authors contend that ineffective child rearers, at minimum, fail to monitor their children's behavior, recognize their children's deviant behavior when it occurs, and punish their children's deviant behavior when it is discovered.[88] Children with low self-control frequently have child rearers with low self-control.[89]

Low self-control adversely affects a person's ability to accurately calculate the consequences of his or her actions. Because everyone has a predisposition toward criminality, according to this theory, those persons with low self-control find it more difficult to resist. For Gottfredson and Hirschi, people with low self-control tend to be "impulsive, insensitive, physical (as opposed to mental), risk-taking, short-sighted, and nonverbal."[90] The lack of self-control, they argue, remains fairly constant over the course of a person's life.

Research testing Gottfredson and Hirschi's General Theory of Crime (GTC) is extensive. Gottfredson argues that "[w]hatever else may be said about the empirical status of control theory in criminology, it most likely holds first place among modern theories for the generation of research."[91] Moreover, much of that research is supportive of its central tenet that low self-control is related to crime as well as a wide range of analogous behavior.[92] Indeed, the consistently strong support leads Unnever, Pratt, and Cullen to conclude that "[low self-control's] relationship to delinquent involvement is a 'fact' for which extant theories must take account."[93]

One of the theory's most controversial propositions is that self-control develops before the age of ten and remains relatively stable over the course of a person's life.[94] Research on this contention is mixed.[95] On one hand, Arneklev, Grasmick, and Bursik, based on a limited convenience sample, found that low self-control "appears to be an invariant latent trait."[96] Tremblay and his colleagues, using data from different periods, different countries, different reporting sources, and different methodologies, also provide empirical support for the proposition that human beings are inherently physically aggressive (i.e., are born with low self-control). Tremblay reports that the frequency of anger outbursts and physical aggression, as well as the frequency of stealing (taking things from others), vandalism (destroying others' belongings), and fraudulent behavior (e.g., lying), "increase rapidly from the first year after birth to approximately the third, and then the frequency decreases."[97] He found that human beings use physical aggression most often between eighteen and forty-two months after birth. He admits that "the physical aggressions by very young children appear qualitatively different from physical aggressions by adolescents and adults, [but] the trajectory of the former appears to lead to the trajectory of the latter."

Tremblay's research shows that the best predictor of chronic physical aggression by preschool children is having an older sibling because "one needs a target to physically aggress." Other key predictors are parent separation before birth; family dysfunction; low income; and having mothers who engaged in frequent antisocial behavior during adolescence, gave birth before twenty-one years of age, did not finish high school, smoked during pregnancy, and were coercive-hostile in their parenting. Tremblay also reports that 80 percent of the variation in the frequency of physical aggression at seventeen months of age could be explained by genetic factors, which he asserts do not determine the trajectories of physical aggression but, instead, determine how human beings react to their environment. Tremblay's conclusion: "Human beings do not appear to need to learn to use physical aggression. As soon as they are in sufficient control of their muscles they use physical aggression to express their anger and to obtain what they desire. The important learning which is going on during the preschool years is *learning not to use physical aggression* and *learning to use alternative strategies* to achieve your aims" (emphasis in original).

On the other hand, findings of a study by Harbin, Simons, and Simons, based on a large, longitudinal sample of African-American children and their caregivers, revealed that low self-control is not "stable and insensitive to social influences after the age of ten."[98] Similarly, Winfree, Taylor, He, and Esbensen contend that "our findings are, for the most part, unequivocally critical of Gottfredson and Hirschi's orienting assumption (or claim) concerning the unchanging nature of self-control after its establishment in preadolescence."[99]

Another fundamental proposition of GTC is that parents with low self-control are more likely to raise children with low self-control. Using a nationwide, longitudinal sample of youth, Nofzinger found that "mothers with low self-control do indeed produce children with lower self-control."[100] She also discovered that the self-control of the mother influenced both her choice of punishment, as well as how she supervised her children.[101]

Policy Implications

One of the appealing aspects of Hirschi's social control theory, and Gottfredson and Hirschi's theory, too, is their seemingly commonsensical crime prevention implication. To prevent delinquency, juveniles must be properly socialized; they must develop a strong moral bond to society (or self-control). For Hirschi, the units of social control most important in the establishment of the bond are the family, the school, and the law. Not surprisingly, then, programs based on social control theories include parent training and functional-family therapies that attempt to reduce family conflict through dispute settlement and negotiation, reduce neglect and abuse, teach moderate discipline, and promote positive interactions between parents and children.[102] Group homes and surrogate families have been proposed for children whose families are unsalvageable.[103] Counseling and problem solving and social skills training have been used with "at-risk" children, especially in school settings.[104]

Critique

Although social control theory is currently very influential in the thinking of many criminologists, it has not escaped extensive criticism. Perhaps the major problem, at least for some criminologists, is the theory's assumption that delinquency will occur if not prevented.[105] Some criminologists find it troublesome that the theory rejects altogether the idea of delinquent motivation.[106] Charles Tittle has addressed this criticism in his integrated control balance theory, which is discussed in Chapter 9.

Another criticism of social control theory is that it rests on the unrealistic assumption that all people have equal skill and ability to commit crime and delinquency.[107]

Hirschi's version of social control theory has also been criticized for underemphasizing the importance of delinquent associates, which has been found to be strongly related to delinquent behavior.[108]

Another criticism of social control theory is that it is a good explanation of only less serious delinquency. It does not explain more serious delinquency or adult criminality very well.[109] Critics claim that self-control theory does not explain many types of white-collar, political, or organized crime that are committed by persons with high levels of self-control.[110]

Regarding serious delinquency, critics point out that Hirschi's survey measure of delinquency consisted of only six "less serious" items: "whether they had stolen anything worth less than $2, stolen anything worth between $2 and $50, stolen anything worth more than $50, taken a car without the owner's permission, damaged or destroyed another person's property, or had beat up or deliberately hurt someone other than a sibling."[111]

The theory may not explain adult criminality very well because subjects in Hirschi's study were several thousand San Francisco area junior and senior high school boys. The subjects in most other tests of social control theory have been junior high and high school boys too.[112] A problem with junior high and high school boys as subjects is the reliability and validity of the data. They could have lied on the surveys by either not confessing to what they had done or claiming to have done more than they had—two likely possibilities with boys that age and an inherent problem with self-report crime surveys.

Another problem is social control theory's tacit assumption that a consensus exists in society about moral values.[113] Not only does the theory ignore the existence of pervasive social conflict about moral values, but it also fails to consider that society, itself, or at least some aspects of society, may be criminogenic.[114]

Another related problem is that social control theory ignores the criminalization process. It fails to consider why certain harmful and destructive behaviors are defined as crime or delinquency, whereas other similar behaviors are not.

Social control theory may also suffer from the problem of overprediction. It may predict too much delinquency. Unless society is much more effective in preventing delinquency than authorities and the media would lead one to believe, there should be much more delinquency than currently is the case.[115] The theory does not explain exceptions well, either. The theory does not allow for delinquency by juveniles who are properly socialized, nor does it allow for conformity by juveniles who are not properly socialized. The theory also has trouble in explaining geographical variations in delinquency (and crime). Are people in one country subject to less social control or do they have less self-control than people in another country? Are there similar differences within countries? Self-control theory has the same problem explaining gender differences in delinquency (and crime). Do females have more self-control than males?

Another problem with social control theory is its trouble with "maturational reform."[116] If juveniles become delinquent because they are not properly socialized (or lack self-control), then why do most delinquents stop their delinquent behaviors in early adulthood and not become criminals as adults? Does effective socialization of those delinquents (or the acquisition of self-control) suddenly occur in young adulthood and continue through the rest of their lives?[117]

A related criticism questions the direction of the purported relationship. In other words, does a weakened bond to society cause delinquency, as Hirschi suggests, or does delinquency produce a weakened bond to society?[118]

Still another problem with social control theory is that it does not explain how juveniles are socialized.[119] For example, how are attachments to others produced and changed?

Perhaps the most difficult question for social control theorists to answer is how people were socialized in the first place. In other words, if people are expected to commit crimes unless they are properly socialized, then who socialized the first people, or how were they socialized? So far, social control theorists have not provided a satisfactory answer to that question.

Study Questions

Learning Theories
1. How would Tarde explain crime?
2. How would Sutherland explain crime?
3. What are problems with Sutherland's theory of differential association?
4. What are the techniques of neutralization?
5. What modification to Sutherland's theory did Glaser make?
6. How would learning theorists explain crime?
7. How would learning theorists prevent crime?
8. What are problems with learning theories of crime?
9. How does learning theory compare with theories described previously in this book?

Subcultural Theories
10. Why are subcultural theories considered micro-level theories of crime?
11. How would Miller explain crime?
12. How would Wolfgang and Ferracuti explain violence?
13. How would Anderson explain crime?
14. What are problems with subcultural theories?

15. How do subcultural theories compare with theories described previously in this book?

Social Control Theories
16. How do social control theorists explain delinquency?
17. How would social control theorists prevent delinquency?
18. What are problems with social control theories?
19. How do social control theories compare with theories described previously in this book?

Notes

1. See Vold and Bernard (1986:208–209).
2. Tarde (1968:256).
3. See Bandura and Walters (1963).
4. Beirne and Messerschmidt (2000:91).
5. See Vold and Bernard (1986:210).
6. Williams and McShane (1994:78).
7. Sutherland (1983).
8. Sutherland and Cressey (1974:75–77).
9. Sutherland and Cressey (1974:77, 89, 93–96); also see Vold and Bernard (1986:213).
10. Sutherland and Cressey (1974:107–109). Because of the importance of the concepts of differential social organization and culture conflict in Sutherland's theory, he is considered a "value-conflict" theorist, albeit an apolitical one, by some (see Davis, 1975:Chap. 6). A political-conflict theory is addressed later in this book.
11. Tittle (1995:3).
12. See National Institute for Juvenile Justice and Delinquency Prevention (NI-JJDP) (1977:31); Kornhauser (1978:189); Martin, Mutchnick, and Austin (1990:164).
13. Curran and Renzetti (1994:188). However, see Andrews (1980) for an explanation of how they can be measured.
14. Sampson (1999:443–444); but see Akers (1999:478–479).
15. Akers and Jensen (2006).
16. Akers and Jensen (2006:51).
17. Lanier and Henry (1998:140).
18. Akers and Sellers (2004).
19. Sampson (1999:441).

20. Beirne and Messerschmidt (2000:136); Sampson (1999:446).
21. Curran and Renzetti (1994:190).
22. Savage (2008:1123).
23. Cullen and Agnew (2006:115).
24. Cohen (1955).
25. Maruna and Copes (2005).
26. Sykes and Matza (1957).
27. Sykes and Matza (1957:664).
28. Sykes and Matza (1957:666).
29. On loyalty and delinquency, also see Warr (2002:55–58).
30. For a critique of this position, see Taylor, Walton, and Young (1974:183–185).
31. Lanier and Henry (1998:151); Beirne and Messerschmidt (2000:162).
32. Maruna and Copes (2005:259).
33. Lanier and Henry (1998:150).
34. Lanier and Henry (1998:151).
35. Maruna and Copes (2005).
36. Maruna and Copes (2005).
37. Curran and Renzetti (1994:190).
38. Glaser (1956).
39. Burgess and Akers (1966); Akers (1985).
40. Jeffery (1965).
41. Wilson and Herrnstein (1985); Akers (1994, 1998); Andrews and Bonta (1994).
42. Akers and Jensen (2006).
43. Akers and Jensen (2006:37).
44. Sampson (1999:443).
45. See Rachlin (1976) for a description of the concepts.
46. In the case of habitual offenders, rewards may also be nonsocial and neu-rophysiological; see Wood, Gove, Wilson, and Cochran (1997).
47. Akers (1994); Andrews and Bonta (1994).
48. Akers (1994).
49. See Jeffery (1977:274–276).
50. This is one reason why so-called intermediate punishments, such as intensive supervision probation and parole, home confinement and electronic monitoring, and day reporting centers have been introduced.
51. See Bandura and Walters (1963:212); Andrews and Bonta (1994:202–205).
52. See Jeffery (1977:275).
53. Wilson and Herrnstein (1985:229–230) maintain that "problem" or "antisocial" children are also a product of ineffective punishment by parents.
54. See Martin et al. (1990:165).

55. Lanier and Henry (1998:144); Sampson (1999:447); Tittle (1995:111); but see Akers (1998:98–101).
56. Tittle (1995:111).
57. See Krohn (1999:470); Tittle (1995:111).
58. Glueck and Glueck (1956); Costello (1997); but see Matsueda (1997).
59. Vold and Bernard (1986:229–230).
60. But see Vold and Bernard (1986:226) for a different view.
61. See Akers (1998). Akers does not present a fully articulated integrated theory. Rather, he simply states that certain social structural factors, primarily drawn from anomie, social disorganization, and conflict theories, affect social psychological processes—that is, social learning concepts, which in turn influence both criminal behavior and crime rates. But which social structural factors are most important? Akers tells us only that the social structural factors strongly related to crime rates will also be strongly related to social learning concepts, and those social structural factors not strongly related to crime rates will not be strongly related to social learning concepts (1998:336). He admits that his theory "does not attempt to explain why a society has the [social structural factors, such as] culture, age structure, class system, race system, family system, economic system, gender/sex role system, or religious system that it has" (1998:336). Nor, for that matter, does his theory, as he again concedes, "explain (by reference to history, social change, or other macro-level variables) why there is social disorganization, conflict, or inequality in society" (1998:336).
62. See the discussion of interactionism in Chapter 8.
63. Cullen ad Agnew (2006:117).
64. Miller (1958).
65. See Vold (1979:224).
66. Kornhauser (1978:205); also see Costello (1997).
67. Ryan (1976:134); also see Kornhauser (1978:206–207).
68. Ryan (1976:134); also see Kornhauser (1978:208).
69. Kornhauser (1978:208).
70. Wolfgang and Ferracuti (1982).
71. Cote (2002:88).
72. Wolfgang and Ferracuti (1982:158–161).
73. Cao, Adams, and Jensen (1997). See Lee, Bankston, Hayes, and Thomas (2007) for a different view.
74. Hawley and Messner (1989).
75. Hayes and Lee (2005:593).
76. Cao et al. (1997:374).
77. Anderson (1999).

78. Cullen and Agnew (2006:151).
79. Stewart and Simons (2006).
80. Brezina, Agnew, Cullen, and Wright (2004).
81. Parker and Reckdenwald (2008).
82. Parker and Reckdenwald (2008:726).
83. Stewart and Simons (2006:1).
84. Lanier and Henry (1998:158) observe that social control theories provide the "missing half" of Sutherland's theory of differential association and other learning theories by suggesting that law-abiding behaviors are learned through a process of socialization. Sutherland's focus was on the learning of law-violating behaviors.
85. See Reiss (1951); Toby (1957); Nye (1958); Reckless (1961).
86. See Hirschi (1969).
87. Gottfredson and Hirschi (1990).
88. Gottfredson and Hirschi (1990:97).
89. Gottfredson and Hirschi (1990:100–101).
90. Gottfredson and Hirschi (1990:90).
91. Gottfredson (2006:77).
92. See for example, Pratt and Cullen (2000).
93. Unnever, Pratt, and Cullen (2003:483).
94. Gottfredson and Hirschi (1990).
95. Arneklev, Grasmick, and Bursik (1999); Burt, Simons, and Simons (2006); Nofzinger (2008); Turner and Piquero (2002).
96. Arneklev et al. (1999:307).
97. Tremblay (2006).
98. Burt, Simons, and Simons (2006:353).
99. Winfree, Taylor, He, and Esbensen (2006:278).
100. Nofzinger (2008:191).
101. Nofzinger (2008).
102. Lanier and Henry (1998:166).
103. Lanier and Henry (1998:166).
104. Lanier and Henry (1998:166).
105. As noted in Chapter 1, the seventeenth-century English philosopher Thomas Hobbes believed that all human beings are basically evil and, therefore, likely to commit crime. This idea may have been derived from the Christian belief that everyone is born into original sin. Similar ideas about human nature are found in Freudian psychoanalytic theory, which is considered a prototype for control theories. In Freud's version of psychoanalytic theory, it is assumed that everyone is capable of committing crime because of the sexual and aggressive drives of the id (see Andrews

and Bonta, 1994:70; Kornhauser, 1978:142). Note, however, that Hirschi is one control theorist who does not believe it is necessary to explain criminal behavior as the result of an uncontrolled id (see Andrews and Bonta, 1994:83). Early social control theorists assumed that all human beings were frustrated in the attempt to satisfy their needs or wants, given scarcity of means, and that need frustration was a "chronic condition of humanity" (see Kornhauser, 1978:47). Criminal behavior is one likely outcome of this chronic condition. Other theorists suggest that control theories do not need to assume that people are basically bad. For them, it is necessary only to assume at least a neutral human nature (see Williams and McShane, 1994:181).

106. NIJJDP (1977:44). Social control theorists do not actually deny delinquent motivation. They deny only a special motivation such as social disorganization or anomie. They assume that individuals are motivated to commit delinquency because of their human nature (but see Williams and McShane, 1994:181, for a different view).

107. Tittle (1995:59).

108. Andrews and Bonta (1994:84).

109. Martin et al. (1990:200); Agnew (1985).

110. Beirne and Messerschmidt (2000:221); Gottfredson and Hirschi (1990) disagree.

111. Curran and Renzetti (1994:200).

112. See Curran and Renzetti (1994:210–212).

113. NIJJDP (1977:43–44).

114. See Schur (1969).

115. Perhaps there is as much delinquency as social control theory predicts, but because most delinquency goes undiscovered and unreported, there is no way of knowing.

116. NIJJDP (1977:43).

117. See Einstadter and Henry (1995:196) and Williams and McShane (1994:192–193) for an affirmative response to this question.

118. Agnew (1985); Liska and Reed (1985).

119. NIJJDP (1977:43).

8

Critical Theories

Origins of Critical Theories

Critical theories are, in part, a product of the demystification of American society that began toward the end of the 1950s. *Demystification* is the correcting of misconceptions or "setting the record straight." At that time, a small group of philosophers and social scientists began to question the activities and priorities of the U.S. government and major American corporations, as well as the functionalist theory that often served as a justification. This questioning and skepticism was due to the revelation about how the American public was being misled about the "true" nature of current events, and about how the interests of the power elite were being served by those actions.[1]

In the political arena, the public's eyes were being opened to McCarthyism, the Bay of Pigs, the Cuban missile crisis, political and racial assassination, the government's abandonment of the civil rights movement, military intervention in Latin America and Asia, the domestic pacification objectives of the War on Poverty, and the destruction of communities for urban renewal. Revelations about corporate misdeeds included price-fixing conspiracies, price gouging, the sale of worthless or dangerous products, deceptive or fraudulent advertising, unsafe working conditions, and pollution and destruction of the environment. Particularly disturbing was evidence of the complicity of social scientists in some of those unsavory and, in some cases, illegal actions under the guise of a "value-free" social science.[2]

145

During the next decades, disclosures about secret and illegal activities of the U.S. government and major U.S. corporations became commonplace. Concepts like racism, sexism, capitalism, imperialism, monopoly, exploitation, and oppression were being employed with greater frequency to describe the social landscape. In the 1960s, the period of naive acceptance of the status quo and the belief in the purely benevolent actions of government ended for many philosophers and social scientists, and the seeds of critical theory began to sprout. For critical criminologists, government and corporate crimes highlight structural causes that are not readily apparent when conventional street crime is examined.[3]

Philosophical Assumptions of Critical Theories

Critical theories, for the most part, are sociological theories. However, not surprisingly, the basic philosophical assumptions of critical theories differ both from those of classical and neoclassical theories and from those of positivist theories. First, unlike classical and neoclassical theories, which are based on the ontological assumption that human beings have free will, and positivist theories, which are based on the ontological assumption that human beings are determined, either in a "hard" or "soft" way, critical theories are based on the ontological assumption that human beings are both determined *and* determining.[4] In other words, critical theorists assume that human beings are the creators of the institutions and structures that ultimately dominate and constrain them. Furthermore, critical theorists believe that as creators, human beings are capable of changing institutions and structures.

Second, in contrast to both classical and neoclassical and positivist theories, which are based on the cosmological assumption that society is characterized fundamentally by a consensus about moral values, whether by social contract in the former or the collective conscience or the division of labor in the latter, critical theories are based on the cosmological assumption that conflict is the norm, that society is characterized primarily by conflict about moral values.

Finally, unlike positivist theories that are based on the assumption that social scientists, including criminologists, can be value-neutral or objective in their work, critical theories are based on the assumption that such a position is impossible. Critical theorists assume that everything they do is value-laden by virtue of their being human. Many critical theorists believe that the most intellectually honest alternative to the value-neutral stance is to be honest and forthright about one's values and let consumers of one's work evaluate that work in light of an explicitly articulated value position.

That said, it is important to note that although many criminologists consider themselves critical, there actually are few critical criminologists.[5] The primary reason is that although most criminologists are typically critical of dissonant theoretical positions, few criminologists, including so-called critical or radical criminologists, are, in the tradition of the Greek philosopher Socrates, critical of their own positions. That is, few criminologists are *reflexive* or self-conscious about their own position.[6] This failure of criminologists to be critical and reflexive about their own theoretical perspectives is one of criminology's major problems.

Interactionism and Labeling Theory

The focus of interactionist and labeling theory is the *meaning* of crime and criminality.[7] Attention is shifted from the positivist concern with the peculiarities of the criminal actor to the *criminalization process*—the way people and actions are defined as criminal.[8] From this perspective, the distinguishing feature of all "criminals" is that they have been the object of a *negative social reaction*.[9] In other words, they have been designated by the state and its agents as different and "bad."[10]

Mead's Theory of Symbolic Interactionism

Interactionism and labeling theory have their roots in the symbolic interactionism of George Herbert Mead (1863–1931), whose ideas on the subject can be summarized in three propositions. First, "human beings act toward things on the basis of the meanings that the things have for them."[11] By this, Mead meant that people often interpret the same event or behavior differently because of the unique meanings that they attach to it.[12] Consider, for example, the Ford Pinto case.[13]

Between 1971 and 1976, Ford Motor Company executives made the decision to sell Ford Pintos (and Mercury Bobcats) to the public, knowing that the placement of the gas tank made the cars susceptible to fiery explosions on rear impact at relatively slow speeds. They also knew that innocent people probably would be killed and injured as a result. Knowing this, they decided that it would be cheaper in the long run to settle the lawsuits initiated by injured drivers and passengers and the families of killed drivers and passengers than to recall the cars and install an $11 metal shield to protect the gas tank. As it turned out, the Ford executives were correct in their belief that people would die and be injured as a result of their decisions. They were wrong, however, in assuming that settling lawsuits would be cheaper than recalling the vehicles and installing the metal shield. In any event, the relevant question for this discussion is whether the Ford executives who made those decisions were guilty of any crimes. Although the courts ultimately decided that they were not, many people believe that they were. The point is that the actions of the Ford executives are interpreted differently by different people, depending on the meaning the event has for them.

Mead's second proposition is that "the meaning of things arises out of the social interaction that one has with one's fellows."[14] By this, Mead meant that meaning resides neither in the thing itself nor exclusively in the sender or the receiver. Meaning is the product of negotiations between the sender, the receiver, and relevant social others.[15] Thus, for example, whether a woman forced to have sexual intercourse against her will has been raped in a legal sense depends on the act's interpretation by police, prosecutors, judges, juries, and especially the woman herself. It may also depend on such things as the amount of resistance offered by the victim, the victim's sexual history, and a host of other factors.

Mead's third proposition is that "these meanings are handled in, and modified through, an interpretative process used by the person in dealing with things he encounters."[16] In other words, in the interpretation of an event, people not only receive meaning but create it as well. Thus, people's actions are, at least to some extent, determined by themselves.[17] This proposition is the basis for the critical theory assumption that people are both determined and determining.[18] For example, according to the Senate Intelligence Committee Report about the CIA's interrogation program, Khalid Sheikh Mohammed, the self-proclaimed mastermind of the 9/11 attacks, was "waterboarded" 183 times, received "rectal hydration," was kept awake for a week, and was made to stand for hours with his hands above his head. Were these actions torture or simply "enhanced interrogation techniques?" Although President Obama and many other people consider waterboarding and other enhanced interrogation techniques torture, former Vice President Dick Cheney adamantly disagrees that Mohammed was tortured.

A lesson to be learned from Mead's theory is that one must be careful not to assume that his or her interpretation of a criminal act is the correct one. Even if the interpretation seems logical to that person, the actor or another independent observer might interpret the act very differently.[19] That may be why many criminal acts are committed by people who do not define themselves as criminals.[20] To truly understand a criminal act, then, it is necessary to understand the act from the perspective of the actor, that is, from the actor's definition of self, situation, and society.[21]

According to Mead, self-image, or conception of self, is constructed by a person's interpretation of the way that person believes other people see him or her.[22] Mead called this self-image "the self as a social construct." Charles Cooley (1864–1929) referred to it as "the looking-glass self."[23] Thus, for example, if a child believes that other people believe he or she is bad or delinquent, then there is a good chance that he or she will believe it too.

People define their situations by the meanings they negotiate with other people. This may explain why two people can have entirely different conceptions of ostensibly the same environment. For one life is interpreted as rosy; for the other, as hell. This difference of interpretation may resolve the problem of over-prediction (i.e., the problem of positivist theories generally accounting for too much crime, and, at the same time, not explaining exceptions well).

Finally, conceptions of society are also formed through an interpretative process. Whether people view society as wonderful and full of opportunity or horrible and oppressive depends on how they interpret society within the context of their social interactions. For Mead, then, human behavior is explained by the meaning people give to self, situation, and society.

Labeling Theory

Labeling theory, or the "societal reaction" approach, uses this theoretical framework to explain why people commit crimes and conceive of themselves as criminals. As Howard Becker (1928–) relates, "Social groups create deviance [crime] by making the rules whose infraction constitutes deviance [crime], and by applying those rules to particular people and labeling them as outsiders."[24]

It is important to note that labeling theorists attempt to explain only what Edwin Lemert (1912–1996) called "secondary deviance."[25] For purposes of this discussion, *secondary deviance* is the commission of crime after the first criminal act, with the acceptance of a criminal label. Secondary deviance begins with an initial criminal act, or what Lemert called "primary deviance." The causes of initial criminal acts are unspecified. Nevertheless, if society, especially official agents of the state such as the police, reacts negatively to an initial criminal act, the offender will likely be *stigmatized*, or negatively labeled. It is possible, even likely, that an initial criminal act will not be reacted to at all, or that the offender will not accept or internalize the negative label. However, if the negative label is successfully applied to the offender, the label may produce a *self-fulfilling prophecy*— a concept created by Robert Merton[26]—in which the offender's self-image is defined by the label. Secondary deviance is the prophecy fulfilled.

Policy Implications

The crime prevention implication of labeling theory is simply not to label or to employ "radical nonintervention."[27] This might be accomplished through decriminalization (the elimination of many behaviors from the scope of the criminal law), diversion (removing offenders from involvement in the criminal justice process), greater due process protections (replacing discretion with the rule of law), and deinstitutionalization (a policy of reducing jail and prison populations and construction).[28]

As is well known, once a person is labeled and stereotyped as a "criminal," he or she will probably be shunned by law-abiding society, have difficulty finding a good job, lose some civil rights (if convicted of a felony), and suffer a variety of other disabilities. The criminal (and delinquent) label is conferred by all of the agencies of criminal justice—the police, the courts, and the correctional apparatus—as well as the media, the schools, churches, and other social institutions. The irony is that in its attempt to reduce crime and delinquency, society may be inadvertently increasing it by labeling people and producing secondary deviance.[29]

A provocative alternative to the nonintervention strategy is John Braithwaite's (1951–) "reintegrative shaming."[30] Reintegrative shaming is a form of restorative justice, an alternative to the punitive justice currently used in the United States and many other countries.[31] The primary goals of restorative justice are to restore the health of the community, repair the harm done, meet victims' needs, and require the offender to contribute to those repairs. In Braithwaite's *reintegrative shaming*, disappointment is expressed for the offender's actions, the offender is shamed and punished, but, what is more important, following the expression of disappointment and shame is a concerted effort on the part of the community to forgive the offender and reintegrate him or her back into society. Throughout this process, the offender is treated respectfully and empathically as a good person, who has committed a bad act, but who deserves to remain a member of the community.[32] In contrast, *stigmatizing shaming*, a characteristic of the current U.S. criminal justice system, occurs when the wrongdoer is treated disrespectfully, labeled a bad person, and shunned, to some degree, by society.[33] Braithwaite contends that the practice of reintegrative shaming is one of the primary reasons for Japan's relatively low crime rate.[34]

Since its introduction in 1989, reintegrative shaming has received a fair amount of attention from researchers.[35] Overall, the results of these studies are mixed.[36] The analyses often compare the outcomes of restorative justice conferences to more traditional court processing. One recent experiment was designed to evaluate the effect of such conferences on recidivism among adult, drunk-driving offenders.[37] Findings suggest that offenders assigned to restorative justice conferences were equally likely to reoffend as those who were assigned to traditional adjudication. However, a lower rate of recidivism and more overall support for the law were discovered for those offenders who believed the conference was procedurally fair, and that they had been truly forgiven and reintegrated.[38] Considerable ethnographic research suggests that the emotional dynamics between the offender and the victim are key to the success of programs based on the ideals of reintegrative shaming.[39]

Critique

Labeling theory has been the subject of several criticisms. First, in taking the side of the "underdog"[40] or adopting what Becker called an "unconventional sentimentality,"[41] labeling theorists have been accused of tending to romanticize the criminal offender as a primitive revolutionary reacting to an unjust society (like Robin Hood). A problem with such a view is that it ignores the very real harm and suffering caused by those offenders. More times than not, offenders and their victims are from the same social groups. Victimizing members of one's own group hardly can be considered liberating.

Labeling theory has also been criticized for not being a theory at all but rather a "sensitizing perspective."[42] This criticism, moreover, has been acknowledged as valid by some of the social scientists (for example, Howard Becker) whose work is identified with the perspective.[43] The criticism, however, in no way diminishes the contribution of labeling ideas.

Another criticism of labeling theory is that it does not explain primary deviance.[44] Critics point out that the label does not create the criminal behavior in the first place. This criticism seems unfair, however, because labeling theorists are quite clear that the object of their theory is secondary and not primary deviance.

A more legitimate problem with labeling theory is that it tends to overemphasize the importance of the official labeling process.[45] On one hand, the impression is given that an oppressive society arbitrarily stigmatizes innocent people and that, as a result, they begin a life of crime.[46] That scenario probably does not happen very often. On the other hand, the impression is given that offenders resist the criminal label and accept it only when they are no longer capable of fighting it.[47] As for the latter, in some communities the label criminal, or some variation of it, is actively sought.[48] In some cases, people develop criminal self-images without ever having been labeled criminal in the first place.[49] Furthermore, if the delinquent label is so stigmatizing, why do most delinquents not engage in adult criminality (the problem of "maturational reform")? For that matter, if the criminal label is so stigmatizing, why do most criminals stop their illegal activities when they reach middle age?[50]

Labeling theory has also been faulted for ignoring individual differences among criminal offenders. For example, critics contend that, whereas radical nonintervention or restorative justice may be appropriate for low-risk cases, it may not be appropriate for high-risk cases.[51]

A major problem with labeling theory is that it holds a simplistic view of the criminalization process.[52] For example, as Becker maintains, "Social groups create deviance [crime] by making the rules whose infraction constitutes deviance [crime], and by applying those rules to particular people and labeling them as outsiders."[53] But what social groups create crime? What is missing in labeling theory is a coherent conception of the interrelationship of power, the state, and law creation.

Perhaps the most telling problem with labeling theory is the question whether the act of stigmatizing someone as criminal or delinquent causes more crime and delinquency than it prevents.[54] To date, the answer is unknown.

Conflict Criminology

Unlike classical or neoclassical and positivist theories, which are based on the assumption that society is characterized primarily by consensus, conflict theory is based on the assumption that society is based primarily on conflict between competing interest groups (for example, the rich against the poor, corporations against labor, Whites against minorities, men against women, adults against children, Protestants against Catholics, Democrats against Republicans). In many cases, competing interest groups are not equal in power and resources, and consequently one group is dominant and the other is subordinate.

Although they did not address crime *per se*, conflict criminology is based on the seminal ideas of the German sociologists Max Weber (1864–1920) and Georg Simmel (1858–1918), whose "liberal" ideas about social conflict, in large part, were a reaction to the more radical ideas of another German social thinker, Karl Marx (1818–1883). (Marx's contribution to radical criminology is addressed in the next section.)

One of the earliest theorists in the United States to apply conflict theory to the study of crime was George B. Vold (1896–1967). For Vold and other conflict theorists, such as Thorsten Sellin (1896–1994), Austin Turk (1934–2014), Richard Quinney (1934–), and William J. Chambliss (1933–2014), many behaviors are defined as crimes because it is in the interests of dominant groups to do so.[55] As for those behaviors that are in everyone's interest to be defined as criminal, members of dominant groups are frequently able to violate them with impunity because of their control of the state. When they cannot escape punitive action, they usually face a civil remedy for administrative or regulatory agency violations. Prison sentences are rarely imposed. They are also able to evade the most punitive penalties for their crimes by being able to hire the best attorneys. For conflict criminologists, people are only labeled as criminals when it is in the interests of dominant groups to do so; and because it is generally not in the interest of dominant groups to label its own members as criminals, members of subordinate groups are more likely to be stigmatized in that way.

Dominant groups use crime and the criminal law, then, to control subordinates. However, the image that is projected for public consumption is quite different. The public image is that the criminal law and the state that administers it are value-neutral institutions.[56] That is, neither the law nor the state is presumed to have a vested interest in which party to a dispute "wins." The only interest of the state and the law, at least as far as the public image is concerned, is in making sure that disputes between competing interest groups are resolved justly and, what is more important, peacefully. This public image allows dominant groups to create the impression that interests of the two groups are the same. This ploy legitimizes the authority and practices of dominant groups and allows them to surreptitiously achieve their own parochial interests, generally at the expense of other groups. Crime also serves the interests of dominant groups by deflecting the attention of subordinate group members from the exploitation they endure from dominant groups and turning that attention to other subordinate group members defined as criminal.[57]

All behavior, including criminal behavior, in this view, is the result of people acting in ways consistent with their social positions. Whether white-collar crime or ordinary street crime, crime is a response to a person's social situation. The reason members of subordinate groups appear in official criminal statistics more frequently than members of dominant groups is that the latter are better able than the former to ensure that the responses of subordinate group members to their social situations will be defined and reacted to as criminal.[58] For conflict theorists, the amount of crime in a society is a function of the extent of conflict generated by *stratification, hierarchical relationships, power differentials*, or the ability of some groups to dominate other groups in that society. Crime, in short, is caused by *relative powerlessness*.[59]

Policy Implications

Conflict theory has two principal crime prevention implications. On one hand, dominant groups could cede some of their power to subordinate groups, making the latter groups more powerful and reducing conflict.[60] Increasing equality in that way might be accomplished by redistributing wealth through a more progressive taxation scheme, for example.

On the other hand, dominant group members could become more effective rulers and subordinate group members better subjects. To do so, dominant groups would have to do a better job of convincing subordinate groups that the current inequitable distribution of power in society is legitimate and in their mutual interests. Members of subordinate groups, in turn, would have to either believe it or resign themselves to their inferior status. Either way, dominant group members hope that over time subordinate group members will learn to follow those who dominate them.

Critique

Psychologists have criticized conflict theory for ignoring individual differences among criminal offenders.[61] Critics charge that conflict theorists ignore the variation in how people respond to relative powerlessness and the conflict that often results. Conflict theorists, according to their critics, fail to explain why criminal offenders choose particular crimes to commit. Ignored in conflict theory, argue critics, are such important factors as the opportunity, intelligence, and skills necessary to commit various crimes.[62]

A related problem is that people, at either the individual or group level, are rarely totally dominated or dominating.[63] At the individual level, people may be dominant in one group (for example, the family) but subordinate in another (for instance, at the workplace). At the group level, people may simultaneously be members of both dominant and subordinate groups. For example, they may be members of a dominant economic or political group but, at the same time, also be members of subordinate religious, racial, or ethnic groups. Furthermore, the status of groups or the status of individuals within groups, as either dominant or subordinate, may change over time.

Conflict theorists may also overestimate the extent of conflict in society about moral values, at least with regard to some types of crime. Numerous studies (albeit older ones) show that the American public, regardless of race or class, almost universally condemns crimes involving theft and violence.[64] Still, while there may be near universal condemnation of crimes such as murder, rape, and robbery, people may nonetheless differ on what they believe constitutes murder, rape, and robbery. For example, were the actions of the Ford Motor Company executives, discussed in the last section, murder? Is euthanasia murder?

Another criticism is that, like positivists, some conflict theorists delude themselves into believing that they can be value-neutral or objective in their work—or at least be able to approximate it.[65] For example, Turk writes:

> Nonpartisan conflict theory and analysis assumes that the ideological bent of theorists or the political utilities of theories are irrelevant for

assessing the validity of knowledge claims.... Recognizing that values can never be totally excluded from the research process, nonpartisan conflict analysts also recognize that approximations to value-neutral procedures and knowledge are possible.[66]

As noted previously, most critical criminologists believe that it is impossible for human beings (including criminologists) to be value-neutral or objective in anything, or even to approximate such a state.

Problems also arise when conflict theory is confused with radical theory, as is frequently the case. (Radical theory is presented in the next section.) The two theories are not the same.[67] For example, conflict theory is less specific than radical theory in the identification of causes of crime. Whereas conflict theory specifies stratification or relative powerlessness as criminogenic factors, radical theory focuses on the political and economic structures of society.[68] In this regard, a problem with conflict theory is that it generally fails to identify the sources of power in society.[69] When those sources are identified, power is usually attributed to the personal characteristics of elites (for example, they are smarter, better educated, luckier, and better able to defer immediate gratification). The problem is that conflict theory ignores the social structural sources of power in society (for example, ownership of private property). Conflict theory presumes, in contrast to radical theory, that power is the basis of private property rather than vice versa.[70]

Another major difference between conflict and radical theories is the erroneous assumption, held by conflict theorists, that radical theorists believe that power in society is the exclusive possession of a "capitalist ruling class." Conflict theorists argue, instead, that different groups in society possess and exercise varying degrees of power.[71] In addition, conflict theorists maintain that conflict is not historically or socially limited to a particular type of society (for instance, capitalism), as they assume radical theorists believe. Conflict theorists maintain that conflict is a fundamental element of all societies.[72] The problem is that conflict theorists fundamentally misunderstand the radical position. First, radical theorists do not deny that conflict is a fundamental element of all societies. Second, radical theorists recognize the existence of many conflicting interest groups that wield varying degrees of power in society. However, for radical theorists, the existence of more or less powerful and oftentimes conflicting interest groups does not preclude the existence of "classes" (especially under capitalism); instead, they are considered two different phenomena. The primary difference between interest groups and classes is that usually an individual may voluntarily align him- or herself with any number of interest groups, whereas his or her class position in society is dictated by his or her relation to the means of production, whether or not he or she owns property, and the type of property he or she owns (see next section on radical theory).[73]

A final difference between conflict and radical theories, and a criticism of conflict theory, is that conflict theory is basically reformist—that is, it is not radical.[74] Politically, conflict theory is liberal. Conflict theorists assume that existing social institutions can correct social problems such as crime. Thus, for example, if only the agencies of criminal justice were more effective, a conflict theorist might argue, crime would be greatly reduced. However, historical evidence suggests that this may be a dubious assumption.

Radical Criminology

Although the German social theorist Karl Marx (1818–1883) wrote very little about crime and criminal justice, radical theories of crime causation are generally based on a Marxist theoretical framework that interrelates the capitalist mode of production, the state, law, crime control, and crime—as well as other relevant factors.[75] Within this view, there are three competing models of society or interpretations of how the aforementioned factors are interrelated: the ruling-class determinist (or instrumentalist), the economic determinist (or structuralist), and the dialectical.

Before examining the three different models of society, however, some definitions and a brief introduction to Marxist theory might prove useful. First, in Marx's methodology for analyzing society, *historical-materialism*, stages of social history are distinguished by different modes or means of production. A *mode* or *means of production* refers to the ways by which people produce the material goods necessary for their existence (for example, slavery, feudalism, capitalism, and socialism). An individual's relationship to the mode or means of production determines his or her *class* position in society (for instance, ruling class or working class) and, ultimately, his or her share of social wealth. Class position is also presumably "an important determinant of such basic life events as social mobility, consciousness, level and types of education and income, leisure patterns, and … the likelihood of incarceration."[76] In capitalist societies, a numerically small *capitalist ruling class* owns the means of production and receives a greatly disproportionate share of social wealth, primarily by means of rent, interest, and profit. A numerically large *working class*, on the other hand, labors for capitalists to earn wages and receives only a small fraction of social wealth.

Returning to the three models of society, in the *ruling-class determinist* or *instrumentalist* model, a mostly homogeneous group of capitalists is able to manipulate the state and the law for its own parochial interests. It is able to do this through, among other things, financially controlling political campaigns, especially at the national level.

In the *economic determinist* or *structuralist* model, by contrast, the functions of the state are presumed to be determined by structures of society (for example, "the market" or "the law") rather than by people who occupy positions of state power or by individual capitalists. In this version, the survival of the capitalist system, even at the expense of individual capitalists or their agents, is of paramount importance.

Finally, the *dialectical* model combines the other two models and adds that which model is a more accurate description of society at any given time is historically contingent. In the dialectical model, moreover, the state and the law are not viewed only as repressive institutions that promote the interests of the capitalist ruling class over those of all others but are also regarded as having liberating potential as well (for example, antidiscrimination legislation and enforcement).

The Dutch socialist, Willem Bonger (1876–1940) introduced one of the earliest versions of a radical theory of crime.[77] Among the first criminologists in the United States to employ one or the other versions of radical criminological theory were Richard Quinney, William J. Chambliss, Anthony M. Platt (1942–), and Raymond Michalowski (1946–).[78] Also influential in the early development of radical criminology were British criminologists Ian Taylor (1944–2001), Paul Walton (1943–2012), and Jock Young (1942–2013).

In general, radical criminologists focus their attention on the social arrangements of society, especially on political and economic structures and institutions (the "political economy") of *capitalism*. They argue that in capitalist societies, a very small percentage of people are the big winners in the individualistic and competitive struggle for material wealth, and the rest of the population are losers (relatively speaking). The winners (the really big winners are members of the ruling class) do everything in their considerable power (which they possess by virtue of their ownership of material wealth) to keep from becoming losers, including taking advantage of other people—preying on them. Losers (members of the working class and the nonworking classes), in an effort to become winners, usually do what the winners do and prey on weaker people. Radical criminologists believe that the more unevenly wealth is distributed in a society, the more likely people are able to find persons weaker than themselves. In fact, it has been argued that "a reasonably strong case can be made that the economic inequality in a society—that is, the gap between the richest and the poorest—has a causal impact on the level of violence in that society."[79]

However, it is important to understand that, for radical criminologists, the destructive effects of capitalism, such as crime, are not caused directly by income or property inequality or poverty *per se*. Rather, crime is a product of the political economy that, in capitalist societies, encourages an individualistic competition among wealthy people and among poor people and between rich and poor people (the intra- and inter*class struggle*) and the practice of taking advantage of other people (*exploitation*). The class struggle and exploitation, in turn, produce crime, income or property inequality, poverty, and many of the other problems that are characteristics of a capitalist society.

In short, for radical criminologists, crime in capitalist societies is often a rational response to the circumstances in which people find themselves in the individualistic and competitive struggle to acquire material wealth. Wilson and Herrnstein, though not radical criminologists themselves, suggest that one of the reasons that Japan has much less crime per capita than the United States, even though Japan too is a capitalist society, is the Japanese emphasis on group achievement, as opposed to the American emphasis on individual achievement.[80] The Japanese emphasis on group achievement is derived from the Confucian principle that "the individual is expected to subordinate his own identity to the interest of the group."[81]

According to radical criminologists, "senseless" violent crime, which most often is committed by poor people against each other, is frequently a product of the demoralizing and brutalizing conditions under which many people are forced to live. As Taylor, Walton, and Young explain, "It is not that man behaves [under capitalism] as an animal because of his 'nature': it is that he is not fundamentally allowed by virtue of the social arrangements of production to do otherwise."[82] Elliott Currie (1942–) has specified seven elements of "market societies" that, in combination, are likely to breed serious violent crime. They are: (1) "the progressive destruction of livelihood" (the absence of steady well-paying work); (2) "the growth of extremes of economic inequality and material deprivation"; (3) "the withdrawal of public services and supports, especially for families and children"; (4) "the erosion of informal and communal networks of mutual support, supervision, and care"; (5) "the spread of a materialistic, neglectful, and 'hard' culture" (the exaltation of "often brutal individual competition and consumption over the values of community, contribution, and productive work"); (6) "the unregulated marketing of the technology of violence" (the absence of public regulation of firearms); and, not least, (7) "the weakening of social and political alternatives" (which inhibits people most "at risk" from defining their problems in collective terms and envisioning a collective response).[83]

None of this means that noncapitalist societies will be crime-free. Rather non-capitalist societies should have different types of crime and much lower rates of crime (as traditionally defined) "because the less intense class struggle should reduce the forces leading to and the functions of crime."[84]

It is important to emphasize that radical criminologists define the concept of crime differently than is the custom of traditional criminologists. Because they assume that criminal law is all too often manipulated to benefit particular interests to the detriment of all others, radical criminologists argue that the legal definition of crime is both too narrow and too broad in scope. Radical criminologists maintain that "crime" should be defined as a violation of human rights. As Platt explains: "A radical perspective defines crime as a violation of politically-defined human rights: the truly egalitarian rights to decent food and shelter, to human dignity and self-determination, rather than the so-called right to compete for an unequal share of wealth and power."[85] A radical definition of crime includes "imperialism, racism, capitalism, sexism and other systems of exploitation which contribute to human misery and deprive people of their human potentiality."[86] Although many behaviors currently proscribed by criminal law would be included in this radical definition, other behaviors now considered crimes would be excluded (such as victimless crimes or crimes of consumption), and some behaviors not now considered crimes would be added (such as racism, sexism, imperialism).[87]

Radical criminologists' definition of crime—as a violation of human rights—is reflected in an impressive body of work yielding support for their theory. In a recent evaluation of the current status of empirical work in this area, Lynch, Schwendinger, and Schwendinger find:

> Over the past fifteen years, radical criminologists have published numerous empirical studies addressing a wide range of factors including: crime and delinquency; public health and safety; violence against women; victimization; racial bias in criminal justice processes; corporate, white collar and state crime; trends in imprisonment, policing and crime; media reporting of crime; and environmental harms, crimes and justice. This research draws on literature from economics, political science, public policy, sociology, anthropology, environmental science, geography, epidemiology, and medicine.[88]

One specific area of research that has garnered the attention of several radical criminologists is the unequal geographic distribution of environmental harms (e.g., exposure to hazardous waste, pesticides, and other environmental toxins) across communities.[89] Exposure to environmental harms has been shown to have detrimental effects on health, including a wide variety of cancers, asthma, birth defects, learning disabilities, and IQ deficits.[90] In a series of studies, Stretesky and Lynch have shown that residents in poor and minority communities are much more likely to live near hazardous waste sites and be exposed to chemical accidents than those residing in more affluent or White areas.[91] This pattern is consistent with respect to public schools as well. Schools with a high percentage of African-American students are more likely than majority White schools to be closer in proximity to hazardous waste sites.[92] Finally, when the Environmental Protection Agency (EPA) fined violating companies, the penalty amounts were lower for violations occurring in minority and poor areas than for those in White or wealthier communities.[93] Findings such as these "indicate that the EPA does a poor job of providing equal protection to racially and economically diverse communities."[94]

Policy Implications

Among the policy implications of radical criminological theory is to reconceptualize the definition of crime in terms of violations of human rights. Another is to demonstrate that the criminal law on which the definition of crime is currently based is "used by the state and the ruling class to secure the survival of the capitalist system, and, as capitalist society is further threatened by its own contradictions, criminal law will be increasingly used in the attempt to maintain domestic order."[95] Among the contradictions of capitalism are structured unemployment (where a 4 or 5 percent peacetime unemployment rate is generally considered "full employment"); the exportation of higher-paying manufacturing jobs to Third World countries and their replacement with lower-paying service-sector jobs (the service-sector jobs also frequently lack the health and retirement benefits commonly available with manufacturing jobs); inflation (which occurs when the supply of goods fails to meet the demand); recession (which is a temporary decline in business activity during a period when such activity has been generally increasing); and depression (which is a period marked by a decrease of business activity, greatly increased unemployment, falling prices and wages, and so forth).

Radical criminologists, following the lead of Marx and Friedrich Engels (1820–1895), point out that criminal law serves the interests of the ruling class in at least three ways.[96] First, it promotes and protects all private property, even though only a small percentage of the population, which includes the ruling class, owns most of the private property. Second, through concepts such as "justice," "the rule of law," and "equality before the law," criminal law gives the impression that it stands above society as an impartial arbiter of conflicts, thus hiding its origins in political and economic interests, especially those of the ruling class. As Beirne and Messerschmidt observe, "To apply law fairly and equally in a society of inequality is merely to perpetuate inequality."[97] Third, the criminal law is a repressive institution, as noted earlier, able to incapacitate (by imprisoning or executing) people who threaten the capitalist system.

Still other implications of radical theory are to expose the criminal justice system as a "state-initiated" and "state-supported" effort to rationalize social control and eventually to replace the criminal justice system with "popular" or "socialist justice."[98]

Contrary to the beliefs of many liberal criminologists, radical criminologists argue that reform of capitalist institutions, especially those of the criminal justice system, cannot legitimately be expected to eradicate the initial causes of crime for two reasons:

> First, capitalism depends quite substantially on the preservation of the conditions of competition and inequality. Those conditions ... will tend to lead almost inevitably to relatively pervasive criminal behavior; without those conditions, the capitalist system would scarcely work at all. Second, as many have argued, the general presence of racism in this country, though capitalists may not in fact have created it, tends to support and maintain the power of the capitalists as a class by providing cheap labor and dividing the working class.[99]

For nearly all radical criminologists (anarchists are exceptions[100]), the solution to the problem of crime is a socialist society in which human diversity would presumably be appreciated as it is not under capitalism.[101] Such a transformation would in turn require the development of a political consciousness among all people who are exploited and alienated by the capitalist system. Perhaps most importantly for radical criminologists, only through *praxis* (human action based on theory) will the new socialist society be achieved.

Currie believes that at present, the most promising lever of change, and at the same time the most effective means to significantly reduce serious violent crime, is "full employment at socially meaningful work at good wages, and with reasonable hours."[102] Such a policy would require "substantially expanding employment in the public and nonprofit sectors of the economy, and developing policies for worksharing and reduction of work time."[103]

Critique

One objection to radical criminological theory is that the radical definition of crime as the violation of human rights is itself too broad and vague. Although that view may be true, in a different context, legal philosopher Edmond Cahn noted that although it is often difficult to determine what is just, most people can easily identify what is unjust.[104] Perhaps in a like manner, it may be equally difficult to determine what a human right is, but radical criminologists generally assume that most people know when a human right has been violated.

A second problem with radical theory is the failure to adequately address the question of how working and nonworking people become conscious of their class interests.[105] In other words, how do people learn that they are in a class struggle? To date, the ruling class has been able to effectively undermine the ability of workers (and the unemployed) to become conscious of their class interests by, among other tactics: (1) the creation of job hierarchies and structures of privileges and promotions; (2) the dispersion and disintegration of working-class communities through suburbanization, increasing homeownership (at least until recent years), and geographic mobility; and (3) the creation by the media of a fear of crime that undermines the organization and solidarity of the groups most victimized by crime and most in need of organization and solidarity to realize their interests.[106] In a longitudinal analysis, Beckett shows that political rhetoric about crime precedes increases in citizen concerns about crime. She suggests that political elites manipulate public perceptions of crime and what should be done about it ("getting tough") ostensibly for political gain.[107]

A related problem is the question of how people realize their class interests once they become conscious of them—that is, what is the relationship between theory and praxis?[108] Presumably, class interests are realized through a synthesis of communicative interaction (knowledge) and labor (action), so that actions occasion consciousness of knowledge which in turn informs subsequent action, and so forth.[109] A problem with this explanation is that it fails to account for obvious constraints on consciousness (for example, false consciousness), theoretical knowledge, and practical choice. As Marx pointed out, "The ideas of the ruling class are in every epoch the ruling ideas."[110]

Psychologists have criticized class-based (that is, radical and some critical) theories for ignoring individual differences in the understanding of crime.[111] The argument is that political economy, social structure, and culture are constants (and not variables) in class-based theories and that they "cannot account for variation in individual conduct within particular social arrangements" (though they do "have important roles to play in establishing the fundamental contingencies that are in effect within each particular social arrangement").[112] In short, for these critics, political economy, social structure, and culture do not vary among individuals and, therefore, cannot adequately explain individual differences in criminality (for example, why one type of crime rather than another is committed). They do, however, determine what stimuli are rewarding or aversive within each particular social arrangement.[113] Many sociologists, on the other hand, believe that social structures and cultures are variables and not constants.[114]

Other criticisms of radical criminological theory are that its adherents are pursuing a political agenda and thus are not objective in their work; that its causal model is wrong—in other words, that social arrangements do not cause people to commit crime, as radical criminologists argue, but rather that crime is committed by people who are born evil and remain evil; that it has not been tested satisfactorily; that it cannot be tested satisfactorily; and that it is utopian in its policy implications.[115]

The accusation of utopianism (*utopia* means "nowhere") is most frequently directed at radical criminology's assumption that socialism is the solution to the crime problem in capitalist societies. At a time when many so-called socialist or communist nations are racing to adopt free-market economies (capitalism), the assumption seems questionable at best. However, radical criminologists maintain that none of the nations that have claimed to be socialist or communist were or are truly socialist or communist, at least as Marx had originally conceived the terms. They say it is unfair to look to the totalitarian nations that were socialist or communist in name only for guidance in dealing with the crime problems of capitalist societies.

Today, it probably makes little sense to speak of capitalist and socialist societies anyway, because no pure societies of either type exist. (They probably never did.) All countries now manifest elements of both capitalism and socialism. In the United States, for example, Social Security, Medicare, Medicaid, and other social programs provided by federal, state, and local governments are clearly socialistic, as is so-called corporate welfare, such as the many subsidies and tax loopholes for corporations. Regarding corporate tax loopholes, the following are three recent examples. In 2009, Exxon Mobil made $19 billion in profits but paid no taxes. Instead, it received a $156 million rebate from the IRS. In 2010, Bank of America made $4.4 billion in profits but paid no taxes. Instead, it received a $1.9 billion tax refund from the IRS. Bank of America had previously received a bailout of nearly $1 trillion from the Federal Reserve and the Treasury Department. Finally, between 2005 and 2010, General Electric made $26 billion in profits just in the United States; yet paid no taxes. Instead, it received a $4.1 billion refund from the IRS.[116]

Thus, in the twenty-first century, we must recognize that all countries have "mixed" economies, with elements of both capitalism and socialism. A key question, then, especially for those people who are interested in reducing the crime problem and improving the overall quality of human life, is, What is the best mix?

Feminist Criminology

Feminism refers to the doctrine—and the political movement based on it—"that women should have the same economic, social, and political rights as men."[117] Feminist theory informs many social sciences including sociology, psychology, anthropology, as well as criminology. The application of feminist theory to criminology, however, is fairly recent,[118] despite the fact that gender is one of the strongest and most consistent correlates of crime.[119] *Feminist criminology* "refers to that body of criminological research and theory that situates the study of crime and criminal justice within a complex understanding that the social world is systematically shaped by relations of sex and gender."[120]

Recognizing that the study of crime has always been androcentric (male-centered), feminist criminologists seek a feminine perspective. Specifically, the focus of feminist analyses is on women's experiences and ways of knowing because, in the past, men's experiences have been taken as the norm and generalized to the population. As a result, women and girls have been omitted almost entirely from general theories of crime and delinquency.

Three areas of inquiry have commanded most of feminist criminologists' attention: (1) the victimization of women, (2) gender differences in criminal offending, and (3) "gendered justice" (that is, the treatment of women and girls by the agencies and agents of the criminal justice system). Regarding gender differences in criminal offending, two questions seem to dominate: Do explanations of male criminality apply to women? Why are women less likely than men to engage in crime?

Policy Implications

Not all feminist criminologists address these areas in the same manner. An early typology identified four different strands of feminist thought: liberal, radical, Marxist, and socialist. Liberal feminism was the earliest form of feminist criminology. Liberal feminists operate within existing social structures (they are not radical) to remove the obstacles to women's full participation in social life. Liberal feminists seek equal opportunity, equal rights, and freedom of choice. As for crime, liberal feminist criminologists, such as Rita Simon (1932–2013) and Freda Adler (1934–), point to gender socialization (that is, the creation of masculine and feminine identities) as the primary culprit.[121]

Radical feminist criminologists, on the other hand, believe that patterns of female offending, female victimization, and the disparate treatment of women by the justice system are the result of the institution of patriarchy. *Patriarchy* is "a deeply entrenched system in which males exert dominance through their power (financial and, if necessary, physical) and a hegemonic culture that defines male ways of doing things as 'normal' and male control of women as legitimate."[122] Radical feminists argue that patriarchal relations predate both class and private property as sources of women's oppression. Consequently, a socialist society that has not eliminated patriarchal relations will do little to emancipate women from their subordinate position. The goal for radical feminists is the abolition of patriarchal relationships.[123]

Marxist feminists combine radical feminism with Marxism.[124] They argue that "the root of male dominance lies in men's ownership and control of the means of economic production [and that] patriarchy is tied to the economic structure of capitalism."[125] Consequently, for them, the solution lies in the transformation of capitalism to socialism. They envision a socialist society where housework and child care are socialized, marriage and other sexual relations based on ideas of private property are abolished, and working-class economic subordination is eliminated.[126]

Finally, socialist feminists combine the positions of radical and Marxist feminists by viewing gender and class relations as coequal sources of oppression that have psychological, cultural, and social roots. According to socialist feminists, women are much more at the mercy of their bodies than men, namely through menstruation, pregnancy, childbirth, and nursing. This renders women dependent upon men for protection and survival, and lays the groundwork for male domination.[127] Socialist feminists argue that to address this inequality, women must take control of their reproductive options, and patriarchal and capitalist class relations must be transformed simultaneously.[128]

Current Feminist Criminology

Today, few feminist criminologists probably identify with any of the four aforementioned types of feminist thought. Still, the typology has at least some value by emphasizing potentially useful concepts, such as patriarchy, and suggesting several promising policies to reduce crime, especially the victimization of women. Currently, feminist criminologists are more attentive to the intersection of race, class, sexual orientation, and gender because of the realization that "women's experiences of gender vary according to their position in racial and class hierarchies."[129] This new focus comes in response to earlier criticisms that the feminist movement was largely about White, middle-class women who, for the most part, ignored women of color and poor women.[130] However, the neglect of women of color may be changing with the development of a "black feminist criminology."[131]

Two other recent developments in feminist criminology are the adoption by some feminist criminologists of a postmodern perspective and/or a "feminist pathways approach." Feminist postmodernism is critical of some feminist criminologists "for assuming that women are a 'clearly defined and uncontroversially given interest group.' "[132] Feminist postmodernists argue "for multiple truths that take context into account."[133] They emphasize "the importance of alternative discourses and accounts and … [examine] the effects of language and symbolic representation, e.g., how legal discourse constructs different 'types of woman' such as 'prostitute' or 'bad mother.' "[134]

The focus of feminist pathways approaches, which share some similarities with life-course and developmental theories (described in Chapter 9), "is how the abuse and oppression of women and girls narrows their options and may place them on a trajectory where crime may be the most logical response."[135] According to those who adopt this position, such as Meda Chesney-Lind (1947–) and Susan Sharp (1951–), "most pathways approaches describe multiple pathways of women into crime."[136]

Feminist criminologists have produced a considerable amount of empirical research.[137] Much of this work, as noted previously, focuses on two areas: (1) the degree to which traditional, male-centered theories apply to female crime and (2) the gender ratio problem (why women are less likely than men to commit crime). With respect to the first concern, several studies demonstrate that the variables that explain male crime also explain crime committed by women and girls.[138] Elements from differential association, control theory, anomie theory, and routine activities theory have been shown to apply to female and male crime, although the nature of the relationships often vary across gender.[139] For example, direct control is more salient in reducing delinquency among boys, while indirect control is more important for girls.[140]

With respect to the gender ratio problem, Heimer and De Coster combine feminist theory with differential association theory in an effort to understand gender differences in violent, adolescent delinquency.[141] In so doing, they are "gendering" differential association theory and exploring how its propositions apply differently to boys and girls. Their results suggest that association with delinquent peers is a significant predictor of delinquency among both boys and girls, but boys are more likely than girls to associate with delinquent peers. Furthermore, boys are more likely than girls to learn definitions favorable to violence because boys are subject to less familial control than girls. Girls, on the other hand, are controlled in more "subtle and covert" ways and are taught that violence is inconsistent with what it means to be feminine.[142] Nonetheless, some criminologists contend that these theories do not adequately explain *why* boys are more likely than girls to associate with delinquent peers, or why boys have less self-control than girls.[143]

Feminist criminologists do not study *only* women. Some of them also study how gender shapes the behavior of both men (and boys) and women (and girls). In his 1993 book, *Masculinities and Crime: Critique and Reconceptualization of Theory*, James Messerschmidt (1951–) calls on criminologists to consider how gender is manifested in male violence. In other words, how does "being male" influence male violence and aggression against women? Although the United States is a patriarchal society, not all men are dominant in every arena. Consequently, some may seek to demonstrate their masculinity (what Messerschmidt calls "doing gender") through crime, especially when legitimate avenues through which masculinity can be demonstrated are blocked.[144]

Critique

One of the principal criticisms of feminist criminology is its tendency to elevate gender to the critical factor in explaining crime, even though it is not the most critical factor always or in all situations. In some cases, race or class, for example, may be equally or more important.[145]

Another problem with feminist criminology is many feminists' contradictory position toward the state. On one hand, several feminists call for greater use of the state and its agents to better protect women from abuse; on the other hand, some feminists concede that giving more power to the state and its agents, under present circumstances, will only lead to further discrimination and harassment of minority males and females.[146] A similar contradictory position is held by many feminists toward using the law to improve gender relations. The law, after all, is almost entirely the product of White males.

British or Left Realism

The focus of many critical criminologists has been on crimes committed by the powerful. While pursuing that area of study, however, they have tended either to ignore or to romanticize working-class crime and criminals. By the mid-1980s, a group of social scientists in Great Britain had begun to criticize that tendency and to argue that critical criminologists needed to redirect their attention to the fear and the very real victimization experienced by working-class individuals.[147] These "left realists" correctly observed that crimes against the working class were being perpetrated not only by the powerful but also by members of the working class. They admonished their critical colleagues to take crime seriously, especially street crime and domestic violence. One of the leading exponents of left realism, Jock Young, who was previously listed as a radical criminologist, has identified relative deprivation as a potent, though not exclusive, cause of crime.[148]

Policy Implications

Not willing to wait for the socialist revolution promised by "left idealists" and, by default, cede criminal justice policy to conservative law-and-order types, left realists have argued that, among other things, police power must be employed to protect people living in working-class communities. Also advocated by left realists are greater community involvement and dealing with structural problems that cause offending. Examples of the latter include reducing unfair income inequities and providing good jobs with a future, neighborhoods of which residents can be proud, and community facilities that enhance a sense of cohesion and belonging.[149]

Critique

Left realism, like feminist criminology, has been criticized for holding a contradictory position toward the state. On one hand, left realists want to give the state more power to combat crime, especially crime committed against the working class. On the other hand, they want to reduce the power of the state to intervene in citizens' lives and make the state more accountable for its actions.[150] Another criticism is that in their effort to focus attention on crimes committed against the working class, left realists have deflected attention from white-collar and government crimes.[151] Left realism's emphasis on the reform of criminal justice practice, rather than on radical change, has been criticized for being little different from traditional, mainstream criminology.[152] Finally, feminists have argued that left realists, like most radical and critical criminologists, have remained "gender blind" and "gender biased," failing to appreciate the "activism, research, and theory drawn from women's experiences."[153]

Peacemaking Criminology

Consisting of a mixture of anarchism, humanism, socialism, and Native American and Eastern philosophies, peacemaking criminology rejects the idea that predatory criminal violence can be reduced by repressive state violence. In this view, "wars" on crime only make matters worse. For peacemaking criminologists, such as Hal Pepinsky (1945–) and Richard Quinney,[154] crime is suffering, and, therefore, to reduce crime, suffering must be reduced.

Policy Implications

Peacemaking criminologists suggest that the solution to all social problems, including crime, is the transformation of human beings, mutual dependence, reduction of hierarchical structures, creation of communities of caring people, and universal social justice. Emphasis is placed on the transformation of human beings, on an inner rebirth or spiritual rejuvenation (inner peace) that enables individuals to experience empathy with those less fortunate and respond to other people's needs. Peacemaking criminologists also advocate "restorative justice," which was discussed previously as a policy implication of interactionism and labeling theories. In short, for peacemaking criminologists, it is necessary for people to first change themselves before they can change the world.

Critique

Peacemaking criminology can be criticized for its extreme idealism and emphasis on the transformation of individuals (as a way of transforming society) rather than the transformation of society (as a way of transforming individuals). It has also been criticized for not providing a blueprint of how such transformations can be achieved.[155]

Postmodern Criminology

Postmodernism originated in the late 1960s as a rejection of the "modern" or Enlightenment belief in scientific rationality as the route to knowledge and progress. Postmodernist ideas first appeared in law and criminology during the late 1980s[156] and emphasize three key issues: (1) the centrality of language; (2) partial knowledge and provisional truth; and (3) deconstruction, difference, and possibility.[157]

First, language (written or spoken) shapes reality.[158] To think of something, anything, without first placing it into words is impossible. Language is necessary to express feelings, ideas, passions, and thoughts; thus, language shapes or "speaks" our reality. Bruce Arrigo (1960–) poses this provocative question: "If words define us, our interaction with others, and the institutions in which we work and play, what implicit values and/or hidden assumptions are contained in the language we use to convey our thoughts?"[159] For postmodernists, language has tremendous power, and some discourses, that is the prevailing ways of describing the world, such as "legalese," medical language, or "professor-speak," are valued over others.

Second, because language structures thought in ways that are neither neutral nor complete, then "rationality, logic, and meaning (components of reality construction) are limited by the (dominant) language in use. Thus, not only are entire fields of understanding devalued or repudiated, but what we come to regard as meaningful is itself forever incomplete.... As a result, what we take to be 'truth,' as an articulated expression of knowledge, can, at best, be defined merely as a provisional, relational, and/or positional reality."[160]

Finally, for postmodernists, because truth is not absolute, but relative to our position, experience, and language, the world is uncertain and random; there is no "real" truth "out there."[161] *Deconstruction* is a method used by many postmodernists to interpret this randomness. Its purpose is to "unveil the implicit assumptions and hidden values ... embedded within a particular narrative" and to expose how certain discourses and ways of knowing are privileged over others.[162] Postmodernists seek to identify the differences in language and to place them all in a valued and respected position. In other words, "postmodernism seeks to include the voices of those whose understanding of the world would otherwise remain dormant and concealed."[163] Further, with respect to criminology, specifically, "the language of possibility means that expressions of law, crime, and justice must reflect the multiple and disparate ways different people (or collectives) come to experience, know, and live reality."[164]

With regard to "the Law," postmodernist criminologists reject the idea "that there is only one true interpretation of a law or for that matter the U.S. Constitution."[165] They argue, instead, that there is a plurality of interpretations that are dependent, in part, on the particular social context in which they arise. As in other critical criminologies, the law, from a postmodernist view, always has a human author and a political agenda.[166]

As for crime theories, postmodernist criminologists typically abandon the usual notion of causation. From the postmodernist perspective:

> crime is seen to be the culmination of certain processes that allow persons to believe that they are somehow not connected to other humans and society. These processes place others into categories or stereotypes and make them different or alien, denying them their humanity. These processes result in the denial of responsibility for other people and to other people.[167]

Policy Implications

Postmodern criminologists would replace the formal criminal justice apparatus with informal social controls so that the current functions of criminal justice are handled by local groups and local communities.[168] This strategy is consistent with the one advocated by peacemaking criminologists.

Critique

A problem with allowing local groups and local communities to handle criminal justice functions is that it places minorities in a precarious position. Who will protect minorities and minority rights from the excesses of local groups and communities without higher-level (state and federal) justice institutions?

Postmodernism and deconstructionist analysis, especially the more radical versions, have been criticized "for not valuing anything, and for a belief that 'anything goes' ... for being an anarchy of knowledge ... [for their] subjectivism, plural relativism, and nihilism."[169] In short, as Einstadter and Henry ask, "If truth is not possible, how can we decide anything?"[170] Some critical criminologists, most notably Stuart Henry (1949–) and Dragan Milovanovic (1948–), have attempted to overcome those charges and have used postmodernist thought to create a "constitutive criminology."[171]

Henry and Milovanovic's Constitutive Criminology

Henry and Milovanovic's *constitutive criminology*, unlike skeptical versions of postmodernism, which they characterize as nihilistic, subjective, and defeatist, offers an affirmative, optimistic, and humanistic approach emphasizing reconstruction and redirection. Ultimately, Henry and Milovanovic hope their theory will inform social policies that produce less, rather than more harm.

Constitutive criminology assumes that human beings socially construct their world primarily through language and symbolic representation but, at the same time, are also shaped by the world they create. Two contradictions of this process are that (1) people come to reify the world they create (that is, they forget, if they ever knew, that they are producers of their social world) and (2) the institutions and structures people create frequently become the sources of social constraint and domination—as do attempts to oppose them. The optimism of Henry and Milovanovic's theory lies in the belief that, as creators, human beings are capable of changing the institutions and structures that dominate and constrain them. In constitutive criminology, people are "coproducers" of reality and their actions can be both constraining and liberating.

Thus, humans are also coproducers of crime — "the ultimate form of reifi-cation"—because of the social and organizational structures they create. Crime, in this theory, is a "socially constructed and discursively constituted category." It is "the power to deny others," "to create harm (pain) in any context," or to render "others powerless to make their own difference." Criminals are " 'ex-cessive investors' in the accumulation and expression of power and control." They are not, however, a distinct category in constitutive criminology as they are in most modernist theories. In constitutive criminology, there is continuity and interrelatedness between law-abiding and law-violating or between harm-re-ducing and harm-producing (see Matza's theory of drift).[172]

Policy Implications

The general policy implications of constitutive criminology are twofold: (1) "crime must be deconstructed as a recurrent discursive [that is, linguistic] process," and (2) "conscious attempts must be made at reconstruction with a view to preventing [crime's] recurrence." The primary way to accomplish those policies is "the development of alternative, 'replacement discourses' that fuel pos-itive social constructions … designed to displace crime as moments in the ex-ercise of power as control." "Discourses," as noted, are the prevailing ways of describing the world. Replacement discourses, created by "cultural revolu-tionaries," will deconstruct prevailing meanings and displace them with "new conceptions, distinctions, words and phrases, which convey alternative mean-ings."[173] A classic example of replacement discourse is Sutherland's concept of "white-collar crime," which he successfully introduced into the criminologi-cal lexicon. Replacement discourses will "tell different stories" about the world as experienced by historically subjugated people. Through their discursive di-versity, replacement discourses celebrate "unofficial, informal, discounted and ignored knowledges." The creation of replacement discourses is an ongoing struggle.

Henry and Milovanovic stress that replacement discourses, once created, must extend beyond the walls of academia to the public arena through such avenues as the news media and popular culture. A primary vehicle for ac-complishing this goal is Gregg Barak's (1948–) "newsmaking criminology," where criminologists proactively demystify or deconstruct crime stories pre-sented by the media and offer more authentic crime stories of their own.[174] Barak's "newsmaking criminology" has been absorbed into a broader "cul-tural criminology," which integrates Mead's symbolic interactionism and sub-cultural theory in an effort to deconstruct crime and crime control during late modernity or late capitalism.[175] For these new cultural criminologists, such as Jeff Ferrell (1954–), "style matters," and so, for them, their replacement discourses are animated by provocative prose and incendiary images designed to be enthralling and persuasive to a late modern audience.[176]

If replacement discourses are to be successful, a transformation or reorganization of the political economy is necessary. For Henry and Milovanovic, the best hope for societal-level or structural transformation is a variant of Roberto Unger's (1947–) "superliberalism" (that is, a practical, political philosophy that aims to maximize diversity and minimize hegemony by creating "a society in which people are more fully empowered through the development of institutional arrangements that both diminish the gap between framework-preserving routine and framework-transforming conflict and weaken the established forms of social division and hierarchy").[177] Henry and Milovanovic expect that such structural transformation will meet with resistance as excessive investors use all means at their disposal (such as cooptation and subversion) to undermine it. Consequently, the societal and cultural transformations advocated in constitutive criminology will require continuous and relentless social struggle.

Critique

Constitutive criminology presumes that crime is the result of powerlessness or power differentials—the position of liberal as opposed to more radical versions of conflict theory. It also incorporates a tenet of early labeling theory that "crime feeds off itself, expanding and consuming the energies intended to control it." A problem with this conceptualization is that, like liberal versions of conflict theory, sources of power and power differentials in constitutive criminology are not fully explained or appreciated. By focusing on the linguistic production of reality, Henry and Milovanovic tend to downplay (but do not ignore) the relationship between power and the material conditions of production, such as the ownership of private property and wealth.

Green or Environmental Criminology

The focus of green or environmental criminology, which emerged during the 1990s, is animal rights, species preservation, and green or environmental harms (the latter is the focus of this section), such as illegal polluting, toxic chemical dumping, timber-clear cutting, the sale of unnecessary and dangerous pesticides and pharmaceuticals banned in developed nations but legally unregulated in Third World countries, and race or class-related hazardous waste siting decisions.[178] (See the description of the latter harm in the section on Radical Criminology.) What these green or environmental harms share in common is that they: (1) may or may not violate existing rules and environmental regulations, (2) have identifiable environmental damage outcomes, and (3) originate in human action generally based on corporate interests. Especially important is the recognition that many of these green or environmental harms are not considered crimes and, therefore, not subject to the criminal law and its enforcement. As a result, many criminologists have neglected a large number of incredibly harmful actions and inactions, and the picture of crime painted by these criminologists distorts the real scope and nature of the crime problem in the United States and throughout the world.

Policy Implications

The purpose of green or environmental criminology, according to proponents Michael Lynch (1958–) and Paul Stretesky (1967–), "is to redirect attention toward serious and widespread environmental harms that, even more than ordinary crimes, threaten human life and community."[179] Grounded in environmental justice principles that emphasize race, class, and gender inequities in society, green or environmental criminologists not only advocate environmental protection but also take a political stance based on the conclusion that the solution to green or environmental harms will likely require economic and political reorganization that eliminates social and economic inequities. Economic and political reorganization are necessary because economic (mostly corporate) interests ultimately determine which or whether environmental harms will be criminalized.

The harms that are not criminalized are those that are most likely to affect politically and economically marginalized groups: the lower classes, minority racial and ethnic groups, and women. Consequently, a green or environmental criminology could benefit from a green or environmental victimology. Equally important as criminalizing green or environmental harms is the enforcement of the laws and regulations prohibiting the harms, which, historically, has been decidedly lax. Corporations have been very clever in avoiding compliance.

Rural Criminology

Because crime has generally been considered an urban phenomenon, relatively few studies on rural crime were published before the mid-1990s.[180] Since then, research on rural crime has been conducted in the United States, Australia, Canada, and Great Britain. Many of these studies have focused on the relationship between rural social structure and crime and have adopted a theoretical perspective based on the early Chicago School's concept of social disorganization and its modern extension of collective efficacy (both discussed in Chapter 6). These studies have been criticized for assuming that rural crime is caused by a lack of cohesion and solidarity rather than different kinds of social and normative structures, which vary greatly across rural localities just as they do across cities.

Some critical criminologists, such as Joseph Donnermeyer (1949–) and Walter DeKeseredy (1959–), have offered a different theoretical perspective on rural crime that rejects "urban-biased perspectives." They also advocate the use of qualitative methods in addition to quantitative methods to study the subject. This new critical theory views rural crime as "a product of inequitable economic relationships in a context of general poverty," as well as patriarchal and ethnic relations. These critical criminologists argue that the dramatic increase in rural drug trafficking, consumption and production and in the problem of male-to-female violence are largely due to an economic crisis characterized by the major decline in the number of family-owned farms because the farmers can no longer make a reasonable living from them; the loss of jobs in rural towns that depended on a few, now-shuttered industries such as sawmills and coalmines; and the "Wal-Marting" of the rural United States that has forced the closing of many locally-owned businesses.

These economic dislocations have challenged the traditional rural patriarchal ideology that maintained the rigid gendered division of labor in which men are the principal "bread winners" and women are relegated to domestic duties such as child rearing and house cleaning. Masculine identity has become fragile as more women have entered the paid workforce because their husbands are unemployed or their farms are less profitable. Research has discovered that some unemployed rural men respond to these masculinity challenges by associating with other men in similar circumstances, who support the view that wife beating, sexual assault, and many other types of abuse are legitimate and effective ways of repairing "damaged patriarchal masculinity." Perhaps not surprisingly, this is why some wives leave or try to leave their husbands—another threat to their husbands' masculinity.

Research also shows that radical-right militia groups are comprised primarily of rural white men who join because they feel under attack, vulnerable, and unsure of their manhood. They are looking for someone else to blame for their problems.

Contrary to popular stereotypes, research indicates that rural communities do not have lower crime rates than urban areas. In some cases, rural communities have higher crime rates than urban areas for some types of crime and for some specific types of rural places.

Convict Criminology

Convict criminology is a new criminology and more of a sensitizing perspective than a theory. Ex-convicts who have become academic faculty, such as John Irwin (1929–2010), founded it in the late 1990s.[181] In addition to ex-convict professors, convict criminology has attracted the interest of ex-convict graduate students, as well as a number of practitioners and criminologists, especially critical criminologists, who have never been incarcerated.

Convict criminology's purpose is twofold: (1) to correct the misrepresentations of scholars, the media, and the government about prisons and jails and convicts and ex-convicts and (2) to revitalize criminological literature and correctional practice with research validated by a convict or insider perspective. Convict criminologists prefer the terms "convicts" or "prisoners" instead of "inmates" because the term inmates is considered a managerial term that is used to insult people who are or have been incarcerated. Convict criminologists explain that when convicts call each other "inmates," they are being disrespectful.

The research agenda of convict criminologists includes the understanding of the convict and ex-convict experience, the forming of the convict identity, issues of survival in the convict world, legal discrimination and social stigma, reduction of the prison population, provision of assistance to prisoners exiting prison to reenter the free society, transforming academic criminology/criminal justice, and proposing realistic policy alternatives.

The preferred methodology of convict criminology is qualitative/ethnographic. Ethnographic research involves observation of and interactions with the people or group being studied in the group's own environment, often for long periods of time.

Arguing that most academic criminologists fail to understand the lived experience of defendants and prisoners, convict criminology challenges what it pejoratively calls "managerial criminology, criminal justice, and corrections" and its emphasis on prison and jail overcrowding, prison gang violence, recidivism, etc.

Queer Criminology

Like convict criminology, queer criminology is another new criminology that is more of a sensitizing perspective than a theory. It focuses on lesbian, gay, bisexual, transgender, and queer/questioning (LGBTQ) populations. Queer criminology has been defined as:

a diverse array of criminology-related researches, critiques, method-ologies, perspectives, and reflections. These projects might engage in some way with the slippery notion of "queer," focus on how people experience or perform sexuality and gender (with particular attention to those whose lives fall outside of what is considered to be "norma-tive"), or challenge other normative orderings and the criminological methods that support and perpetuate them. These studies might also include empirical projects that chart the experiences of queer popu-lations within criminal justice institutions. Most often, these studies would lead to critiques of mainstream criminology, further theoreti-cal reflection, and political projects that seek to address injustice and inequality.[182]

Among the benefits of queer criminology, according to its proponents, are ex-panding the criminological and criminal justice imagination to populations and problems that have largely been ignored; contributing meaningfully to justice policy and practice by promoting human rights, democratic participa-tion, and social justice; and, from a pedagogical standpoint, preparing stu-dents, especially criminal justice students, to work with LGBTQ populations and communities.

Queer criminologists believe that viewing crime through a "queer lens" might enhance criminological and criminal justice theorizing, research, and policy. The consideration of LGBTQ populations can force crime theorists to question the het-eronormative assumptions that guide their own research. Research with LGBTQ populations can help assess a crime theory's explanatory power by determining whether the theory applies adequately to people with different sexual orienta-tions and gender identities. Finally, queer criminology can sensitize criminal jus-tice personnel to the unique needs and challenges of LGBTQ offenders and victims.

Study Questions

Critical Theories
1. What are the origins of critical theory in the United States?
2. How do critical theories differ from classical/neoclassical and positivist theories?

Interactionism and Labeling Theory
3. What contribution to crime causation theory does interactionism make?
4. How would interactionist and labeling theorists explain crime?

5. How would they prevent crime?
6. What are problems with interactionist and labeling theories?
7. How do interactionist and labeling theories compare with theories described in previous chapters?

Conflict Criminology
8. How do conflict criminologists explain crime?
9. How would conflict criminologists prevent crime?
10. What are problems with conflict criminology?
11. How does conflict criminology compare with theories described previously in this book?

Radical Criminology
12. What are the three models of society for radical criminologists?
13. How do radical criminologists explain crime?
14. How would radical criminologists prevent crime?
15. What are problems with radical theories of crime causation?
16. How does radical criminological theory compare with theories described previously in this book?

Feminist Criminology
17. What is feminism?
18. What are the primary areas of interest for feminist criminologists?
19. Describe six different types of feminist thought.
20. How is the work of Messerschmidt different from that of other feminist criminologists?
21. What are problems with feminist criminology?
22. How does feminist criminology compare with theories described previously in this book?

British or Left Realism
23. What is the focus of British or Left Realism?
24. What are some of the policy implications of British or Left Realism?
25. What are problems with British or Left Realism?
26. How does British or Left Realism compare with theories described previously in this book?

Peacemaking Criminology
27. What is crime for peacemaking criminologists?
28. What are some of the policy implications of peacemaking criminology?

29. What are problems with peacemaking criminology?
30. How does peacemaking criminology compare with theories described previously in this book?

Postmodern Criminology

31. What are three key issues in postmodern criminology?
32. How do Henry and Milovanovic explain crime?
33. What are some of the policy implications of postmodern criminology?
34. What are problems with postmodern criminology?
35. How does postmodern criminology compare with theories described previously in this book?

Green or Environmental Criminology

36. What is the focus of green or environmental criminology?
37. What are some policy implications of green or environmental criminology?
38. How does green or environmental criminology compare with theories described previously in this book?

Rural Criminology

39. How does critical rural criminology explain rural crime?
40. How does rural criminology compare with theories described previously in this book?

Convict Criminology

41. What is the purpose of convict criminology?
42. Of what does the research agenda of convict criminology consist?
43. How does convict criminology compare with theories described previously in this book?

Queer Criminology

44. What are the benefits of queer criminology, according to its proponents?
45. How does queer criminology compare with theories described previously in this book?

Notes

1. See Mills (1970, originally published in 1956); also see Gouldner (1971); Zinn (1990); Simon (2006).
2. See Chomsky (1969); also see Gouldner (1971).

3. Lanier and Henry (1998:236).
4. See Taylor, Walton, and Young (1974:213).
5. See Bohm (1981); Howe (1997).
6. See Gouldner (1971:Chap. 13).
7. Vold and Bernard (1986:250).
8. See Vold (1979:253).
9. See Vold (1979:254).
10. Vold (1979:254).
11. Blumer (1969:2).
12. See Vold (1979:255–256).
13. See Dowie (1977).
14. Blumer (1969:2).
15. See Vold (1979:256).
16. Blumer (1969:2).
17. See Vold (1979:256).
18. See Vold (1979:256).
19. Vold (1979:258).
20. Vold and Bernard (1986:253–254).
21. See Vold (1979:256–257).
22. Vold (1979:257); Taylor et al. (1974:142).
23. Cooley (1964); also see Vold (1979:257).
24. Becker (1963:9). Lanier and Henry (1998:167) observe that whereas social control theories view clear moral labeling of behavior as important, labeling theory views such labeling as the problem.
25. Lemert (1951).
26. Martin, Mutchnick, and Austin (1990:216).
27. Schur (1973).
28. Lilly, Cullen, and Ball (1989:131–135).
29. Vold and Bernard (1986:255); National Institute for Juvenile Justice and Delinquency Prevention (1977:136); Taylor et al. (1974:140–141).
30. Braithwaite (1989).
31. Another form of restorative justice is "participatory justice," see Stephens (1987).
32. Braithwaite, Ahmed, and Braithwaite (2006:402).
33. Braithwaite et al. (2006).
34. Braithwaite (1989:61–65).
35. Braithwaite et al. (2006).
36. Bergseth and Bouffard (2007).
37. Tyler, Sherman, Strang, Barnes, and Woods (2007).
38. Tyler et al. (2007).

39. Braithwaite et al. (2006).
40. See Davis (1975:165).
41. Becker (1963).
42. Martin et al. (1990:371).
43. Martin et al. (1990:372).
44. See Taylor et al. (1974:153–155).
45. Vold and Bernard (1986:256); also see Akers (1967).
46. Vold and Bernard (1986:256).
47. Vold and Bernard (1986:256).
48. Vold and Bernard (1986:256).
49. Vold and Bernard (1986:256).
50. Martin et al. (1990:369).
51. Andrews and Bonta (1994:197); Hudson (1997).
52. See Davis (1975:179).
53. Becker (1963:9).
54. See Vold (1979:266).
55. Vold (1958); Sellin (1938); Turk (1969); Quinney (1970); Chambliss and Seidman (1971). Sellin's is a theory of culture conflict and not the conflict of competing interest groups. Sellin has been criticized for overemphasizing the extent of culture conflict in society (see Kornhauser, 1978:182–186). Quinney and Chambliss were considered conflict theorists before they became identified with radical theory. Quinney has since moved on to peacemaking criminology (which is presented in a later section of this chapter).
56. See Davis (1975:193).
57. See Vold and Bernard (1986:293).
58. Vold and Bernard (1986:294).
59. Vold and Bernard (1986:294).
60. See Vold and Bernard (1986:295–296).
61. Andrews and Bonta (1994:95–96).
62. Tittle (1995:7).
63. See Dahrendorf (1959:171); Messerschmidt (1997:71).
64. Skogan (1990:5).
65. Bohm (1981).
66. Turk (1979:464).
67. The two theories are sometimes distinguished as "pluralistic-conflict theory" and "class-conflict theory." The former refers to the conflict theory presented in this section; the latter refers to the radical theory presented in the next section.
68. See Bohm (1982).

69. See Bohm (1982).
70. See Bohm (1982).
71. See Bohm (1982).
72. See Bohm (1982).
73. See Bohm (1982).
74. See Bohm (1982).
75. Much of the following discussion is from Bohm (1982); also see Lynch and Groves (1989).
76. Beirne and Messerschmidt (2000:102).
77. See Bonger (1916).
78. See note 55.
79. Bernard, Snipes, and Gerould (2010:106).
80. Wilson and Herrnstein (1985:455–456).
81. Wilson and Herrnstein (1985:455–456).
82. Taylor, Walton, and Young (1975:23).
83. Currie (1997a); also see Currie (1997b).
84. Chambliss (1976:9).
85. Platt (1975:103).
86. Platt (1975:103); also see Schwendinger and Schwendinger (1975) for a similar definition.
87. Although racism and sexism are not explicitly illegal, hate-crime legislation has been enacted that enhances the penalties for crimes that are motivated by an offender's bias against a race, a religion, an ethnic/national origin group, or a sexual-orientation group. See Jacobs (1998).
88. Lynch, Schwendinger, and Schwendinger (2006:193–194).
89. Lynch et al. (2006).
90. Lynch and Stretesky (2001); Lanphear, Vorhees, and Bellinger (2005).
91. Stretesky and Lynch (1999a, 1999b, 2003).
92. Stretesky and Lynch (2003).
93. Lynch, Stretesky, and Burns (2004).
94. Lynch et al. (2006:200).
95. Quinney (1974:16); also see Michalowski and Bohlander (1976).
96. See Beirne and Messerschmidt (2000:105).
97. Beirne and Messerschmidt (2000:105).
98. Quinney (1977:10, 22–23).
99. D. Gordon (1976:206).
100. For a description of "anarchist criminology," see Ferrell (1997, 1999).
101. Taylor et al. (1974:282).
102. Currie (1997a:168).
103. Currie (1997a:168).

104. Cahn (1966).
105. Bohm (1981).
106. Regarding the first two tactics, see Wright (1978:100–101). Regarding the third tactic, see Beckett (1997).
107. Beckett (1997).
108. See Bohm (1981).
109. See Gouldner (1976).
110. Marx and Engels (1970:64).
111. Andrews and Bonta (1994:95–96); also see Tittle (1995:7).
112. Andrews and Bonta (1994:113–114).
113. See criticisms of learning theories.
114. See, for example, Kornhauser (1978:Chap. 1).
115. See Lynch and Groves (1989) for a discussion of those criticisms; also see Einstadter and Henry (1995:253–257).
116. Sanders (2011).
117. Feminism (n.d.).
118. For excellent reviews and examples, see Daly and Chesney-Lind (1988); Simpson (1989); Daly and Maher (1998); Chesney-Lind and Bloom (1997); also see Williams and McShane (1994:230–240) and Beirne and Messerschmidt (2000:202–209).
119. Bernard et al. (2010).
120. Miller and Mullins (2006).
121. See Simon (1975); Adler (1975).
122. Cullen and Agnew (2006:348).
123. For an example of radical feminist theory, see Stanko (1985).
124. Bernard et al. (2010).
125. Bernard et al. (2010:290).
126. For examples of Marxist feminist theory, see Balkan, Berger, and Schmidt (1980) and Schwendinger and Schwendinger (1983).
127. Bernard et al. (2010).
128. For examples of socialist feminist theory, see Messerschmidt (1986); Jurik (1999).
129. Miller (2003:15); Flavin (2001:273).
130. Einstadter and Henry (1995:275).
131. Chesney-Lind and Morash (2013); Potter (2006).
132. Flavin (2001:274).
133. Flavin (2001:274).
134. Flavin (2001:274).
135. Sharp (2014:12).
136. Sharp (2014:12).

137. Miller and Mullins (2006).
138. Cullen and Agnew (2006).
139. Hubbard and Pratt (2002); Lanctot and Le Blanc (2002).
140. Costello and Mederer (2003); Heimer and De Coster (2006).
141. Heimer and De Coster (2006).
142. Heimer and De Coster (2006:381).
143. Miller and Mullins (2006); Lanctot and Le Blanc (2002).
144. Messerschmidt (1993).
145. Messerschmidt (1997:70–71).
146. Einstadter and Henry (1995:275).
147. See, for example, Lea and Young (1984); Kinsey, Lea, and Young (1986); Matthews and Young (1986); also see Schwartz and DeKeseredy (1991) for a review and critique of this position.
148. Young (1997:30).
149. Young (1997:30, 35).
150. Einstadter and Henry (1995:256).
151. Einstadter and Henry (1995:256); Michalowski (1990).
152. Einstadter and Henry (1995:257); Michalowski (1990).
153. Cited in Einstadter and Henry (1995:257).
154. See Pepinsky and Quinney (1991, 1997); Pepinsky (1999); Sullivan (1980).
155. Beirne and Messerschmidt (2000:237).
156. Einstadter and Henry (1995:278).
157. This discussion is taken largely from Arrigo (2003).
158. Arrigo (2003).
159. Arrigo (2003:45).
160. Arrigo (2003:46).
161. Arrigo (2003).
162. Arrigo (2003:48).
163. Arrigo (2003:49).
164. Arrigo (2003:49).
165. Cited in Einstadter and Henry (1995:287).
166. Arrigo and Young (1997:77).
167. Einstadter and Henry (1995:291).
168. Einstadter and Henry (1995:294).
169. Einstadter and Henry (1995:280).
170. Einstadter and Henry (1995:280).
171. Henry and Milovanovic (1991, 1996); also see Barak, Henry, and Milovanovic (1997).
172. Matza (1964).
173. Also see Arrigo and Young (1997:81–82).

174. Barak (1988, 1994).
175. Ferrell, Hayward, and Young (2008).
176. Ferrell et al. (2008).
177. Unger (1987).
178. Information in this section is from Lynch and Stretesky (2003).
179. Lynch and Stretesky (2003:231).
180. Information in this section is from Donnermeyer and DeKeseredy (2008).
181. Information in this section is from Jones, Ross, Richards, and Murphy (2009); Ross and Richards (2003).
182. Ball, Buist, and Woods (2014:2). Additional information about queer criminology is from Panfil and Miller (2014).

9

Conclusion: Integrated Theories, Developmental Theories, and Beyond

Integrated Theories
Developmental Theories
A Further Critique of Integrated and
   Developmental Theories
Conclusion

Because theories of crime and delinquency have been produced by scholars representing several different academic disciplines, the review of theories in this book is reminiscent of the story about the blind people and the elephant. The story goes something like this: Several blind people encountered an elephant. Attempting to describe it, each of the blind people felt a different part. One person felt the elephant's tail and described the elephant as long and hairy. Another felt the elephant's ear and described the elephant as rough and leathery. Still another blind person felt the elephant's tusk and described the elephant as smooth and long. Get the idea? Each of the blind people felt only a part of the elephant and believed that what they felt described the elephant as a whole. However, none of the blind people actually described the elephant accurately. In an analogous way, scholars trying to understand criminality and delinquency generally have examined only a part of the phenomenon and only from the vantage of their particular discipline. None of them probably has explained the phenomenon completely, which would be an imposing task even if they could agree on what the phenomenon they are trying to explain really is.

The multidisciplinary nature of crime theory production is both a benefit and a curse. The benefit stems from the many different perspectives and bodies of knowledge that are applied to the subject matter. The causes of crime probably have been analyzed with a greater disciplinary breadth than most other academic subject matters. The curse, as already noted, is that analyses of the causes of crime generally have not been interdisciplinary. The questions that have been asked and the answers that have been given, for the most part, have remained within the province of a particular academic discipline. The result has been biological reductionism, psychological reductionism, socio-logical reductionism, and so forth. In this context, *reductionism* is the discipline-specific use of concepts that are considered to cause criminal or delinquent behavior.[1]

Charles Tittle, whose control balance theory is examined later in this chapter, calls the resulting theories "simple theories," which he characterizes as consisting of "one or two explanatory principles involving only a few variables that are assumed to apply to all instances of the particular form of deviance [crime] being explained."[2] Most of the theories of crime and delinquency presented in Chapters 1 to 8 are simple theories, according to Tittle. The problem with simple theories, observes Tittle, is that they may seem reasonable, have some (but never compelling) empirical support, and have attracted followers, but none of them has much explanatory power (see the discussion in Chapter 1). Thus, to increase explanatory power, overcome charges of reductionism, and for other reasons (such as reducing the number of competing theories), "integrated" theories of crime causation have been created. Of course, if a single factor, such as low IQ, lack of self-control, or economic inequality, causes crime and that factor is present at birth or acquired early in life and remains with a person throughout his or her life, then theoretical integration is unnecessary. Such single-factor theories are sometimes referred to as *latent trait theories* in which opportunity is generally the key to whether or not a person actually commits crime.[3]

What Tittle calls simple theories are, for the most part, really simple integrated theories because, as he defines them, they are typically comprised of at least two explanatory principles and a few variables. As noted in Chapter 3, early positivists long ago advocated and employed multifactor approaches; some even recognized the need for theorists to integrate biological, psychological, and sociological influences. Many recent positivists and some critical theorists have followed this trend. What distinguishes simple integrated theories from more elaborate integrated theories are the number of concepts (and variables) employed, the degree of specification of how those concepts (and variables) are combined or interact, and, oftentimes, the range of crime types to be explained.

Integrated Theories

For discussion purposes, it may prove useful to consider three different types of integrated theories. First are theories that integrate or synthesize concepts from different theories within the same discipline, for example, some combination of concepts from the following sociological theories: social disorganization theory, anomie theories, learning theories, and social control theories.

A second type of integrated theories combines theories or concepts from different disciplines within the same paradigm, for instance, the integration of theories or concepts from biological positivism, psychological positivism, and sociological positivism. This type of integration usually requires the synthesis of theories or concepts at different levels of analysis, for example, the integration of concepts from biological and psychological theories (individual level of analysis) with concepts from sociological theories (aggregate, group, or societal level of analysis). Many of these theories were described in earlier chapters, for example, Akers (1998); Cloward and Ohlin (1960); Cohen (1955); Glueck and Glueck (1930, 1934, 1950, 1967); Goring (1913); Gottfredson and Hirschi (1990); Halleck (1967); Henry and Milovanovic (1996); Hirschi and Gottfredson (1987, 1989); Lombroso (1968); Maslow (1970); Merton (1938); and Wilson and Herrnstein (1985).

A third type of integrated theories is theories that attempt to integrate concepts from different paradigms or to combine all of the different types of integration, for example, theories that attempt to synthesize classical, positivist, or critical theories or concepts.[23] Some of these theories are quite elaborate.

Elliott et al.'s Theory of Delinquency and Illegal Drug Use

An example of the first type of integrated theory is Delbert Elliott (1933–) and his colleagues' theory of delinquency and illegal drug use. In *Explaining Delinquency and Drug Use* (1985), the authors contend that social disorganization, strain, and inadequate socialization combine to weaken conventional bonding and strengthen delinquent bonding. Specifically, they define two major pathways to delinquency. First, among those who are subject to low levels of social control, the likelihood of their association with delinquent peers is high, which increases their likelihood of delinquency.[4]

Second, when individuals who are subjected to high levels of social control experience strain, their level of social control is reduced, which consequently increases their likelihood of association with delinquent peers.[5] Association with delinquent peers increases the likelihood of delinquency and drug use. In fact, in a subsequent study, Elliott et al. found that association with delinquent peers was the best predictor of later delinquency, especially among those with weak social control.[6] The social control components of the theory are emphasized over the social learning components.[7]

Tittle's Control Balance Theory

An example of the second type of integrated theory is Charles Tittle's (1939–) control balance theory, which integrates elements from several positivist theories.[8] According to Tittle, the probability that a person will commit delinquency, including specific types of delinquency (his theory is about deviance, which includes crime and delinquency), is primarily a result of the interplay of deviant motivation and control. *Control*, or *the limiting of behavioral options*, refers to both the amount of control that a person can exercise and the amount of control to which a person is exposed and that is likely to be exercised (that is, the "control ratio"). For Tittle, delinquency is a means by which "people escape deficits and extend surpluses of control."[9]

Four factors are key to Tittle's theory.[10] First is the predisposition toward delinquent motivation, which varies from person to person and from situation to situation. This predisposition is a function of a desire for autonomy, basic biological and psychological needs, and an unbalanced control ratio.[11] *A desire for autonomy* refers to "escaping control over oneself and exercising more control over the social and physical world than one experiences."[12] Because nearly everyone has a desire for autonomy, as well as basic biological and psychological needs, an imbalance in the control ratio is of paramount importance.[13] The second key factor in the theory is provocation or the situational stimulant of delinquent motivation. *Provocations* are contextual features and include such things as verbal insults, challenges, or displays of weaknesses.[14] The third and fourth factors are the *opportunity to commit delinquency*, which is most important in explaining specific types of delinquency, and *constraint*, which refers to the likelihood that a delinquent behavior will activate restraining responses by others. When these four factors converge in a certain way, delinquency is likely. In general, the greater the control ratio imbalance, the greater the likelihood of delinquency. Differences in the magnitude of control imbalances determine the seriousness of specific types of delinquent behavior. When the amount of control exercised relative to the amount of control experienced is balanced—and the other factors are benign—people are likely to conform.

Critique

Among problems with Tittle's control balance theory is the calculation of the control ratio, which varies according to the number and types of relationships. So, for example, a father may have a control surplus in relation to a child, but a control deficit in relation to his employer. Depending on the time or situation a husband and wife, for example, may experience either a control surplus or a control deficit. The problem is how to determine the net control ratio from all of an individual's different relationships. Because (1) the number of a person's relationships is almost limitless, (2) some relationships are more influential than others, and (3) the control ratio in any relationship may vary by time and situation, calculating the net control ratio may turn out to be impossible.

Despite the problem of calculating the net control ratio, several researchers have examined the applicability of control balance theory to various types of criminal and deviant behavior.[15] Generally, results have been supportive of various parts of the theory. For example, some results suggest that both control balance deficits and surpluses are related to serious theft,[16] assault,[17] drug use,[18] deviant sexual practices,[19] and cheating.[20] Other results indicate that only control deficits are related to deviance,[21] while still other results show that only control surpluses are significantly related to exploitative corporate crime.[22]

Vila's Evolutionary Ecological Theory

An example of the third type of integrated theories is Bryan Vila's (1947–) "holistic theory" comprised of ecological, micro-level, and macro-level factors which, he argues, interact and influence a wide range of criminal behaviors depending on individual developmental factors over the life course and across generations.[24] He also maintains that a statistical model based on mathematical nonlinear chaos theory rather than on more traditional statistical analytic models may be a more useful and accurate way to test his integrated theory.

Hagan's Power-Control Theory

In "A Power Control-Theory of Common Delinquent Behavior," John Hagan (1946–) and his colleagues formulate and test a neo-Marxian, class-based, power-control theory of gender and delinquency—another example of the third type of integrated theories. Power, in this theory, refers to the "relations of dominance that derive from control over the means of production."[25] Hagan et al.'s specific interest is with parents' power in the workplace, which, according to Hagan and his colleagues, varies by class position: owners have more power than managers who have more power than workers who have more power than the unemployed. A parent's power in the workplace, in turn, translates into a parent's power in the family. Families, for Hagan et al., can be described along a continuum from patriarchal to egalitarian. A patriarchal family is defined as one in which the husband is employed in an authority position in the workplace, and the wife does not work outside the home.[26] An egalitarian family is one in which both parents have authority positions in the workplace.[27]

Control, on the other hand, refers to "dominance established within the family."[28] Borrowing from control theory, Hagan and his colleagues contend that mothers, rather than fathers, are the primary instruments of control in the household and that daughters, rather than sons, are the primary objects of that control.[29] Consequently, daughters enjoy less autonomy than do sons, and are "taught to avoid risks generally and the risk of legal sanctions specifically."[30]

Integrating the concepts of power and control, power-control theory proposes that "positions of power in the workplace are translated into power relations in the household and that the latter, in turn, influence the gender-determined control of adolescents, their preferences for risk taking, and the patterning of gender and delinquency."[31] Borrowing a proposition espoused by Marxist Willem Bonger more than a half a century earlier, Hagan and his colleagues propose that the effect of gender on delinquency is contingent upon class structure.[32] Specifically, they predict that while sons consistently engage in more delinquency than daughters, that gender difference diminishes as a family moves from more patriarchal to more egalitarian. In more patriarchal families, mothers exert more control over their daughters than they do over their sons, while in egalitarian families, mothers are more likely to administer control equally between sons and daughters. In other words, "as mothers gain power relative to husbands [in the workplace], daughters gain freedom relative to sons."[33] Consequently, in egalitarian families, by reducing the amount of control placed on daughters, mothers provide them with more freedom to engage in delinquency; thus, reducing the gender gap in delinquency.[34]

Power-control theory predicts that "patriarchal families will be characterized by large gender differences in common delinquent behavior, while egalitarian families will be characterized by smaller gender differences in delinquency."[35] Power-control theory is one of the first theories to directly address this gender-ratio issue.[36]

When Hagan et al. tested their theory, they found general support for its propositions.[37] While boys engage in more delinquency than girls overall, that gap is narrowest at the egalitarian end of the family structure spectrum. Daughters in egalitarian homes are more likely to be treated like sons, more likely to take risks, and more likely to engage in delinquency than their counterparts in patriarchal homes.

Results of other, more recent studies, however, have been mixed with some aspects of the theory receiving more support than others.[38] For example, studies that use a class-based measure of patriarchy tend to show greater support for the theory than do those tests utilizing a proxy measure of class.[39] Evidence also suggests that in patriarchal families, daughters are more likely than sons to be the object of maternal control.

Critique

Several studies indicate that power-control theory may be *underspecified*. An underspecified theory is missing important concepts. For example, Blackwell and Piquero found that Gottfredson and Hirschi's concept of self-control is an important mediating factor in the relationship between parental control and delinquency. Among daughters in egalitarian households, "low self-control actually significantly suppressed the effect of parental control on intentions to offend."[40]

Agnew's General Theory of Crime and Delinquency

Robert Agnew, whose *General Strain Theory* was discussed previously in Chapter 6, has more recently presented *Why Do Criminals Offend: A General Theory of Crime and Delinquency*, which attempts to integrate concepts from biological theories, psychological theories, social control theories, self-control theories, strain theories, social learning theories, social support theories, and labeling theories.[41] He maintains that the idea underlying most of these theories is that "crime is most likely when the constraints against crime are low and the motivations for crime are high."[42] The theory attempts to explain why "some *individuals* are more likely than others to engage in *behaviors that are generally condemned* and that *carry a significant risk of sanction* by the state if detected."[43] Agnew notes that his theory best explains "street crime," such as homicide, robbery, rape, and illicit drug use, but that it also explains other types of crime, including white-collar crime. He adds that his theory also can be extended to explain "group differences in crime rates."[44]

To simplify his theory and, according to Agnew, make it more manageable than other attempts at integrated theory, he organizes his theory's explanatory variables into five "life domain" clusters: self, family, school, peers, and work.[45] Variables and indicators of each of these clusters are listed below:

- Self: (irritability/low self-control) easily upset, quick to blame others, intense emotional reactions to stressors, low empathy, impulsivity, sensation seeking, lack of motivation or perseverance, and beliefs favorable to crime.
- Family: (poor parenting practices) negative parent/juvenile bonding, poor supervision/discipline, family conflict and child abuse, absence of positive parenting (instruction in social, academic, and problem-solving skills;

provision of social support), and criminal parents/siblings. (no/bad marriages) unmarried or, if married, negative bonding to spouse/partner, negative bonding to children, family conflict, poor spouse/partner supervision, criminal/spouse partner, and low social support.

- School: (negative school experiences/limited education) negative bonding to teachers and school, poor academic performance, little time spent on homework, low educational and occupational goals, poor supervision/discipline, negative treatment by teachers, absence of positive teaching, and limited education (for adults out of school).
- Peers: (peer delinquency) close friends engage in crime, peer conflict/abuse, and spend much time with peers in unstructured, unsupervised activities.
- Work: (unemployment/bad jobs) long-term unemployment, poor supervision/discipline, negative bonding to work, poor work performance, poor working conditions, and criminal coworkers.[46]

Describing the dynamics of his theory, Agnew explains that "the life domains have reciprocal effects on one another, although some effects are stronger than others and effect sizes sometimes vary over the life course."[47] He gives the example that poor parenting has a large effect on peer delinquency, while peer delinquency has a small or moderate effect on poor parenting, and that this is probably true only during childhood and adolescence. Among other dynamics, Agnew argues that (1) "crime affects the life domains and that prior crime has a direct effect on subsequent crime," and (2) "life domains interact in affecting crime and one another."[48]

Critique

Agnew's claim that his integrated theory is simpler than other integrated theories belies the obvious complexity of his theory, as it is briefly described here. Another problem with the theory is that the life domains omit potentially important variables, such as levels of inequality, relative deprivation, government assistance, and patriarchy in society.

Agnew's Unified Criminology

In 2011, a new book by Agnew was published—*Toward a Unified Criminology*: *Integrating Assumptions about Crime, People, and Society*—that begins with Agnew's assessment that his earlier *Why Do Criminals Offend: A General Theory of Crime and Delinquency* (described above) is "quite solid" but that "it is built on a weak foundation." The earlier book's problem, according to Agnew, is that it fails to devote sufficient attention to foundational issues or, what was described in Chapter 1 of this book, as philosophical assumptions. This is a problem, states Agnew, endemic to "mainstream criminologists," that is, non-critical criminologists, such as himself.[49]

After studying the philosophical assumptions that inform criminological theories, Agnew concludes that "the [philosophical] assumptions that criminologists make ... have a fundamental impact on their work: they largely determine what criminologists study, the causes they examine, the control strategies they recommend, and how they test their theories and evaluate crime-control strategies."[50] Coming late to this realization, as Agnew does, is obviously better than not realizing the importance of a theory's philosophical assumption at all—as is the case with most "mainstream criminologists."

In any event, Agnew sets as his ambitious task the integration of the seemingly contradictory philosophical assumptions of criminological theories. His major conclusion is that "there is some truth to each of the underlying [philosophical] assumptions made by criminologists, but that each assumption only captures a part of the truth."[51]

He begins with the ontological assumption that pits determinism against free will or human agency. Agnew believes that "behaviors fall along a continuum, ranging from fully determined to somewhat agentic" or freewilled.[52] Agnew adds that "individuals exercise greater agency when they (a) are motivated to alter their behavior, (b) believe they can produce desired change, (c) have the traits and resources necessary to exercise agency (e.g., creativity, broad knowledge, autonomy, power), and (d) are in environments that have weak or countervailing constraints, provide numerous opportunities for agency, and encourage agency."[53] He advises that "we cannot blame individuals for their behavior unless we assume that they have at least some responsibility for it, which is to say that they exercise some agency."[54]

His next target is the ontological assumption about human nature—whether human beings are basically good, bad, or a blank slate. Agnew concludes that "people show evidence of social concern [people are basically good], self-interest [people are basically bad], and social learning [people are basically a blank slate and respond to their experiences]—with the strength of these traits varying across individuals and social circumstances."[55]

He continues with the cosmological assumption about the nature of society— whether society is based primarily on consensus or conflict about moral values. Agnew argues that "there is reason to believe that all functioning societies are characterized by a core consensus; with people condemning the unconditional use of personal violence and theft and cooperating in certain areas, such as defense from external threats."[56] "Beyond that," he adds, "the extent and nature of consensus and conflict vary."[57]

Finally, he addresses the metaphysical assumption about the nature of reality. Agnew asserts that "there is reason to believe that there is an objective reality that affects behavior including crime."[58] "At the same time," he continues, "it is difficult to accurately measure this reality, particularly since individual reports of it are biased for several reasons."[59] He warns that "it is also important to consider the subjective views of different types of respondents."[60]

Critique

Agnew should be commended for considering issues that most "mainstream criminologists" fail to appreciate. His attempt at theory integration and the integration of philosophical assumptions is provocative but, in the end, is influenced by positivist biases. These biases are discussed in the following section on problems with integrated theories. Here, we only note that critical theorists, who assume that "reality" is socially constructed, reject Agnew's belief in an objective reality. Thus, successfully integrating positivist and critical theories may prove to be an impossible task.

Barak's Post-Postmodern Synthesis

A final example of this third type of integrated theory is Gregg Barak's "post-postmodern synthesis."[61] Barak, whose "newsmaking criminology" was discussed in the section on postmodern criminology in the previous chapter, advocates combining, in a truly interdisciplinary approach, the different types of knowledges that have something to say about crime and criminality. He lists knowledges from "economics, philosophy, anthropology, biochemistry, psychology, law, sociology, cultural studies, ethnic studies, gender studies, media studies, political economy, and social history" as prime candidates for this type of integration.[62] At the same time, Barak also doubts whether different theories and concepts can ever be successfully integrated,[63] so it remains to be seen what is to be integrated from the different knowledges if not theories and concepts.

Developmental Theories

Developmental or life-course theories are different from the aforementioned integrated theories because of their emphasis on individual development. Developmental theories posit that different factors (sometimes from different disciplines and different levels of analysis) affect people's propensity for crime at different times in their lives. So, for example, during childhood, the family may be the most important influence in determining whether a child engages in delinquency; during adolescence, peer group influences may be most important; and during adulthood, marital and occupational relations may predominate. Any factor that is influential at one point in a person's life may be irrelevant at another time.

Sampson and Laub's Age-Graded Theory of Informal Social Control

Several criminologists have examined crime from a developmental, or life-course, perspective.[64] One example is Robert Sampson (1956–) and John Laub's (1953–) age-graded theory of informal social control.[65] Like Hirschi and other social control theorists, Sampson and Laub argue that crime and delinquency are likely to occur when an individual's bond to society is weakened or broken. What is unique about their theory is that the important elements of the social bond change over the life course.

Specifically, Sampson and Laub contend that a wide variety of individual and social structural factors (such as socioeconomic disadvantage, broken homes, family disruption, parental criminality, household crowding, large family size, residential mobility, and mother's employment) affect both informal social controls and social capital, which, in turn, affect crime and delinquency. *Social capital* refers to social relationships (for example, parent–child, teacher–student, or employer–employee) that can become social and psychological resources that can reduce the chances of criminal or delinquent behavior. Thus, for Sampson and Laub, adolescent delinquency is often the product of individual and social structural factors mediated by little social capital and weakened social controls (inadequate family socialization and school attachment and the influence of delinquent siblings and peers).

Adult deviance and criminality, for Sampson and Laub, are sometimes, but not always, a function of antisocial and delinquent behavior in childhood. The critical factors in adult crime and deviance are again the social bond and social capital. Strong social bonds (for example, strong social ties to jobs and family) and social capital reduce the likelihood of crime and deviance; conversely, weak social bonds and little social capital increase the likelihood of crime and deviance.

Crime Over the Life Course

In explaining crime over the life course, developmental theorists examine a number of stages and characteristics of criminal development. First, *onset* refers to the initial entry into crime or delinquency. Most developmental theorists contend that criminal behavior, especially serious criminal behavior begins in childhood as any number of "conduct problems" such as bullying, lying, and cheating.[66]

Second, an individual's pathway through life can be characterized by *continuity*, in which his or her behavior patterns (either criminal or not) are relatively stable. For example, according to some developmental theorists, individuals with particular traits (such as low self-control or neuropsychological deficits) will display a continuous, high rate of offending throughout their lives.[67] Developmental theorists frequently refer to people who persistently commit crime over their life course as *career criminals*. Only a very small percentage of all offenders are believed to be career criminals. For most offenders, criminal behavior can begin or end anytime during their lives, though, for most offenders, it is likely to end by the time they reach their late thirties or early forties.

Third, an individual's life can be marked by *change* or *turning points* in which behavior on a particular pathway changes and heads in a different direction.[68] For example, many developmental theorists examine the "age–crime curve" in an attempt to explain why crime peaks in adolescence and decreases in the mid-twenties. The answer to this question varies, but can include peer pressure, mimicry, increased opportunity, or changes in social bonds.[69]

Finally, some developmental theorists also examine *desistance* or the process through which an offender stops offending. In an update of their earlier work on age-graded theory, Laub and Sampson examined how adult, persistent offenders desist from crime.[70] They found that "social controls, structured routine activities, and purposeful human agency are the causal elements in explaining persistent offending and desistance from crime in adulthood."[71] Generally, desistance occurs though a series of life-changing events.[72] For example, a persistent offender may experience a significant, structural turning point (such as marriage, birth of a child, or military service), then is placed under increased social controls (for instance, a wife, the responsibility of a new job, childcare), then experiences a change in routine activities (e.g., spends less time out with the guys and more time at home with his wife and children) and finally, almost by "default," is committed to a new life.[73] This commitment to a new life, a noncriminal pathway, is dependent upon the former offender's willingness to exercise what Laub and Sampson call human agency. *Human agency* refers to choice exercised within the context of given circumstances or what in Chapter 3 was called "soft determinism" or "conditional free will."

Since their emergence in the early 1990s, developmental theories have garnered considerable attention from researchers.[74] Because developmental theories focus on changes across the life course, much of this research is based on the analysis of longitudinal data. With respect to Sampson and Laub's original work[75] and their more recent revisions,[76] evidence is supportive: "A growing body of empirical evidence supports the empirical propositions of the age-graded theory of informal social control. These results support the theoretical explanation of the onset of delinquency as well as the dual concern of the theory with continuity and change in behavior over the life course."[77]

A Further Critique of Integrated and Developmental Theories

Despite empirical support, integrated and developmental theories are not without their detractors.[78] Some critics argue that, at the extreme, theory integration is sometimes little more than an exercise in throwing into a statistical model everything including the kitchen sink to explain more of the variation in the dependent variable crime.[79] Although combining factors such as gender, race, age, place of residence, IQ, aggressiveness, level of self-control, conditions of childhood training, prior offenses, peer relationships, and social bonds, allows a researcher to predict criminal behavior with a fair degree of accuracy, it does not begin to answer the questions of why or how those factors are related either to each other or, more importantly, to criminal behavior.[80] It is also impossible to determine whether or not the relationships in such models are spurious. Such statistical modeling, then, is really not theory integration at all.

Two methodological problems with some attempts at theory integration are (1) the failure to specify the sequencing or the temporal ordering of concepts, and (2) the failure to consider reciprocal effects or interactions among concepts.[81] So, for example, does a bad family life determine whether a child drops out of school and, as a result, engages in delinquency? Or does delinquency cause a child to drop out of school and, consequently, have a bad family life? Or does dropping out of school reduce the quality of family life, which causes delinquency? And so forth. Research suggests that in all cases the relationships are probably reciprocal or interactive. In other words, dropping out of school, a bad family life, and delinquency may each be cause and effect of the other (but not necessarily for all people and at all times during the life course). In short, there may not be any correct ordering of factors. Thus, in this example, it is probably inaccurate to argue that either dropping out of school or a bad family life necessarily precedes delinquency in time. On this point, Barak argues that "in all likelihood, criminologists will never be able to definitely ascertain the correct ordering of all the complex variables and how, over time, these influence each other."[82] However, rather than abandon efforts at integration, Barak calls for a different type of integration, which, as noted previously, he calls a "post-postmodern synthesis."

Some critics contend that the combining of certain concepts or assumptions produces logical inconsistencies. They ask, for example, how is it possible "that crime is caused by successful and unsuccessful socialization, control and lack of control, individualistic and group goals, social and nonsocial reinforcement, and contact with deviant and conventional others?"[83] They also wonder how criminal behavior can be both freewilled and determined at the same time, or how both consensus and conflict over moral values can simultaneously characterize society.[84] This is especially true of integrations that attempt to bridge different paradigms (for example, integrating anomie and radical theories). For that matter and more broadly, they wonder whether crime is the response of an abnormal individual to a normal environment, or whether crime is the response of a normal individual to an abnormal environment. How could it be both? Critics, in short, argue that the integration of some theories has been accomplished only by ignoring philosophical assumptions or misrepresenting or distorting the theories or concepts to be combined.

These presumed logical inconsistencies, moreover, are crucial when it comes to policy. For example, if crime is the response of a freewilled or abnormal individual to a normal environment, then it makes sense to focus crime control policy on individuals (for example, deterrence or rehabilitation). On the other hand, if crime is the response of a determined or normal individual to an abnormal environment, then it makes sense to direct crime control policy to changing the environment (for instance, providing opportunity or strengthening communities). It makes little sense to do both.

The charge of logical inconsistency, however, only applies to positivist or classical/neoclassical syntheses, in which the conceptual or philosophical dichotomies or categories are presumed to accurately represent phenomena in the real world. To the critical theorist, conceptual or philosophical dichotomies or categories are at best heuristic devices that necessarily distort reality. They are false dichotomies. For the critical theorist, human beings are neither freewilled nor determined but are both freewilled and determined. In other words, human beings are free to choose within biological, psychological, and sociological constraints. Human beings not only shape the world, but are also shaped by it. Likewise, for critical theorists, society is characterized by neither consensus nor conflict over moral values but is instead a reflection of both consensus and conflict over moral values (though conflict is likely to predominate).

Finally, neither individuals nor societies are normal or abnormal. To the extent that the two concepts have any meaning at all, individuals and societies manifest both normal and abnormal qualities along a continuum. In short, for critical theorists, there is always a dialectical relationship between invented categories of individuals or societies.

As for policy implications, if the dialectic more accurately describes the relationships between individuals and the societies in which they live, then the choice of policies may depend primarily on utility. In other words, since policies can be directed toward individuals, social institutions, or both, one of three choices must prevail if anything is going to be done at all. First, policies could be directed toward individuals. Such a choice would require the changing of individuals—in many cases, one person at a time—which seems like an incredibly inefficient way of producing change. Second, policies could be directed toward changing social institutions which seems like a less intrusive and much more efficient strategy for changing large numbers of people. Such a policy, however, would have to be sensitive to individual differences and undoubtedly would allow some individuals to "fall through the cracks." Third, policies could be directed toward changing individuals and social institutions simultaneously. However, this policy seems less efficient than the second one and is likely to squander scarce resources if the ultimate goal is to change the behavior of large numbers of people.

Conclusion

Probably the best way to make sense of the various theories examined in this book is to begin with a consideration of their philosophical assumptions. As mentioned in Chapter 1, whether a theory is accepted or rejected often depends on whether one believes in a theory's philosophical assumptions rather than on the scientific support (or lack of support) for the theory. A principal reason for this state of affairs, as noted in Chapter 1, is that scientific research into the causes of crime almost never offers a critical test that supports one competing theory over another.

As for philosophical assumptions, do you believe that human beings are freewilled and completely responsible for their behavior? Do you believe that they are motivated by pleasure–pain, risk–reward, or cost–benefit rationality? Do you believe that society is based on a social contract? If your answer to those three questions is yes, then you probably find classical theory most compelling. Even if you believe that human beings are not completely freewilled and responsible for their behavior, but you still believe in hedonistic or other cal-

culating kind of rationality as the basis of human motivation and social contract as the basis of society, then you probably find the neoclassical revision
most compelling.

On the other hand, if you believe that human beings are determined (either
in a "hard" or "soft" way) and that society is based primarily on a consensus
(by either the collective conscience or division of labor, but not a social contract), then you probably find one of the positivist theories most compelling.
If so, then you can narrow your choice or choices of theories by critically assessing the problems associated with each of the theories. Ask yourself, Are
any of the problems critical enough to disqualify the theory? If your answer is
yes, then reject the theory. If any theory survives this exercise, then it must be
compelling to you. Note that this is more than a counting exercise. Just because one theory has been criticized more than another theory, it does not
necessarily follow that the theory with the fewest criticisms is the better theory. Not all criticisms are equally condemning; some criticisms are more telling
than others. Some theories may be criticized more than other theories simply
because they have commanded more interest than other theories. If more than
one theory survives the exercise, ask yourself which theory has greater explanatory power, testability, and empirical validity. The theory with the greater
explanatory power, testability, and empirical validity probably is the better
theory. If you cannot make a choice between two or more compelling theories,
then you might consider theory integration. Determine whether the integrated
theory is more compelling than any of the theories that were combined taken
by itself.

Finally, if you believe that human beings are both determined and determining and that society is characterized fundamentally by conflict rather than
by consensus, then you probably find critical theories more compelling. If
this is the case, then ask yourself which model of society (the conflict model
or the radical model) is the more accurate one. Consider theory integration.
Decide what contributions, if any, from left realism, peacemaking criminology, feminist criminology, postmodern criminology, and the other newer,
critical criminologies would enhance your theory. Ponder the question of
whether classical/neoclassical, positivist, and critical theories can be successfully integrated.

By engaging in these exercises, you may be able to draw some informed
conclusions about the causes of crime and delinquency. Remember, however,
that theories must be evaluated in relation to other theories. As noted in Chapter 1, theories are more or less compelling, convincing, or believable *in relation to other theories*. It is not correct to say that theories are good or bad or
right or wrong, in and of themselves.

Study Questions

1. Why have integrated theories been produced?
2. What are some different types of integrated theory?
3. Why have developmental theories been produced?
4. To what stages and characteristics of offending do developmental theorists focus?
5. What are problems with integrated and developmental theories?
6. What are some of the policy implications of integrated and developmental theories?
7. How do integrated and developmental or life-course theories compare with theories described in previous chapters?
8. What is a useful method for evaluating theories?

Notes

1. See Babbie (1992:97).
2. Tittle (1995:1). Tittle's book is about deviance, which includes crime and delinquency.
3. See Gottfredson and Hirschi (1990).
4. Cullen and Agnew (2006).
5. Cullen and Agnew (2006).
6. Elliott, Huizinga, and Menard (1989).
7. Elliott, Huizinga, and Ageton (1985). Also see Elliott, Ageton, and Cantor (1979); Elliott et al. (1989); and Wolfgang and Ferracuti (1982) for other examples of this type of theory.
8. Tittle (1995).
9. Tittle (1995:142).
10. Tittle (1995:142).
11. Tittle (1995:147–148).
12. Tittle (1995:145).
13. Tittle (1995:148).
14. Tittle (1995:163).
15. Baron and Forde (2007).
16. Baron and Forde (2007).
17. Piquero and Hickman (1999, 2003).
18. Curry and Piquero (2003).
19. Piquero and Hickman (1999).
20. Curry (2005).

21. Hickman, Piquero, Lawton, and Greene (2001).
22. Piquero and Piquero (2006).
23. Examples include Colvin and Pauly (1983); Pearson and Weiner (1985); Vold and Bernard (1986); Groves and Sampson (1987); Braithwaite (1989); Hagan (1989); and Messner and Rosenfeld (2001).
24. Vila (1994).
25. Hagan, Gillis, and Simpson (1985:1154).
26. Hagan, Gillis, and Simpson (1987:791).
27. Hagan, Gillis, and Simpson (1987:792).
28. Hagan, Gillis, and Simpson (1985:1154).
29. Blackwell (2010).
30. Hagan, Gillis, and Simpson (1985:1156).
31. Hagan, Gillis, and Simpson (1987:812).
32. Hagan, Gillis, and Simpson (1985:1170).
33. Hagan, Gillis, and Simpson (1987:792).
34. Hagan, Gillis, and Simpson (1985:1157).
35. Hagan, Gillis, and Simpson (1987:793).
36. Blackwell (2010).
37. Hagan, Gillis, and Simpson (1985, 1987).
38. Blackwell (2010).
39. Blackwell (2010).
40. Blackwell and Piquero (2005:13).
41. Agnew (2005:213–214).
42. Agnew (2005:17).
43. Agnew (2005:12, emphasis in original).
44. Agnew (2005:13).
45. Agnew (2005:209).
46. Agnew (2005:209).
47. Agnew (2005:210).
48. Agnew (2005:211–212).
49. Agnew (2011:vii).
50. Agnew (2011:vii–viii).
51. Agnew (2011:194).
52. Agnew (2011:195).
53. Agnew (2011:195).
54. Agnew (2011:196).
55. Agnew (2011:196). For an examination of the evidence for social concern and the relationship between social concern and crime, see Agnew (2014).
56. Agnew (2011:197).
57. Agnew (2011:197).

58. Agnew (2011:197).
59. Agnew (2011:197).
60. Agnew (2011:198).
61. Barak (1998).
62. Barak (1998:231–232).
63. Barak (1998:212).
64. See Farrington (2006) for an excellent overview.
65. Sampson and Laub (1992, 1993); other examples are Thornberry (1987); Patterson, DeBaryshe, and Ramsey (1989); and McCord (1991).
66. Cullen and Agnew (2006).
67. See Gottfredson and Hirschi (1990); Moffitt (1993).
68. Cullen and Agnew (2006).
69. See Moffitt (1993); Sampson and Laub (1993); Cullen and Agnew (2006).
70. Laub and Sampson (2003).
71. Laub, Sampson, and Sweeten (2006).
72. Laub and Sampson (2003).
73. Cullen and Agnew (2006:522).
74. Cullen and Agnew (2006); Bernard, Snipes, and Gerould (2010).
75. Sampson and Laub (1993).
76. Laub and Sampson (2003).
77. Laub et al. (2006:320–321).
78. See Barak (1998:Chap. 9); Einstadter and Henry (1995:301–310); Tittle (1995:89–123); Gibbons (1994); Bohm (1987); Hirschi (1979); Kornhauser (1978:46–50).
79. See Tittle (1995:90).
80. Tittle (1995:93).
81. See Hirschi (1979); Tittle (1995).
82. Barak (1998:212).
83. Costello (1997:424); also see Hirschi (1979).
84. See Hirschi (1979).

References

Abrahamsen, David. 1944. *Crime and the Human Mind*. New York: Columbia University Press.

Abrahamsen, David. 1960. *The Psychology of Crime*. New York: Columbia University Press.

Adler, Freda. 1975. *Sisters in Crime: The Rise of the New Female Criminal*. New York: McGraw-Hill.

Agnew, Robert. 1985a. "Social Control Theory and Delinquency: A Longitudinal Test." *Criminology* 23:47–61.

Agnew, Robert. 1985b. "A Revised Strain Theory of Delinquency." *Social Forces* 64:151–167.

Agnew, Robert. 1992. "Foundation for a General Strain Theory of Crime and Delinquency." *Criminology* 30:47–87.

Agnew, Robert. 2005. *Why Do Criminals Offend: A General Theory of Crime and Delinquency*. Los Angeles, CA: Roxbury.

Agnew, Robert. 2006a. "Pressured Into Crime: General Strain Theory." Pp. 201–209 in Francis T. Cullen and Robert Agnew (Eds.), *Criminological Theory Past to Present: Essential Readings*. New York: Oxford University Press.

Agnew, Robert. 2006b. "General Strain Theory: Current Status and Directions for Further Research." Pp. 101–123 in Francis T. Cullen, John Paul Wright & Kristie R. Blevins (eds.), *Taking Stock: The Status of Criminological Theory: Advances in Criminological Theory*, Volume 15. New Brunswick: Transaction.

Agnew, Robert. 2011. *Toward a Unified Criminology: Integrating Assumptions about Crime, People, and Society*. New York: New York University Press.

Agnew, Robert. 2014. "Social Concern and Crime: Moving Beyond the Assumption of Simple Self-Interest." *Criminology* 52:1–32.

Aichorn, August. 1935. *Wayward Youth*. New York: Viking.

Akers, Ronald L. 1967. "Problems in the Sociology of Deviance: Social Definitions and Behavior." *Social Forces* 46:455–465.

Akers, Ronald L. 1985. *Deviant Behavior: A Social Learning Approach*. 3d ed. Belmont, CA: Wadsworth.

Akers, Ronald L. 1994. *Criminological Theories: Introduction and Evaluation*. Los Angeles, CA: Roxbury.

Akers, Ronald L. 1998. *Social Learning and Social Structure: A General Theory of Crime and Deviance*. Boston: Northeastern University Press.

Akers, Ronald L. 1999. "Social Learning and Social Structure: Reply to Sampson, Morash, and Krohn." *Theoretical Criminology* 3:477–493.

Akers, Ronald L. and Gary F. Jensen. 2006. "The Empirical Status of Social Learning Theory of Crime and Deviance: The Past, Present, and Future." Pp. 37–76 in Francis T. Cullen, John Paul Wright & Kristie R. Blevins (eds.), *Taking Stock: The Status of Criminological Theory: Advances in Criminological Theory*, Volume 15. New Brunswick: Transaction.

Akers, Ronald L. and Christine S. Sellers. 2004. *Criminological Theories: Introduction, Evaluation and Application*. New York: Oxford University Press.

Akers, Ronald L. and Christine S. Sellers. 2013. *Criminological Theories: Introduction, Evaluation and Application*, 6th ed. New York: Oxford University Press.

Alexander, Franz and William Healy. 1935. *Roots of Crime*. New York: Knopf.

Anderson, Elijah. 1999. *Code of the Street: Decency, Violence, and the Moral Life of the Inner City*. New York: Norton.

Anderson, Gail. 2006. *Biological Influences on Criminal Behavior*. Boca Raton, FL: CRC Press.

Andrews, D. A. 1980. "Some Experimental Investigations of the Principles of Differential Association Through Deliberate Manipulations of the Structure of Service Systems." *American Sociological Review* 45:448–462.

Andrews, D. A. and James Bonta. 1994. *The Psychology of Criminal Conduct*. Cincinnati, OH: Anderson.

Archer, John. 2006. "Testosterone and Human Aggression: An Evaluation of the Challenge Hypothesis." *Neuroscience and Biobehavioral Reviews* 30:319–345.

Arneklev, Bruce J., Harold G. Grasmick, and Robert J. Bursik, Jr. 1999. "Evaluating the Dimensionality and Invariance of 'Low Self-Control.'" *Journal of Quantitative Criminology* 15:307–331.

Arrigo, Bruce A. 2003. "Postmodern Justice and Critical Criminology: Positional, Relational, and Provisional Science." Pp. 43-55 in Martin D. Schwartz and Suzanne E. Hatty (eds.), *Controversies in Critical Criminology*, Cincinnati, OH: Anderson Publishing Co.

Arrigo, Bruce and T. R. Young. 1997. "Chaos, Complexity, and Crime: Working Tools for a Postmodern Criminology." Pp. 77–84 in Brian D. MacLean and Dragan Milovanovic (eds.), *Thinking Critically About Crime*. Vancouver, BC: Collective Press.

Aseltine, Robert H., Jr., Susan Gore, and Jennifer Gordon. 2000. "Life Stress, Anger and Anxiety, and Delinquency: An Empirical Test of General Strain Theory." *Journal of Health and Social Behavior* 41:256–275.

Babbie, Earl. 2007. *The Practice of Social Research*, 11th ed. Belmont, CA: Thompson Learning.

Baker, Laura A., Serena Bezdjian, and Adrian Raine. 2006. "Behavioral Genetics: The Science of Antisocial Behavior." *Law and Contemporary Problems* 69:7–46.

Balkan, Sheila, Ronald J. Berger, and Janet Schmidt. 1980. *Crime and Deviance in America: A Critical Approach*. Belmont, CA: Wadsworth.

Ball, Matthew, Carrie L. Buist, and Jordan Blair Woods. 2014. "Introduction to the Special Issue on Queer/ing Criminology: New Directions and Frameworks." *Critical Criminology* 22:1–4.

Bandura, Albert and Richard H. Walters. 1963. *Social Learning and Personality Development*. New York: Holt, Rinehart and Winston.

Banner, Stuart. 2002. *The Death Penalty: An American History*. Cambridge: Harvard University Press.

Barak, Gregg. 1988. "Newsmaking Criminology: Reflections on the Media, Intellectuals, and Crime." *Justice Quarterly* 5:565–587.

Barak, Gregg (ed.). 1994. *Media, Process and the Social Construction of Crime: Studies in Newsmaking Criminology*. New York: Garland.

Barak, Gregg. 1998. *Integrating Criminologies*. Boston: Allyn and Bacon.

Barak, Gregg, Stuart Henry, and Dragan Milovanovic. 1997. "Constitutive Criminology: An Overview of an Emerging Postmodernist School." Pp. 93–99 in Brian D. MacLean and Dragan Milovanovic (eds.), *Thinking Critically About Crime*. Vancouver, BC: Collective Press.

Baron, Stephen W. 2004. "General Strain, Street Youth and Crime: A Test of Agnew's Revised Theory." *Criminology* 42:457–484.

Baron, Stephen W. and David R. Forde. 2007. "Street Youth and Crime: A Test of Control Balance Theory." *Justice Quarterly* 24:335–355.

Bartol, Carl, R. 1991. *Criminal Behavior: A Psychological Approach*, 3rd. ed. Englewood Cliffs, NJ: Prentice-Hall.

Baumer, Eric P. and Regan Gustafson. 2007. "Social Organization and Instrumental Crime: Assessing the Empirical Validity of Classic and Contemporary Anomie Theories." *Criminology* 45:617–664.

Beccaria, Cesare. 1975. *On Crimes and Punishments*. Tr., with introduction, by Harry Paolucci. Indianapolis, IN: Bobbs-Merrill.

Becker, Carl L. 1932. *The Heavenly City of the Eighteenth Century Philosophers.* New Haven, CT: Yale University Press.

Becker, Gary. S. 1968. "Crime and Punishment: An Economic Approach." *Journal of Political Economy*, 169–217.

Becker, Howard S. 1963. *Outsiders: Studies in the Sociology of Deviance.* New York: Free Press of Glencoe.

Beckett, Katherine. 1997. *Making Crime Pay: Law and Order in Contemporary American Politics.* New York: Oxford University Press.

Bedau, Hugo Adam. 1982. *The Death Penalty in America*, 3d ed. New York: Oxford University Press.

Beirne, Piers. 1991. "Inventing Criminology: The 'Science of Man' in Cesare Beccaria's Dei Delitti E Delle Pene (1764)." *Criminology* 29:777–820.

Beirne, Piers and James Messerschmidt. 2000. *Criminology*, 3d ed. Boulder, CO: Westview Press.

Bentham, Jeremy. 1996, originally 1789. *An Introduction to the Principles of Morals and Legislation.* New York: Oxford University Press.

Bernard, Thomas J. and Jeffrey B. Snipes. 1996. "Theoretical Integration in Criminology." Pp. 301–348 in Michael Tonry (ed.), *Crime and Justice: A Review of Research* (Vol. 20). Chicago: University of Chicago Press.

Bernard, Thomas J., Jeffrey B. Snipes and Alexander L Gerould. 2010. *Vold's Theoretical Criminology.* New York: Oxford University Press.

Berofsky, Bernard. 1973. "Free Will and Determinism." Pp. 236–242 in Philip P. Wiener (ed.), *Dictionary of the History of Ideas: Studies of Selected Pivotal Ideas* (Vol. II). New York: Charles Scribner's Sons.

Blackwell, Brenda Sims. 2010. "Hagan, John: Power Control Theory." Pp. 413–417 in Francis T. Cullen and Pamela Wilcox (eds.), *Encyclopedia of Criminological Theory* (Vol. I). Los Angeles: Sage.

Blackwell, Brenda Sims and Alex R. Piquero. 2005. "On the Relationships between Gender, Power control, Self-Control, and Crime." *Journal of Criminal Justice* 33:1–17.

Blumer, Herbert. 1969. *Symbolic Interactionism.* Englewood Cliffs, NJ: Prentice-Hall.

Bohm, Robert M. 1981. "Reflexivity and Critical Criminology." Pp. 29–47 in Gary F. Jensen (ed.), *Sociology of Delinquency: Current Issues.* Beverly Hills, CA: Sage.

Bohm, Robert M. 1982. "Radical Criminology: An Explication." *Criminology* 19:565–589.

Bohm, Robert M. 1987. "Comment on 'Traditional Contributions to Radical Criminology' by Groves and Sampson." *Journal of Research in Crime and Delinquency* 24:324–331.

Bonger, Willem. 1916. *Criminology and Economic Conditions*. Boston: Little, Brown.

Boomsma, Dorret, Andreas Busjahn and Leena Peltonen. 2002. "Classical Twin Studies and Beyond." *Nature Reviews Genetics* 3:872–882.

Botchkovar, Ekaterina V., Charles R. Tittle, and Olena Antonaccio. 2009. "General Strain Theory: Additional Evidence using Cross-Cultural Data." *Criminology* 47:131–173

Bouffard, Jeffrey A. 2002. "The Influence of Sexual Arousal on Rational Decision Making in Sexual Aggression." *Journal of Criminal Justice* 30:121–134.

Braithwaite, John. 1989. *Crime, Shame and Reintegration*. Cambridge: Cambridge University Press.

Braithwaite, John, Eliza Ahmed, and Valerie Braithwaite. 2006. "Shame, Restorative Justice, and Crime." Pp. 397–417 in Francis T. Cullen, John Paul Wright & Kristie R. Blevins (eds.), *Taking Stock: The Status of Criminological Theory: Advances in Criminological Theory*, Volume 15. New Brunswick, NJ: Transaction.

Brantingham, Paul J. and Patricia L. Brantingham. 1984. *Patterns of Crime*. New York: Macmillan.

Brantingham, Paul J. and Patricia L. Brantingham. 1991. *Environmental Criminology*. Prospect Heights, IL: Waveland.

Brennan, Joseph G. 1953. *The Meaning of Philosophy*, 2d ed. New York: Harper & Row.

Brezina, Timothy, Robert Agnew, Francis T. Cullen, and John Paul Wright. 2004. "Code of the Street: A Quantitative Assessment of Elijah Anderson's Subculture of Violence Thesis and Its Contribution to Youth Violence Research." *Youth Violence and Juvenile Justice* 2:303–328.

Bromberg, Walter and Charles B. Thompson. 1937. "The Relation of Psychosis, Mental Defect, and Personality Types to Crime." *Journal of Criminal Law and Criminology* 28:70–89.

Bruder, Carl E. G., Arkadiusz Piotrowski, Antoinet A. C. J. Gijsbers, Robin Andersson, Stephen Erickson, Teresita Diaz de Stahl, Uwe Menzel, Johanna Sandgren, Desiree von Tell, Andrzej Poplawski, Michael Crowley, Chiquito Crasto, E. Christopher Partridge, Hemant Tiwan, David B. Allison, Jan Komorowski, Gert-Jan B. van Ommen, Dorret I. Boomsma, Nancy L. Pedersen, Johan T. den Dunnen, Karin Wirdefeldt, and Jan P. Dumanski. 2008. "Phenotypically Concordant and Discordant Monozygotic Twins Display Different DNA Copy-Number-Variation-Profiles." *American Journal of Human Genetics* 82:763–771.

Burgess, Robert L. and Ronald L. Akers. 1966. "A Differential Association-Reinforcement Theory of Criminal Behavior." *Social Problems* 14:128–147.

Bursik, Robert. 1984. "Urban Dynamics and Ecological Studies of Delinquency." *Social Forces* 63:393–413.

Burt, Callie H. and Ronald L. Simons. 2014. "Pulling Back the Curtain on Heritability Studies: Biosocial Criminology in the Postgenomic Era." *Criminology* 52:223–262.

Burt, Callie Harbin, Ronald L. Simons and Leslie G. Simons. 2006. "A Longitudinal Test of the Effects of Parenting and the Stability of Self-control: Negative Evidence for the General Theory of Crime." *Criminology* 44:353–396.

Cahn, Lenore (ed.). 1966. *Confronting Injustice*. Boston: Little, Brown.

Caspi, Avshalom, Terrie E. Moffitt, Phil A. Silva, Magda Stouthamer-Loeber, Robert F. Frueger and Panela S. Schmutte. 1994. "Are Some People Crime-Prone? Replications of the Personality-Crime Relationship Across Countries, Genders, Races, and Methods." *Criminology* 32:163–195.

Chambliss, William J. 1976. "Functional and Conflict Theories of Crime: The Heritage of Emile Durkheim and Karl Marx." Pp. 1–28 in William J. Chambliss and Milton Mankoff (eds.), *Whose Law What Order?* New York: Wiley.

Chambliss, William J. and Robert B. Seidman. 1971. *Law, Order, and Power*. Reading, MA: Addison-Wesley.

Chamlin, Mitchell and John Cochran. 1997. "Social Altruism and Crime." *Criminology* 35:203–227.

Chesney-Lind, Meda and Barbara Bloom. 1997. "Feminist Criminology: Thinking About Women and Crime." Pp. 45–55 in Brian D. MacLean and Dragan Milovanovic (eds.), *Thinking Critically About Crime*. Vancouver, BC: Collective Press.

Chesney-Lind, Meda and Merry Morash. "Transformative Feminist Criminology: A Critical Re-thinking of a Discipline." *Critical Criminology* 21:287–304.

Chesney-Lind, Meda and Randall G. Shelden. 2004. *Girls, Delinquency, and Juvenile Justice*. Belmont, CA: Wadsworth.

Chisholm, Roderick M. 1966. *Theory of Knowledge*. Englewood Cliffs, NJ: Prentice-Hall.

Chomsky, Noam. 1969. *American Power and the New Mandarins: Historical and Political Essays*. New York: Vintage Books.

Christian, James L. 1977. *Philosophy*, 2d ed. New York: Holt, Reinhart and Winston.

Cisneros, Henry G. 1995. *Defensible Space: Deterring Crime and Building Community*. Rockville, MD: U.S. Department of Housing and Urban Development.

Clarke, Ronald V. 1980. "'Situational' Crime Prevention: Theory and Practice." *British Journal of Criminology* 20:136–147.

Clarke, Ronald. 1992. *Situational Crime Prevention: Successful Case Studies*. Albany, NY: Harrow and Heston.

Cleckley, Hervey. 1982. *The Mask of Sanity*. 4th ed. St. Louis, MO: Mosby.

Cloninger, C. Robert, Dragan M. Svrakic, and Thomas R. Przybeck. 1993. "A Psychobiological Model of Temperament and Character." *Archives of General Psychiatry* 50:975–990.

Cloward, Richard A. and Lloyd E. Ohlin. 1960. *Delinquency and Opportunity: A Theory of Delinquent Gangs*. New York: Free Press.

Coccaro, Emil F., Richard J. Kavoussi and Brian McNamee. 2000. "Central Neurotransmitter Function in Criminal Aggression." Pp. 6–16 in Diane H. Fishbein (ed.), *The Science, Treatment, and Prevention of Antisocial Behaviors*. Kingston NJ: Civic Research Institute.

Cohen, Albert K. 1955. *Delinquent Boys: The Culture of the Gang*. New York: Free Press.

Cohen, Lawrence E. and Marcus Felson. 1979. "Social Change and Crime Rate Trends: A Routine Activity Approach." *American Sociological Review* 44:588–608.

Colvin, Mark and John Pauly. 1983. "A Critique of Criminology: Toward an Integrated Structural-Marxist Theory of Delinquency Production." *American Journal of Sociology* 89:513–551.

Comte, Auguste. 1974. *The Positive Philosophy*. New York: AMS Press.

Connor, Steve. 2006. "Genetic Breakthrough Reveals Differences Between Humans." *The Independent* (November 23) at www.anapsid.org/cnd/diffdx/geneticvariance.html (accessed September 6, 2009).

Cooley, Charles H. 1964. *Human Nature and the Social Order*. New York: Schocken.

Cornish, Derek and Ronald Clarke (eds.). 1986. *The Reasoning Criminal: Rational Choice Perspectives on Offending*. New York: Springer-Verlag.

Cortes, Juan B. with Florence M. Gatti. 1972. *Delinquency and Crime: A Biopsychological Approach*. New York: Seminar Press.

Costello, Barbara. 1997. "On the Logical Adequacy of Cultural Deviance Theories." *Theoretical Criminology* 1:403–428.

Costello, Barbara and Helen J. Mederer, 2003. "A Control theory of Gender Differences in Crime and Delinquency." Pp. 77–108 in Chester L. Britt and Michael R. Gottfredson (eds.), *Control Theories of Crime and Delinquency*. New Brunswick, NJ: Transaction.

Cote, Suzette. 2002. *Criminological Theories: Bridging the Past to the Future*. Thousand Oaks, CA: Sage.

Cullen, Francis T. 1984. *Rethinking Crime and Deviance Theory: The Emergence of Structuring Tradition.* Totowa, N.J.: Rowman and Littlefield.

Cullen, Francis T. 1994. "Social Support as an Organizing Concept for Criminology: Presidential Address to the Academy of Criminal Justice Sciences." *Justice Quarterly* 11:527–559.

Cullen, Francis T. and Robert Agnew. 2006. *Criminological Theory: Past to Present. Essential Readings,* 3rd ed. New York: Oxford Publishing.

Cullen, Francis T., Paul Gendreau, G. Roger Jarjoura, and John Paul Wright. 1997. "Crime and the Bell Curve: Lessons from Intelligent Science." *Crime & Delinquency* 43:387–411.

Cullen, Francis T. and Steven F. Messner. 2007. "The Making of Criminology Revisited: An Oral History of Merton's Anomie Paradigm." *Theoretical Criminology* 11:5–37.

Cullen, Francis T. and John Paul Wright. 1997. "Liberating the Anomie-Strain Paradigms: Implications from Social-Support Theory." Pp. 187–206 in Nikos Passas and Robert Agnew (eds.), *The Future of Anomie Theory.* Boston: Northeastern University Press.

Curran, Daniel J. and Claire M. Renzetti. 1994. *Theories of Crime.* Boston: Allyn and Bacon.

Currie, Elliott. 1997a. "Market, Crime and Community: Toward a Mid-Range Theory of Post-Industrial Violence." *Theoretical Criminology* 1:147–172.

Currie, Elliott. 1997b. "Market Society and Social Disorder." Pp. 37–42 in Brian D. MacLean and Dragan Milovanovic (eds.), *Thinking Critically About Crime.* Vancouver, BC: Collective Press.

Curry, Theodore. 2005. "Integrating Motivating and Constraining Forces in Deviance Causation: A Test of Causal Chain Hypotheses in Control Balance Theory." *Deviant Behavior* 26:571–599.

Curry, Theodore and Alex R. Piquero. 2003. "Control Rations and Defiant Acts of Deviance: Assessing Additive and Conditional Effects with Constraints and Impulsivity." *Sociological Perspectives* 46:397–415.

Dahrendorf, Ralf. 1959. *Class and Class Conflict in Industrial Society.* Stanford, CA: Stanford University Press.

Dalgard, Odd S. and Einar Kringlen. 1976. "A Norwegian Twin Study of Criminology." *British Journal of Criminology* 16:213–232.

Daly, Kathleen and Meda Chesney-Lind. 1988. "Feminism and Criminology." *Justice Quarterly* 5:497–538.

Daly, Kathleen and Lisa Maher (eds.). 1998. *Criminology at the Crossroads: Feminist Readings in Crime and Justice.* New York: Oxford University Press.

Davis, Kingsley. 1971. "Prostitution." In Robert K. Merton and Robert Nisbit (eds.), *Contemporary Social Problems*. New York: Harcourt Brace Jovanovich.

Davis, Nanette J. 1975. *Sociological Constructions of Deviance: Perspectives and Issues in the Field*. Dubuque, IA: Wm. C. Brown.

Death Penalty Information Center. Retrieved June 1, 2009 from http://www.deathpenaltyinfo.org/states-and-without-death-penalty.

DeFronzo, James. 1997. "Welfare and Homicide." *Journal of Research in Crime and Delinquency* 34:395–406.

Denno, Deborah. 1985. "Sociological and Human Developmental Explanations of Crime: Conflict or Consensus." *Criminology* 23:711–741.

DNA Learning Center. n.d. "Copy Number Variants" at http://www.dnalc.org/view/552-Copy-Number-Variants.html (accessed September 27, 2014).

Donnellan, M. Brent, R. Chris Fraley, and Robert F. Krueger. 2007. "Not So Situational." Letter to the Editor, *Association for Psychological Science Observer*, Vol. 20, No. 6 (June/July) at www.psychologicalscience.org/observer/getArticle.cfm?id=2171 (accessed September 6, 2009).

Donnermeyer, Joseph F. and Walter DeKeseredy. 2008. "Toward a Rural Critical Criminology." *Southern Rural Sociology* 23:4–28.

Dowie, Mark. 1977. "Pinto Madness." *Mother Jones* 2:18–22.

Dubin, Robert. 1959. "Deviant Behavior and Social Structure: Continuities in Social Theory." *American Sociological Review* 24:147–164.

Dugdale, Richard L. 1877. *The Jukes: A Study in Crime, Pauperism, Disease and Heredity*. New York: Putnam.

Durkheim, Emile. 1997, originally 1893. *The Division of Labor in Society*. Tr. by W. D. Halls. New York: Free Press.

Durkheim, Emile. 1964, originally 1895. *The Rules of Sociological Method*. Tr. by Sarah A. Solovay and John H. Mueller; Ed. by George E. G. Catlin. New York: Free Press.

Einstadter, Werner and Stuart Henry. 1995. *Criminological Theory: An Analysis of Its Underlying Assumptions*. Fort Worth, TX: Harcourt Brace.

Elliott, Delbert S., Suzanne S. Ageton, and Rachelle J. Cantor. 1979. "An Integrated Theoretical Perspective on Delinquent Behavior." *Journal of Research in Crime and Delinquency* 16:3–27.

Elliott, Delbert S., David Huizinga, and Suzanne S. Ageton. 1985. *Explaining Delinquency and Drug Use*. Beverly Hills, CA: Sage.

Elliott, Delbert S., David Huizinga, and Scott Menard. 1989. *Multiple Problem Youth: Delinquency, Substance Abuse, and Mental Health Problems*. New York: Springer-Verlag.

Elliott, Frank A. 2006. "A Neurological Perspective of Violent Behavior." Pp. 19-1–19-21 in Diana H. Fishbein (Ed.), *The Science, Treatment, and Preven-*

tion of Antisocial Behaviors: Application to the Criminal Justice System.
Kingston NJ: Civic Research Institute, Inc.

Ellis, Lee and Anthony Walsh. 1997. "Gene-Based Evolutionary Theories in Criminology." *Criminology* 35:229–276.

Estabrook, Arthur H. 1916. *The Jukes in 1915.* Washington, DC: Carnegie Institute of Washington.

Eysenck, Hans J. 1977. *Crime and Personality.* London, UK: Routledge and Kegan Paul.

Eysenck, Hans J. 1997. "Personality and the Biosocial Model of Antisocial and Criminal Behavior." Pp. 21–38 in Adrian Raine, Patricia Brennan, David P. Farrington and Sarnoff A. Mednick (eds.), *Biosocial Bases of Violence.* New York: Plenum.

Farrington, David P. 1997. "The Relationship between Low Resting Heart Rate and Violence." Pp. 89–105 in Adrian Raine, Patricia A. Brennan, David P. Farrington, and Sarnoff A. Mednick (eds.), *Biosocial Bases of Violence.* New York: Plenum.

Farrington, David P. 2006. "Building Developmental and Life-Course Theories of Offending." Pp. 335–364 in Francis T. Cullen, John Paul Wright and Kristie R. Blevins (eds.), *Taking Stock: The Status of Criminological Theory: Advances in Criminological Theory,* Volume 15. New Brunswick, NJ: Transaction Publishers.

Feminism. (n.d.). *The American Heritage® New Dictionary of Cultural Literacy, Third Edition* at http://dictionary.reference.com/browse/feminism (accessed November 25, 2009).

Ferrell, Jeff. 1993. *Crimes of Style: Urban Graffiti and the Politics of Criminality.* New York: Garland.

Ferrell, Jeff. 1997. "Against the Law: Anarchist Criminology." Pp. 146–154 in Brian D. MacLean and Dragan Milovanovic (eds.), *Thinking Critically About Crime.* Vancouver, BC: Collective Press.

Ferrell, Jeff. 1999. "Anarchist Criminology and Social Justice." Pp. 93–108 in Bruce A. Arrigo (ed.), *Social Justice/Criminal Justice: The Maturation of Critical Theory in Law, Crime, and Deviance.* Belmont, CA: West/Wadsworth.

Ferrell, Jeff, Keith Hayward, and Jock Young. 2008. *Cultural Criminology.* Thousand Oaks, CA: Sage.

Ferrero, Guglielmo. 2000. "Savages and Criminals." Pp. 95–99 in David M. Horton, *Pioneering Perspectives in Criminology: The Literature of 19th Century Criminological Positivism.* Incline Village, NV: Copperhouse. [Originally published in *The Independent,* Vol. 52 (November 8, 1900), pp. 2688–2690].

Finckenauer, James O. 1982. *Scared Straight! and the Panacea Phenomenon.* Englewood Cliffs, NJ: Prentice-Hall.

Fishbein, Diana H. 1990. "Biological Perspectives in Criminology." *Criminology* 28:27–72.

Fishbein, Diana H. 2000. *The Science, Treatment, and Prevention of Antisocial Behaviors: Application to the Criminal Justice System.* Kingston, NJ: Civic Research Institute.

Fishbein, Diana H. and Robert Thatcher. 1986. "New Diagnostic Methods in Criminology: Assessing Organic Sources of Behavioral Disorders." *Journal of Research in Crime and Delinquency* 23:240–267.

Fitz Round, William Marshall. 2000. "Criminal Not the Victims of Heredity." Pp. 227–238 in David M. Horton, *Pioneering Perspectives in Criminology: The Literature of 19th Century Criminological Positivism.* Incline Village, NV: Copperhouse. [Originally published in *Forum*, Vol. 16 (September 1893), pp. 48–59].

Flavin, Jeanne. 2001. "Feminism for the Mainstream Criminologist: An Invitation." *Journal of Criminal Justice* 29:271–285.

"Footnotes." 1987. *The Chronicle of Higher Education* (October 21), p. A6.

Foucault, Michel. 1977. *Discipline and Punish: The Birth of the Prison.* New York: Pantheon Books.

Fradella, Henry F. 2007. "From Insanity to Beyond Diminished Capacity: Mental Illness and Criminal Excuse in the Post-*Clark* Era." *University of Florida Journal of Law and Public Policy* 18:7–92.

Freud, Sigmund. 1953. *A General Introduction to Psychoanalysis.* New York: Permabooks.

Friedlander, Kate. 1947. *The Psychoanalytical Approach to Juvenile Delinquency.* London: International Universities Press.

Friedrichs, David O. 1996. *Trusted Criminals: White Collar Crime in Contemporary Society.* Belmont, CA: Wadsworth.

Gibbons, Don C. 1994. *Talking About Crime and Criminals: Problems and Issues in Theory Development in Criminology.* Englewood Cliffs, NJ: Prentice-Hall.

Glaser, Daniel. 1956. "Criminality Theories and Behavioral Images." *American Journal of Sociology* 61:433–444.

Glueck, Shelden. 1956. "Theory and Fact in Criminology: A Criticism of Differential Association." *British Journal of Delinquency* 7:92–109.

Glueck, Shelden and Eleanor Glueck. 1930. *500 Criminal Careers.* New York: Knopf.

Glueck, Shelden and Eleanor Glueck. 1934. *One Thousand Juvenile Delinquents.* Cambridge: Harvard University Press.

Glueck, Shelden and Eleanor Glueck. 1950. *Unraveling Juvenile Delinquency.* Cambridge: Harvard University Press.

Glueck, Shelden and Eleanor Glueck. 1956. *Physique and Delinquency*. New York: Harper.

Glueck, Shelden and Eleanor Glueck. 1967. *Predicting Delinquency and Crime*. Cambridge: Harvard University Press.

Goddard, Henry H. 1914. *Feeblemindedness: Its Causes and Consequences*. New York: Macmillan.

Goldman, David and Diana H. Fishbein. 2000. "Genetic Bases for Impulsive and Antisocial Behaviors—Can Their Course Be Altered?" Pp. 9-1–9-18 in Diana H. Fishbein (ed.), *The Science, Treatment, and Prevention of Antisocial Behaviors: Application to the Criminal Justice System*. Kingston, NJ: Civic Research Institute, Inc.

Gordon, David M. 1976. "Class and the Economics of Crime." Pp. 193–214 in William J. Chambliss and Milton Mankoff (eds.), *Whose Law What Order?* New York: Wiley.

Gordon, Robert. 1976. "Prevalence: The Rare Datum in Delinquency Measurement and Its Implications for the Theory of Delinquency." Pp. 201–284 in Malcolm W. Klein (ed.), *The Juvenile Justice System*. Beverly Hills, CA: Sage.

Goring, Charles. 1913. *The English Convict: A Statistical Study*. London: HMSO (reprinted by Patterson Smith, Montclair, NJ, 1972).

Gottfredson, Michael R. 2006. "The Empirical Status of Control Theory in Criminology." Pp. 77–100 in Francis T. Cullen, John Paul Wright & Kristie R. Blevins (eds.), *Taking Stock: The Status of Criminological Theory: Advances in Criminological Theory*, Volume 15. New Brunswick: Transaction.

Gottfredson, Michael R. and Travis Hirschi. 1990. *A General Theory of Crime*. Stanford, CA: Stanford University Press.

Gould, Stephen Jay. 1996. *The Mismeasure of Man*. New York: Norton.

Gouldner, Alvin W. 1971. *The Coming Crisis of Western Sociology*. New York: Avon.

Gouldner, Alvin W. 1976. *The Dialectic of Ideology and Technology: The Origins, Grammar, and Future of Ideology*. New York: Seabury Press.

Gove, Walter. 1985. "The Effect of Age and Gender on Deviant Behavior: A Biopsychological Perspective." Pp. 115–144 in Alice S. Rossi (ed.), *Gender and the Life Course*. New York: Aldine.

Greenfeld, Lawrence A. 1998. *Alcohol and Crime: An Analysis of National Data on the Prevalence of Alcohol Involvement in Crime (NCJ 168632)*. Washington, D.C.: Bureau of Justice Statistics.

Groves, W. Byron and Robert J. Sampson. 1987. "Traditional Contributions to Radical Criminology." *Journal of Research in Crime and Delinquency* 24:181–214.

"Guerry on the Statistics of Crime in France, Being an Abstract of His *Essai Sur La Statistique Morale De La France, Avec Cartes*." 2000. Pp. 255–268 in David

M. Horton, *Pioneering Perspectives in Criminology: The Literature of 19th Century Criminological Positivism*. Incline Village, NV: Copperhouse. [Originally published in *Westminister Review*, Vol. 18, No. 36 (April 1833), pp. 353–366].

Hagan, John. 1989. *Structural Criminology*. New Brunswick, NJ: Rutgers University Press.

Hagan, John, A. R. Gillis, and John Simpson. 1985. "The Class Structure of Gender and Delinquency: Toward a Power-Control Theory of Common Delinquent Behavior." *American Journal of Sociology* 90:1151–1178.

Hagan, John, A. R. Gillis, and John Simpson. 1987. "Class in the Household: A Power-Control Theory of Gender and Delinquency." *American Journal of Sociology* 92:788–816.

Hall, Calvin S. 1954. *A Primer of Freudian Psychology*. New York: World Publishing Co.

Halleck, Seymour L. 1967. *Psychiatry and the Dilemmas of Crime*. New York: Harper and Row.

Hare, Robert D. 1999. *Without Conscience: The Disturbing World of the Psychopaths among Us*. New York: Guilford Press.

Hawley, F. Frederick and Steven F. Messner. 1989. "The Southern Violence Construct: A Review of Arguments, Evidence, and the Normative Context." *Justice Quarterly* 6:481–511.

Hayes, Timothy C. and Matthew R. Lee. 2005. "The Southern Culture of Honor and Violent Attitudes." *Sociological Spectrum* 25:593–617.

Healy, William and Augusta Bonner. 1926. *Delinquents and Criminals: Their Making and Unmaking*. New York: Macmillan.

Healy, William and Augusta Bonner. 1936. *New Light on Delinquency and Its Treatment*. New Haven, CT: Yale University Press.

Heimer, Karen and Stacy De Coster. 2006. "The Gendering of Violent Delinquency." Pp. 374–382 in Francis T. Cullen and Robert Agnew (eds.), *Criminological Theory: Past to Present. Essential Readings*, 3rd ed. New York: Oxford Publishing.

Henry, Stuart and Dragan Milovanovic. 1991. "Constitutive Criminology: The Maturation of Critical Theory." *Criminology* 29:293–315.

Henry, Stuart and Dragan Milovanovic. 1996. *Constitutive Criminology: Beyond Postmodernism*. London: Sage.

Herrnstein, Richard J. and Charles Murray. 1994. *The Bell Curve: Intelligence and Class Structure in American Life*. New York: Free Press.

Hickman, Matthew J, Alex R. Piquero, Brian A. Lawton and Jack R. Greene. 2001. "Applying Tittle's Control Balance Theory to Police Deviance." *Policing: An International Journal of Police Strategies and Management* 24:497–519.

Hirschi, Travis. 1969. *Causes of Delinquency*. Berkeley, CA: University of California Press.

Hirschi, Travis. 1979. "Separate but Unequal Is Better." *Journal of Research in Crime and Delinquency* 16:34–38.

Hirschi, Travis and Michael Gottfredson. 1987. "Causes of White-Collar Crime." *Criminology* 25:949–974.

Hirschi, Travis and Michael Gottfredson. 1989. "The Significance of White-Collar Crime for a General Theory of Crime." *Criminology* 27:359–372.

Hirschi, Travis and Michael J. Hindelang. 1977. "Intelligence and Delinquency: A Revisionist Review." *American Sociological Review* 42:572–587.

Honer, Stanley and Thomas C. Hunt. 1968. *Invitation to Philosophy*. Belmont, CA: Wadsworth.

Horkheimer, Max. 1996. *Critique of Instrumental Reason*. New York: Continuum.

Horney, Julie. 2006. "An Alternative Psychology of Criminal Behavior: The American Society of Criminology 2005 Presidential Address." *Criminology* 44:1–16.

Howe, Adrian. 1997. "Criminology Meets Postmodern Feminism (and Has a Nice Day)." Pp. 85–92 in Brian D. MacLean and Dragan Milovanovic (eds.), *Thinking Critically About Crime*. Vancouver, BC: Collective Press.

Hubbard, Dana Jones and Travis C. Pratt. 2002. "A Meta-Analysis of the Predictors of Delinquency Among Girls." *Journal of Offender Rehabilitation* 34:1–13.

Hudson, Barbara. 1997. "Punishment or Redress: Current Themes in European Abolitionist Criminology." Pp. 131–138 in Brian D. MacLean and Dragan Milovanovic (eds.), *Thinking Critically About Crime*. Vancouver, BC: Collective Press.

Hutchins, Robert Maynard (ed.). 1952. *The Major Works of Sigmund Freud*. Chicago: Encyclopedia Britannica.

Jacobs, James B. 1998. "Emergence and Implications of American Hate Crime Jurisprudence." Pp. 150–176 in Robert J. Kelly and Jess Maghan (eds.), *Hate Crime: The Global Politics of Polarization*. Carbondale, IL: Southern Illinois University Press.

Jeffrey, C. Ray. 1965. "Criminal Behavior and Learning Theory." *Journal of Criminal Law, Criminology, and Police Science* 56:294–300.

Jeffrey, C. Ray. 1977. *Crime Prevention Through Environmental Design*. Beverly Hills, CA: Sage.

Jensen, Arthur R. 1998. *The g Factor: The Science of Mental Ability*. Westport, CT: Praeger.

Jensen, Gary, 2002. "Institutional Anomie and Societal Variations in Crime: A Critical Appraisal." *International Journal of Sociology and Social Policy* 22:45–74.

Jones, David A. 1987. *History of Criminology: A Philosophical Perspective*. New York: Greenwood.

Jones, Owen D. 2006. "Behavioral Genetics and Crime, in Context." *Law and Contemporary Problems* 69:81–100.

Jones, Richard S., Jeffrey Ian Ross, Stephen C. Richards, and Daniel S. Murphy. 2009. "The First Dime: A Decade of Convict Criminology." *The Prison Journal* 89:151–171.

Jurik, Nancy C. 1999. "Socialist Feminism, Criminology, and Social Justice." Pp. 31–50 in Bruce A. Arrigo (ed.), *Social Justice/Criminal Justice: The Maturation of Critical Theory in Law, Crime, and Deviance*. Belmont, CA: West/Wadsworth.

Kahler, Erich. 1967. *The Tower and the Abyss: An Inquiry into the Transformation of Man*. New York: Viking Press.

Katz, Jack. 1988. *Seductions of Crime: Moral and Sensual Attractions in Doing Evil*. New York: Basic Books.

Kerlinger, Fred N. 1964. *Foundations of Behavioral Research: Educational and Psychological Inquiry*. New York: Holt, Rinehart and Winston.

Kinsey, Richard, John Lea, and Jock Young. 1986. *Losing the Fight Against Crime*. London: Basil Blackwell.

Kornhauser, Ruth Rosner. 1978. *Social Sources of Delinquency: An Appraisal of Analytic Models*. Chicago: University of Chicago Press.

Krohn, Marvin D. 1999. "Social Learning Theory: The Continuing Development of a Perspective." *Theoretical Criminology* 3:462–476.

Lanctot, Nadine, and Mark Le Blanc. 2002. "Explaining Deviance by Adolescent Females." *Crime and Justice: A Review of Research* 29:113–202.

Lane, Scott D. and Don R. Cherek. 2000. "Biological and Behavioral Investigation of Aggression and Impulsivity." Pp. 5-1–5-21 in Diana H. Fishbein (ed.), *The Science, Treatment, and Prevention of Antisocial Behaviors: Application to the Criminal Justice System*. Kingston, NJ: Civic Research Institute, Inc.

Lanier, Mark M. and Stuart Henry. 1998. *Essential Criminology*. Boulder, CO: Westview Press.

Lanphear, Bruce P., Charles V. Voorhees and David C. Bellinger. 2005. "Protecting Children from Environmental Toxins." *Public Library of Science Journal of Medicine* 2: e61 at http://medicine.plosjournals.org/perlserv?request=get-document&doi=10.1371/journal.pmed.0020061 (accessed May 16, 2008).

Laub, John H. and Robert J. Sampson. 1991. "The Sutherland-Glueck Debate: On the Sociology of Criminological Knowledge." *American Journal of Sociology* 96:1402–1440.

Laub, John H. and Robert J. Sampson. 2003. *Shared Beginnings, Divergent Lives: Delinquent Boys at Age 70.* Cambridge, MA: Harvard University Press.

Laub, John H., Robert J. Sampson, and Gary A. Sweeten. 2006. "Assessing Sampson and Laub's Life-Course Theory of Crime." Pp. 313–333 in Francis T. Cullen, John Paul Wright and Kristie R. Blevins (eds.), *Taking Stock: The Status of Criminological Theory: Advances in Criminological Theory*, Volume 15. New Brunswick, NJ: Transaction Publishers.

Lea, John and Jock Young. 1984. *What Is to Be Done about Law and Order?* Harmondsworth, England: Penguin.

Lee, Matthew, R., William B. Bankston, Timothy C. Hayes, and Shaun A. Thomas. 2007. "Revisiting the Southern Culture of Violence." *The Sociological Quarterly* 48:253–275.

Lemert, Edwin M. 1951. *Social Pathology: A Systematic Approach to the Theory of Sociopathic Behavior.* New York: McGraw-Hill.

Levin, Michael. 1973. "Social Contract." Pp. 251–263 in Philip P. Wiener (ed.), *Dictionary of the History of Ideas.* New York: Charles Scribner's Sons.

Levin, Michael. 1997. *Why Race Matters: Race Differences and What They Mean.* Westport, CT: Praeger.

Lilienfeld, Scott O. and Hal Arkowitz. December 2007–January 2008. "What 'Psychopath' Means: It Is Not Quite What You May Think." *Scientific American Mind* 18:80–81.

Lilly, J. Robert, Francis T. Cullen, and Richard A. Ball. 1989. *Criminological Theory: Context and Consequences.* Newbury Park, CA: Sage.

Lilly, J. Robert, Francis T. Cullen, and Richard A. Ball. 2007. *Criminological Theory: Context and Consequences*, 4th edition. Thousand Oaks, CA: Sage.

Link, Bruce, Howard Andrews, and Francis Cullen. 1992. "The Violent and Illegal Behavior of Mental Patients Reconsidered." *American Sociological Review* 57:275–292.

Liska, Alan E. and M. D. Reed. 1985. "Ties to Conventional Institutions and Delinquency: Estimating Reciprocal Effects." *American Sociological Review* 50:547–560.

Lobo, Ingrid. 2008. "Copy Number Variation and Genetic Disease." Nature Education 1 at http://www.nature.com/scitable/topicpage/copy-number-variation-and-genetic-disease-911 (accessed September 27, 2014).

Lombroso, Cesare. 1968. *Crime, Its Causes and Remedies.* Tr. by Henry P. Horton. Montclair, NJ: Patterson Smith.

Lombroso, Cesare. 2000. "Criminal Anthropology: Its Origin and Application." Pp. 65–81 in David M. Horton, *Pioneering Perspectives in Criminology: The Literature of 19th Century Criminological Positivism.* Incline

Village, NV: Copperhouse. [Originally published in *Forum*, Vol. 20 (September 1895), pp. 33–49].

Lowenkamp, Christopher T., Francis T. Cullen, and Travis C. Pratt. 2003. "Replicating Sampson and Grove's Test of Social Disorganization Theory: Revisiting a Criminological Classic." *Journal of Research in Crime and Delinquency* 40:351–373.

Lynch, Michael J. and Ronald G. Burns. 2004. "Slippery Business: Race, Class and Legal Determinants of Penalties Against Petroleum Refineries." *Journal of Black Studies* 34:421–440.

Lynch, Michael J. and W. Byron Groves. 1989. *A Primer in Radical Criminology*, 2d ed. New York: Harrow and Heston.

Lynch, Michael J. and Raymond Michalowski. 2006. *Primer in Radical Criminology: Critical Perspectives on Crime, Power and Identity*, 4th ed. Monsey, New York: Criminal Justice Press.

Lynch, Michael J. and Paul Stretesky. 2001. "Toxic Crimes: Examining Corporate Victimization of the General Public Employing Medical and Epidemiological Evidence." *Critical Criminology* 10:153–171.

Lynch, Michael J. and Paul B. Stretesky. 2003. "The Meaning of Green: Contrasting Criminological Perspectives." *Theoretical Criminology* 7:217–238.

Lynch, Michael J., Herman Schwendinger, and Julia Schwendinger. 2008. "The Status of Empirical Research in Radical Criminology" Pp. 191–215 in Francis T. Cullen, John Paul Wright & Kristie R. Blevins (eds.), *Taking Stock: The Status of Criminological Theory: Advances in Criminological Theory*, Volume 15. New Brunswick, NJ: Transaction.

MacLean, Brian D. and Dragan Milovanovic (eds.). 1997. *Thinking Critically About Crime*. Vancouver, BC: Collective Press.

Mark, Vernon H. and Frank R. Ervin. 1970. *Violence and the Brain*. New York: Harper & Row.

Martin, Randy, Robert J. Mutchnick, and W. Timothy Austin. 1990. *Criminological Thought: Pioneers Past and Present*. New York: Macmillan.

Maruna, Shadd and Heith Copes. 2005. "What Have We Learned from Five Decades of Neutralization Research?" *Crime and Justice* 32:419–463.

Marx, Karl and Frederick Engels. 1970. *The German Ideology*. New York: International.

Maslow, Abraham H. 1970. *Motivation and Personality*, 2d ed. New York: Harper & Row.

Matsueda, Ross L. 1997. "'Cultural Deviance Theory': The Remarkable Persistence of a Flawed Term." *Theoretical Criminology* 1:429–452.

Matthews, Roger and Jock Young (eds.). 1986. *Confronting Crime*. London: Sage.

Matza, David. 1964. *Delinquency and Drift*. New York: Wiley.

Matza, David. 1969. *Becoming Deviant.* Englewood Cliffs, NJ: Prentice-Hall.

Mazerolle, Paul and Jeff Maahs. 2000. "General Strain Theory and Delinquency: An Alternative Examination of Conditioning Influences." *Justice Quarterly* 17:753–778.

McCarthy, Bernie and John Hagan. 2005. "Danger and the Decision to Offend." *Social Forces* 83:1065–1096.

McCord, Joan. 1991. "Family Relationship, Juvenile Delinquency, and Adult Criminality." *Criminology* 29:397–417.

McCrae, Robert R. and Paul T. Costa. 1990. *Personality in Adulthood.* New York: Guilford Press.

Mead, Hunter. 1959. *Types and Problems of Philosophy.* New York: Henry Holt.

Merton, Robert K. 1938. "Social Structure and Anomie." *American Sociological Review* 3:672–682.

Messerschmidt, James W. 1986. *Capitalism, Patriarchy, and Crime: Toward a Socialist Feminist Criminology.* Totowa, NJ: Rowman and Littlefield.

Messerschmidt, James W. 1993. *Masculinities and Crime: Critique and Reconceptualization of Theory.* Lanham, MD: Rowman and Littlefield.

Messerschmidt, James W. 1997. "Structured Action Theory: Understanding the Interrelation of Gender, Race, Class, and Crime." Pp. 67–74 in Brian D. MacLean and Dragan Milovanovic (eds.), *Thinking Critically About Crime.* Vancouver, BC: Collective Press.

Messner, Steven F. and Richard Rosenfeld. 2001. *Crime and the American Dream.* Belmont, CA: Wadsworth.

Messner, Steven F. and Richard Rosenfeld. 2006. "The Present and Future of Institutional-Anomie Theory." Pp. 127–148 in Francis T. Cullen, John Paul Wright, and Kristie R. Blevins (eds.), *Taking Stock: The Status of Criminological Theory—Advances in Criminological Theory*, Volume 15, New Brunswick, NJ: Transaction.

Michalowski, Ray. 1990. "Niggers, Welfare Scum, and Homeless Assholes: The Problems of Idealism, Consciousness, and Context in Left Realism." *The Critical Criminologist* 2:5–6, 17–18.

Michalowski, Raymond J. and Edward W. Bohlander. 1976. "Repression and Criminal Justice in America." *Sociological Inquiry* 46:95–106.

Milgram, Stanley. 1974. *Obedience to Authority.* New York: Harper & Row.

Miller, Jody. 2003. "Feminist Criminology." Pp. 15–28 in Martin D. Schwartz and Suzanne E. Hatty (eds.), *Controversies in Critical Criminology*, Cincinnati, OH: Anderson.

Miller, Jody and Christopher W Mullins. 2006. "The Status of Feminist Theories in Criminology." Pp. 217–249 in Francis T. Cullen, John Paul Wright, and Kristie R. Blevins (eds.), *Taking Stock: The Status of Criminological*

Theory—Advances in Criminological Theory. Volume 15, New Brunswick, NJ: Transaction.

Miller, Joshua D. and Donald Lynam. 2001. "Structural Models of Personality and their Relation to Antisocial Behavior: A Meta-Analysis." *Criminology* 39:765–798.

Miller, J. Mitchell, Christopher Schreck, and Richard Tewksbury. 2008. *Criminological Theory: A Brief Introduction.* Boston: Pearson.

Miller, Walter B. 1958. "Lower Class Culture as a Generating Milieu of Gang Delinquency." *Journal of Social Issues* 14:5–19.

Mills, C. Wright. 1942. "The Professional Ideology of Social Pathologists." *American Journal of Sociology* 49:165–180.

Mills, C. Wright. 1970. *The Power Elite.* New York: Oxford University Press.

Moffitt, Terrie E. 1993. "Life-Course-Persistent and Adolescence-Limited Antisocial Behavior: A Developmental Taxonomy." *Psychological Review* 100:674–701.

Monahan, John and Henry J. Steadman. 1983. "Crime and Mental Disorder: An Epidemiological Approach." In Michael Tonry and Norval Morris (eds.), *Crime and Justice* (Vol. 4). Chicago: University of Chicago Press.

Montague, William Pepperell. 1953. *The Ways of Knowing.* New York: MacMillan.

Moon, Byongook, Merry Morash, Cynthia Perez McCluskey, and Hye-Won Hwang. 2009. "A Comprehensive Test of General Strain Theory: Key Strains, Situational- and Trait-Based Negative Emotions, Conditioning Factors, and Delinquency." *Journal of Research in Crime and Delinquency* 46:182–212.

Morenoff, Jeffrey D., Robert J. Sampson, and Stephen W. Raudenbush. 2001. "Neighborhood Inequality, Collective Efficacy, and the Spatial Dynamics of Urban Violence." *Criminology* 39:517–559.

Morris, Charles G. with Albert A. Maisto. 1998. *Psychology: An Introduction,* 10th ed. Upper Saddle River, NJ: Prentice-Hall.

Mountain, Joanna L. and Neil Risch. 2004. "Assessing Genetic Contributions to Phenotypic Differences Among 'Racial' and 'Ethnic' Groups." *Nature Genetics Supplement* 36:S48–S53.

Mumola, Christopher J. and Jennifer C. Karberg. 2006. *Drug Use and Dependence, State and Federal Prisoners, 2004 (NCJ No. 213530).* Washington, DC: Bureau of Justice Statistics.

"Musings on Physiognomy." 2000. Pp. 5–8 in David M. Horton, *Pioneering Perspectives in Criminology: The Literature of 19th Century Criminological Positivism.* Incline Village, NV: Copperhouse. [Originally published in *Britannia Monthly Magazine,* Vol 2 (March 1836), pp. 227–230].

National Institute for Juvenile Justice and Delinquency Prevention. 1977. *Preventing Delinquency* (Vol. 1). U.S. Department of Justice, Office of Juvenile Justice and Delinquency Prevention, Law Enforcement Assistance Administration. Washington, DC: U.S. Government Printing Office.

Neufeldt, Victoria (Ed.). 1988. *Webster's New World Dictionary of American English*, 3rd college ed. Cleveland: Webster's New World.

Newman, Oscar. 1976. *Defensible Space: Crime Prevention Through Urban Design*. New York: Collier.

Nisbet, Robert A. 1965. *Emile Durkheim*. Englewood Cliffs, NJ: Prentice Hall.

Nofzinger, Stacey, 2008. "The 'Cause' of Low Self-Control: The Influence of Maternal Self-Control." *Journal of Research in Crime and Delinquency* 45:191–224.

Nye, F. Ivan. 1958. *Family Relationships and Delinquent Behavior*. New York: Wiley.

Ortiz, Jame and Adrian Raine. 2004. "Heart Rate Level and Antisocial Behavior in Children and Adolescents: A Meta-Analysis." *Journal of the American Academy of Child and Adolescent Psychiatry* 43:154–162.

Pallone, Nathaniel and James Hennessy. 1998. "Brain Dysfunction and Criminal Violence." *Society* 35:21–27.

Panfil, Vanessa R. and Jody Miller. 2014. "Beyond the Straight and Narrow: The Import of Queer Criminology for Criminology and Criminal Justice." *The Criminologist* 39:1, 3–8.

Park, Madison. 2012. "Using Chemical Castration to Punish Child Sex Crimes." CNNHealth at http://www.cnn.com/2012/09/05/health/chemical-castra tion-science/ (accessed September 21, 2014).

Park, Robert E., Ernest W. Burgess, and Roderick D. McKenzie. 1928. *The City*. Chicago: University of Chicago Press.

Parker, Karen F. and Amy Reckdenwald. 2008. "Concentrated Disadvantage, Traditional Male Role Models, and African-American Juvenile Violence." *Criminology* 46:711–735.

Paternoster, Raymond. 1987. "The Deterrent Effect of Perceived Certainty and Severity of Punishment: A Review of the Evidence and Issues." *Justice Quarterly* 4:173–217.

Paternoster, Raymond and Robert Brame. 2008. "Reassessing Race Disparities in Maryland Capital Cases." *Criminology* 46:971–1008.

Paternoster, Raymond and Alex R. Piquero. 1995. "Reconceptualizing Deterrence: An Empirical Test of Personal and Vicarious Experiences." *Journal of Research in Crime and Delinquency* 32:251–286.

Patrinos, Ari. 2004. "'Race' and the Human Genome." *Nature Genetics Supplement* 36:S1–S2.

Patterson, G. R., Barbara DeBaryshe, and Elizabeth Ramsey. 1989. "A Developmental Perspective on Antisocial Behavior." *American Psychologist* 44:329–335.

Pearson, Frank S. and Neil Alan Weiner. 1985. "Toward an Integration of Criminological Theories." *Journal of Criminal Law and Criminology* 76:116–150.

Pepinsky, Hal. 1999. "Peacemaking Primer." Pp. 52–70 in Bruce A. Arrigo (ed.), *Social Justice/Criminal Justice: The Maturation of Critical Theory in Law, Crime, and Deviance*. Belmont, CA: West/Wadsworth.

Pepinsky, Harold E. 1997. "Thinking Critically About Peacemaking: Reflections from Two Proponents." Pp. 109–117 in Brian D. MacLean and Dragan Milovanovic (eds.), *Thinking Critically About Crime*. Vancouver, BC: Collective Press.

Pepinsky, Harold E. and Richard Quinney (eds.). 1991. *Criminology as Peacemaking*. Bloomington, IN: Indiana University Press.

Peskin, Melissa, Yu Gao, Andrea L. Glenn, Anna Rudo-Hutt, Yaling Yang, and Adrian Raine. 2014. "Biology and Crime." Pp. 76–85 in Francis T. Cullen, Robert Agnew, and Pamela Wilcox (eds.) *Criminological Theory: Past to Present*. New York: Oxford University Press.

Pfohl, Stephen and Avery Gordon. 1986. "Criminological Displacements: A Sociological Deconstruction." *Social Problems* 33:94–113.

"Phrenology Epitomized." 2000. Pp. 17–24 in David M. Horton, *Pioneering Perspectives in Criminology: The Literature of 19th Century Criminological Positivism*. Incline Village, NV: Copperhouse. [Originally published in *Continental Repository*, Vol 2 (August 1841), pp. 156–159].

Piquero, Alex. 2002. "The Rational Choice Implications of Control Balance Theory." Pp. 85–107 in Alex R. Piquero and Stephen G. Tibbetts (eds). *Rational Choice and Criminal Behavior*. New York: Routledge.

Piquero, Alex and Matthew Hickman. 1999. "An Empirical Test of Tittle's Control Balance Theory." *Criminology* 37:319–341.

Piquero, Alex and Raymond Paternoster. 1998. "An Application of Stafford and Warr's Reconceptualization of Deterrence to Drinking and Driving." *Journal of Research in Crime and Delinquency* 35:3–39.

Piquero, Alex and Greg Pogarsky. 2002. "Beyond Stafford and Warr's Reconceptualization of Deterrence: Personal and Vicarious Experiences, Impulsivity, and Offending Behavior." *Journal of Research in Crime and Delinquency* 39:153–186.

Piquero, Alex and Stephen G. Tibbetts. 1999. "The Impact of Pre/Perinatal Disturbances and Disadvantaged Familial Environment in Predicting Criminal Offending." *Studies on Crime and Crime Prevention* 8:52–70.

Piquero, Nicole L., A. R. Gover, J. M. MacDonald, and Alex R. Piquero. 2005. "The Influence of Delinquent Peers on Delinquency: Does Gender Matter?" *Youth & Society* 36:251–275.

Piquero, Nicole L. and Alex Piquero. 2006. "Control Balance and Exploitative Corporate Crime." *Criminology* 44:397–430.

Platt, Tony. 1975. "Prospects for a Radical Criminology in the USA." Pp. 95–112 in Ian Taylor. Paul Walton, and Jock Young (eds.), *Critical Criminology*. Boston: Routledge & Kegan Paul.

Potter, Hillary. 2006. "An Argument for Black Feminist Criminology: Understanding African-American Women's Experiences with Intimate Partner Abuse Using an Integrated Approach." *Feminist Criminology* 1:106–124.

Pratt, Travis C. and Francis T. Cullen. 2005. "Assessing Macro-Level Predictors and Theories of Crime: A Meta-Analysis." Pp. 373–450 in Michael Tonry (ed.), *Crime and Justice: A Review of Research*, Volume 32. Chicago: University of Chicago Press.

Pratt, Travis C., Francis T. Cullen, Kristie R. Blevins, Leah E. Daigle, and Tamara D. Madensen. 2006. "The Empirical Status of Deterrence Theory: A Meta-analysis." Pp. 367–395 in Francis T. Cullen, John P. Wright and Kristie R. Blevins (eds.), *Taking Stock: The Status of Criminological Theory*. New Bruswick: Transaction Publishers.

"Quetelet on the Laws of the Social System." 2000. Pp. 269–273 in David M. Horton, *Pioneering Perspectives in Criminology: The Literature of 19th Century Criminological Positivism*. Incline Village, NV: Copperhouse. [Originally published in *Littell's Living Age*, Vol. 21, No. 260 (May 12, 1849), pp. 241–244].

Quinney, Richard. 1970. *The Social Reality of Crime*. Boston: Little, Brown.

Quinney, Richard. 1974. *Critique of Legal Order: Crime Control in Capitalist Society*. Boston: Little, Brown.

Quinney, Richard. 1977. *Class, State and Crime*. New York: McKay.

Rachlin, Howard. 1976. *Introduction to Modern Behaviorism*, 2d ed. San Francisco: W.H. Freeman.

Rafter, Nicole Hahn. 1997. "Psychopathy and the Evolution of Criminological Knowledge." *Theoretical Criminology* 1:235–259.

Rafter, Nicole Hahn. 2004. "The Unrepentant Horse-Slasher: Moral Insanity and the Origins of Criminological Thought." *Criminology* 42:979–1008.

Rafter, Nicole Hahn. 2007. "Somatotyping, Antimodernism, and The Production of Criminological Knowledge." *Criminology* 45:805–833.

Rafter, Nicole Hahn. 2008. *The Criminal Brain: Understanding Biological Theories of Crime*. New York: New York University Press.

Raine, Adrian. 1993. *The Psychopathology of Crime: Criminal Behavior as a Clinical Disorder*. San Diego, CA: Academic Press.

Raine, Adrian. 2002a. "Biosocial Studies of Antisocial and Violent Behavior in Children and Adults: A Review." *Journal of Abnormal Child Psychology* 30:311–326.

Raine, Adrian. 2002b. "The Biological Basis of Crime." Pp. 43–74 in James Q. Wilson & Joan Petersilia (eds.), *Crime: Public Policies for Crime Control.* Oakland, CA: ICS Press.

Raine, Adrian, Patricia Brennan, and Sarnoff A. Mednick. 1997. "Birth Complications Combined with Early Maternal Rejection at Age 1 Year Predispose to Violent Crime at Age 18 Years." *Archives of General Psychiatry* 51:984–988.

Raine, Adrian, Monte Buchsbaum, and Lori LaCasse. 1997. "Brain Abnormalities in Murderers Indicated by Positron Emission Tomography." *Biological Psychiatry* 42:495–508.

Reckless, Walter C. 1961. "A New Theory of Delinquency and Crime." *Federal Probation* 25:42–46.

Redl, Fritz and David Wineman. 1951. *Children Who Hate.* New York: Free Press.

Redl, Fritz and David Wineman. 1952. *Controls from Within.* New York: Free Press.

Reiss, Albert J. 1951. "Delinquency as the Failure of Personal and Social Controls." *American Sociological Review* 16:196–207.

Reynolds, Paul Davidson. 1971. *A Primer in Theory Construction.* Indianapolis and New York: Bobbs-Merrill.

Ritzer, George. 1975. *Sociology: A Multiple Paradigm Science.* Boston: Allyn and Bacon.

Robinson, Matthew B. 1999. "The Theoretical Development of Crime Prevention Through Environmental Design (CPTED)." Pp. 427–462 in William Laufer and Freda Adler (eds.), *Advances in Criminological Theory*, Vol. 8. New Brunswick, NJ: Transaction.

Robinson, Matthew B. and Tom Kelley. 2000. "The Identification of Neurological Correlates of Brain Dysfunction in Offenders by Probation Officers." Pp. 12-1–12-20 in Diane H. Fishbein (ed.), *The Science, Treatment, and Prevention of Antisocial Behaviors.* Kingston, NJ: Civic Research Institute.

Rosenfeld, Richard and Steven F. Messner. 2006. "Crime and the American Dream." Pp. 191–200 in Francis T. Cullen and Robert Agnew (eds.), *Criminological Theory Past to Present: Essential Readings.* New York: Oxford University Press.

Rosner, Richard. 1979. "Adolescents Accused of Murder and Manslaughter: A Five-Year Descriptive Study." *Bulletin of the American Academy of Psychiatry and the Law* 7:342–351.

Rowe, David C. 2007. *Biology and Crime*, 2nd ed. New York: Oxford.

Ross, Jeffery Ian and Stephen C. Richards. 2003. *Convict Criminology*. Belmont, CA: Wadsworth/Thomson Learning.

Runes, Dagobert D. (ed.). 1968. *Dictionary of Philosophy*. Totowa, NJ: Littlefield, Adams.

Rushton, J. Philippe. 1995. *Race, Evolution, and Behavior: A Life History Perspective*. New Brunswick, NJ: Transaction.

Ryan, William. 1976. *Blaming the Victim*. New York: Vintage.

Saint-Simon, Henri De. 1964. *Social Organization, the Science of Man and Other Writings*. Ed. and Tr. by Felix Markham. New York: Harper Torchbooks.

Salopek, Paul. 1997. "What's Next for Mankind?" *The Orlando Sentinel* (from the *Chicago Tribune*) (June 1), p. G-1.

Sampson, Robert J. 1999. "Techniques of Research Neutralization." *Theoretical Criminology* 3:438–451.

Sampson, Robert J. 2006. "Collective Efficacy Theory: Lessons Learned and Directions for Future Inquiry." Pp. 149–187 in Francis T. Cullen, John Paul Wright, and Kristie R. Blevins (eds.), *Taking Stock: The Status of Criminological Theory: Advances in Criminological Theory,* Volume 15. New Brunswick, NJ: Transaction.

Sampson, Robert J. and W. Byron Groves. 1989. "Community Structure and Crime: Testing Social Disorganization Theory." *American Journal of Sociology* 94:774–802.

Sampson, Robert J. and John H. Laub. 1992. "Crime and Deviance in the Life Course." *Annual Review of Sociology* 24:509–525.

Sampson, Robert J. and John H. Laub. 1993. *Crime in the Making: Pathways and Turning Points Through Life*. Cambridge: Harvard University Press.

Sampson, Robert J., Stephen W. Raudenbush, and Felton Earls. 1997. "Neighborhoods and Violent Crime: A Multilevel Study of Collective Efficacy." *Science*: 277: 918–924.

Sanders, Bernie. 2011. "Release: Tax Time? Not for Giant Corporations." Available at http://www.sanders.senate.gov/newsroom/press-releases/release-tax-time-not-for-giant-corporations (accessed August 25, 2014).

Savage, Joanne. 2008. "The Role of Exposure to Media Violence in the Etiology of Violent Behavior: A Criminologist Weighs In." *American Behavioral Scientist* 51:1123–1136.

Scarpa, Angela and Adrian Raine. 2003. "The Psychophysiology of Antisocial Behavior: Interactions with Environmental Experiences." Pp. 209–225 in Anthony Walsh and Lee Ellis (eds.), *Biosocial Criminology: Challenging Environmentalism's Supremacy*. Hauppauge, NY: Nova Science Publishers.

Schlossman, Steven, Gail Zellman, and Richard Shavelson, with Michael Sedlak and Jane Cobb. 1984. *Delinquency Prevention in South Chicago: A Fifty-Year Assessment of the Chicago Area Project*. Santa Monica, CA: Rand.

Schuessler, Karl F. and Donald R. Cressey. 1950. "Personality Characteristics of Criminals." *American Journal of Sociology* 55:476–484.

Schur, Edwin M. 1969. *Our Criminal Society*. Englewood Cliffs, NJ: Prentice-Hall.

Schur, Edwin M. 1973. *Radical Nonintervention*. Englewood Cliffs, NJ: Prentice-Hall.

Schwartz, Martin D. 1989. "The Undercutting Edge of Criminology." *The Critical Criminologist* 1:1, 2, 5.

Schwartz, Martin D. and Walter DeKeseredy. 1991. "Left Realist Criminology: Strengths, Weaknesses and the Feminist Critique." *Crime, Law and Social Change* 15:51–72.

Schwendinger, Herman and Julia Schwendinger. 1975, originally 1970. "Defenders of Order or Guardians of Human Rights?" Pp. 113–146 in Ian Taylor, Paul Walton, and Jock Young (eds.), *Critical Criminology*. Boston: Routledge & Kegan Paul.

Schwendinger, Herman and Julia Schwendinger. 1983. *Rape and Inequality*. Beverly Hills, CA: Sage.

Sellin, Thorstein. 1938. *Culture, Conflict and Crime*. New York: Social Science Research Council.

Shah, Saleem and Loren H. Roth. 1974. "Biological and Psychophysiological Factors in Criminality." Pp. 101–173 in Daniel Glaser (ed.), *Handbook of Criminology*. Chicago: Rand.

Sharp, Susan F. 2014. *Mean Lives, Mean Laws: Oklahoma's Women Prisoners*. New Brunswick, NJ: Rutgers University Press.

Shaw, Clifford R. 1929. *Delinquency Areas*. Chicago: University of Chicago Press.

Shaw, Clifford R. 1930. *The Jackroller*. Chicago: University of Chicago Press.

Shaw, Clifford R. 1931. *The Natural History of a Delinquent Career*. Chicago: University of Chicago Press.

Shaw, Clifford R. 1938. *Brothers in Crime*. Chicago: University of Chicago Press.

Shaw, Clifford R. 1942. *Juvenile Delinquency and Urban Areas*. Chicago: University of Chicago Press.

Shaw, Clifford R. and Henry D. McKay. 1931. *Social Factors in Juvenile Delinquency*. Chicago: University of Chicago Press.

Sheldon, William H. 1949. *Varieties of Delinquent Youth*. New York: Harper.

Siegel, Larry J. 2010. *Criminology: Theories, Patterns, and Typologies*. Belmont, CA: Wadsworth.

Simon, David R. 1996. *Elite Deviance*, 5th ed. Boston: Allyn and Bacon.

Simon, Rita. 1975. *Women and Crime*. Lexington, MA: D.C. Heath.

Simpson, Sally S. 1989. "Feminist Theory, Crime, and Justice." *Criminology* 27:605–631.

Sitren, Alicia H. and Brandon K. Applegate. 2007. "Testing the Deterrent Effects of Personal and Vicarious Experience with Punishment and Punishment Avoidance." *Deviant Behavior* 28:29–55.

Skogan, Wesley G. 1990. *Disorder and Decline: Crime and the Spiral of Decay in American Neighborhoods*. New York: Free Press.

Smedley, Audrey and Brian D. Smedley. 2005. "Race as Biology Is Fiction, Racism as a Social Problem Is Real: Anthropological and Historical Perspectives on the Social Construction of Race." *American Psychologist* 60:16–26.

Smith, Samuel G. 2000. "Relation of Crime to Economics." Pp. 357–366 in David M. Horton, *Pioneering Perspectives in Criminology: The Literature of 19th Century Criminological Positivism*. Incline Village, NV: Copperhouse. [Originally published in *Lend A Hand*, Vol. 17 (June 1896), pp. 408–4419].

Stafford, Mark C. and Mark Warr. 1993. "A Reconceptualization of General and Specific Deterrence." *Journal of Research in Crime and Delinquency* 30:123–128.

Stanko, Elizabeth. 1985. *Intimate Intrusions: Women's Experience of Male Violence*. Boston: Routledge & Kegan Paul.

Stark, Rodney. 1987. "Deviant Places: A Theory of the Ecology of Crime." *Criminology* 25:893–909.

Stephens, Gene. 1987. "Crime and Punishment: Forces Shaping the Future." *The Futurist* (January-February):18–26.

Stern, Simon (forthcoming) "William Blackstone, *Commentaries on the Laws of England*, vol. 4 (1769)." In Markus Dubber, *Foundational Texts in Modern Law*. Oxford: Oxford University Press. (Accessed September 21, 2014, SSRN-id2296451.pdf).

Sternberg, Robert J., Elena L. Grigorenko, and Kenneth K. Kidd. 2005. "Intelligence, Race and Genetics." *American Psychologist* 60:46–59.

Steury, Ellen Hochstedler. 1993. "Criminal Defendants with Psychiatric Impairment: Prevalence, Probabilities and Rates." *Journal of Criminal Law and Criminology* 84:354–374.

Stewart, Eric A. and Ronald L. Simons. 2006. "Structure and Culture in African American Adolescent Violence: A Partial Test of the 'Code of the Street' Thesis." *Justice Quarterly* 23:1–33.

Straton, James. 2000. "The Correspondence Between the Characters and Heads of Two Murderers Lately Executed at Newgate." Pp. 27–40 in David M.

Horton, *Pioneering Perspectives in Criminology: The Literature of 19th Century Criminological Positivism*. Incline Village, NV: Copperhouse. [Originally published in *Zoist*, Vol. 13 (July 1856), pp. 202–218].

Stretesky, Paul B. and Michael J. Lynch. 1999a. "Environmental Justice and the Prediction of Distance to Accidental Chemical Releases in Hillsborough County, Florida." *Social Science Quarterly* 80:830–846.

Stretesky, Paul B. and Michael J. Lynch. 1999b. "Corporate Environmental Violence and Racism." *Crime, Law and Social Change* 30:163–184.

Stretesky, Paul B. and Michael J. Lynch. 2003. "Environmental Hazards and School Segregation in Hillsborough, 1987–1999." *Sociological Quarterly* 43:553–573.

Sullivan, Dennis. 1980. *The Mask of Love: Corrections in America, Toward a Mutual Aid Alternative*. Port Washington, NY: Kennikat Press.

Sutherland, Edwin H. 1983. *White Collar Crime: The Uncut Version*. New Haven: Yale University Press.

Sutherland, Edwin H. and Donald R. Cressey. 1974. *Criminology*, 9th ed. Philadelphia: J. B. Lippincott. Reprinted by permission of the Estate of R. Cressey.

Suttles, Gerald D. 1968. *The Social Order of the Slum: Ethnicity and Territory in the Inner City*. Chicago: University of Chicago Press.

Sweet, William. n.d. "Jeremy Bentham." Internet Encyclopedia of Philosophy: A Peer-Reviewed Academic Resource at www.iep.utm.edu/bentham/ (accessed September 3, 2014).

Sykes, Gresham and David Matza. 1957. "Techniques of Neutralization: A Theory of Delinquency." *American Sociological Review* 22:664–670.

Tappan, Paul W. (ed.). 1951. *Contemporary Correction*. New York: McGraw-Hill.

Tarde, Gabriel. 1968. *Penal Philosophy*. Tr. by Rapelje Howell. Montclair, NJ: Patterson Smith.

Taylor, Ian, Paul Walton, and Jock Young. 1974. *The New Criminology: For a Social Theory of Deviance*. New York: Harper & Row.

Taylor, Ian, Paul Walton, and Jock Young. 1975. *Critical Criminology*. Boston: Routledge & Kegan Paul.

Tellegen, Auke. 1985. "Structures of Mood and Personality and their Relevance to Assessing Anxiety with an Emphasis on Self-Report." In A. Hussain Tuma and Jack D. Maser (eds.), *Anxiety and the Anxiety Disorders*. Hillsdale, N.J.: Lawrence Erlbaum Associates.

Thompson, Edward P. 1975. *Whigs and Hunters: The Origin of the Black Act*. New York: Pantheon.

Thornberry, Terence P. 1987. "Towards an Interactional Theory of Delinquency." *Criminology* 25:863–891.

Tittle, Charles R. 1995. *Control Balance: Toward a General Theory of Deviance*. Boulder, CO: Westview Press.

Toby, Jackson. 1957. "Social Disorganization and Stake in Conformity: Complementary Factors in the Predatory Behavior of Hoodlums." *Journal of Criminal Law, Criminology and Police Science* 48:12–17.

Tremblay, Richard E. 2006. "Tracking the Origins of Criminal Behaviour: Back to the Future." *The Criminologist* 31:1, 3–7.

Turk, Austin. 1969. *Criminality and Legal Order*. Chicago: Rand.

Turk, Austin. 1979. "Analyzing Official Deviance: For Nonpartisan Conflict Analyses in Criminology." *Criminology* 4:459–476.

Turner, Michael G. and Alex R. Piquero. 2002. "The Stability of Self-Control." *Journal of Criminal Justice* 30:457–71.

Tyler, Tom R., Lawrence Sherman, Heather Strang, Geoffrey C. Barnes, and Daniel Woods. 2007. "Reintegrative Shaming, Procedural Justice, and Recidivism: The Engagement of Offenders' Psychological Mechanisms in the Canberra RISE Drinking-and-Driving Experiment." *Law and Society Review* 41:553–585.

Unger, Roberto Mangabeira. 1987. *False Necessity*. New York: Cambridge University Press.

Unnever, James D., Travis C. Pratt, and Francis T. Cullen. 2003. "Parental Management, ADHD, and Delinquent Involvement: Reassessing Gottfredson and Hirschi's General Theory." *Justice Quarterly* 20:471–500.

Van Wilsem, Johan, Karin Wittebrood, and Nan Dirk De Graaf. 2006. "Socioeconomic Dynamics of Neighborhoods and the risk of Crime Victimization: A Multilevel Study of Improving, Declining, and Stable Areas in the Netherlands." *Social Problems* 53:226–247.

Vila, Bryan. 1994. "A General Paradigm for Understanding Criminal Behavior: Extending Evolutionary Ecological Theory." *Criminology* 32:311–359.

Vila, Bryan and Cynthia Morris (eds.). 1997. *Capital Punishment in the United States: A Documentary History*. Westport, CT: Greenwood.

Vold, George B. 1958. *Theoretical Criminology*. New York: Oxford.

Vold, George B. 1979. *Theoretical Criminology*. 2d ed. New York: Oxford.

Vold, George B. and Thomas J. Bernard. 1986. *Theoretical Criminology*. 3d ed. New York: Oxford.

Wakschlag Lauren S., Kate E. Pickett, Edwin Cook Jr., Neal L. Benowitz, and Bennett L. Leventhal. 2002. "Maternal Smoking During Pregnancy and Severe Antisocial Behavior in Offspring: A Review." *American Journal of Public Health* 92:966–974.

Waldo, Gordon P. and Simon Dinitz. 1967. "Personality Attributes of the Criminal: An Analysis of Research Studies, 1950–1965." *Journal of Research in Crime and Delinquency* 4:185–202.

Walsh, Anthony. 2000. "Behavior Genetics and Anomie/Strain Theory." *Criminology* 38:1075–1107.

Walsh, Anthony and Lee Ellis. 1999. "Political Ideology and American Criminologists' Explanations for Criminal Behavior." *The Criminologist* 24 (No. 6, November/December):1, 14, 26–27.

Walters, Glenn. 1992. "A Meta-Analysis of the Gene-Crime Relationship." *Criminology* 30:595–613.

Walters, Glenn and Thomas White. 1989. "Heredity and Crime: Bad Genes or Bad Research." *Criminology* 27:455–486.

Walters, Glenn, D. 2000. "Disposed to Aggress? In Search of the Violence-Prone Personality," *Aggression and Violent Behavior* 5:177–190.

Warr, Mark. 2002. *Companions in Crime: The Social Aspects of Criminal Conduct.* Cambridge, UK: Cambridge University Press.

Williams, Frank P. III and Marilyn D. McShane. 1994. *Criminological Theory,* 2d ed. Englewood Cliffs, NJ: Prentice-Hall.

Wilson, James Q. and Richard J. Herrnstein. 1985. *Crime and Human Nature.* New York: Simon and Schuster.

Wilson, William Julius. 1987. *The Truly Disadvantaged.* Chicago: University of Chicago Press.

Winfree, L. Thomas and Howard Abadinsky. 2010. *Understanding Crime: Essentials of Criminological Theory,* 3rd ed. Belmont, CA: Wadsworth Cengage Learning.

Winfree, L. Thomas, Terrance J. Taylor, Ni He, and Finn-Aage Esbensen. 2006. "Self-Control and Variability Over Time: Multivariate Results Using a 5-Year, Multisite Panel of Youths." *Crime & Delinquency* 52:253–286.

Wolfgang, Marvin E. and Franco Ferracuti. 1982. *The Subculture of Violence.* Beverly Hills, CA: Sage.

Wong, Siu Kwong. 2007. "Disorganization [Precursors?], the Family and Crime: A Multi-year Analysis of Canadian Municipalities." *Western Criminology Review* 8:48–68.

Wood, Peter B., Walter R. Gove, James A. Wilson, and John K. Cochran. 1997. "Nonsocial Reinforcement and Habitual Criminal Conduct: An Extension of Learning Theory." *Criminology* 35:335–366.

Woodworth, Robert S. and Mary R. Sheehan. 1964. *Contemporary Schools of Psychology,* 3d ed. New York: Ronald Press.

Wortley, Richard. 2011. *Psychological Criminology: An Integrated Approach.* New York: Routledge.

Wright, Erik Olin. 1978. *Class, Crisis and the State.* New York: NLB.

Yochelson, Samuel and Stanton E. Samenow. 1976. *The Criminal Personality* (Vol. 1: *A Profile for Change*). Northvale, NJ: Jason Aronson.

Young, Jock. 1997. "Left Realism: The Basics." Pp. 28–36 in B.D. MacLean and D. Milovanovic (eds.), *Thinking Critically About Crime.* Vancouver, BC: Collective Press.

Zeitlin, Irving M. 1968. *Ideology and the Development of Sociological Theory.* Englewood Cliffs, NJ: Prentice-Hall.

Zhang, Lening, Steven F. Messner, and Jianhong Liu. (2007). "A Multilevel Analysis of the Risk of Household Burglary in the Ciry of Tianjin, China."*British Journal of Criminology* 47: 918–937.

Zimbardo, Philip. 2008. *The Lucifer Effect: Understanding How Good People Turn Evil.* New York: Random House.

Zinn, Howard. 1990. *A People's History of the United States.* New York: Harper Perennial.

Zucchino, David. 2012. "The State Raped Me All Over Again." *The Orlando Sentinel* (January 29), p. A8.

Index

Names of books are in italic font.

A

achievement, group *vs.* individual, 158

activism, oppression and, 82

ADHD (attention deficit/hyperactivity disorder), 58–59

Adler, Freda, 164

adoption studies, 54–55

"age-crime curve," 198

age-graded theory of informal social control (Sampson and Laub), 197

"Age of Reason," 19

aggression. *See* violence, criminality and

Agnew, Robert, theories by
General Strain Theory (GST), 109–10
general theory of crime and delinquency, 193–94
unified criminology, 194–96

Aid to Families with Dependent Children, policy implications of, 70

Akers, Ronald L., learning theory of, 127–31, 142n. 61

alcoholism, 72, 106, 150–51

American Anthropological Association, 71, 103

anal stage (Freud), 72–73

Anderson, Elijah, 133–34

Andrews, D.A., 127

animal rights. *See* green/environmental criminology

anomie theories, 105–13
anomie, definitions, 92
anomie theory (Merton), 105–6
anomie *vs.* strain theory, 108–9
critique of, 111–13
differential opportunity theory (Cloward and Ohlin), 107–8
failure *vs.* success, 113

237

of evolutionary biopsychological theories, 70–71
of feminist criminology,
164–65
of functional theory (structural-functional theory), 104
of green/environmental criminology, 174
of integrated theories, 200, 201
of intelligence-and-crime theories, 70–71
of labeling theory, 149–51
of learning theories, 128–30
of needs theory (Maslow),
81–82
of oppression/psychological advantages of crime theories
(Halleck), 83
of peacemaking criminology,
169
of politics, 6, 34, 98, 104–5,
145–46, 156, 163
of postmodern criminology,
171
of psychoanalytic theories,
75–76
of race-IQ-crime theories,
70–71
of radical criminology, 160–61
of routine activity theory,
101–2
of situational crime prevention
(opportunity theory),
100–101
of social control theories, 137
of system-situation-person theory (Zimbardo), 85
pollution. See green/environmental
criminology

positive reinforcement, 128,
129–30
positivist theories, 33–39. See also
psychological theories
classicism/neoclassicism vs.,
36–38
critical theories vs., 146
critique of, 38–39, 50
empirical/experimental science,
influence of, 35–36
Italian school of criminology
and, 49–50
positive philosophy, 33–35
simple integrated theories and,
188
post-postmodern synthesis (Barak),
196, 199–200
postmodern criminology, 169–73
constitutive criminology
(Henry and Milovanovic),
171–73
critique of, 171
feminist postmodernism, 166
policy implications of, 171
postmodernism, definition,
169
poverty, crime and
collective efficacy and, 96–97
Marxist theory and, 156–58
positivists and, 35–36
rural crime and, 175
War on Poverty, 108
power-control theory (Hagan),
191–93
"A Power Control-Theory of Common Delinquent Behavior"
(Hagan), 191
power differentials, in constitutive
criminology, 173

criminal anthropology in, 48
criminal justice model in,
29–30
cultural goals *vs.* social structure in, 105–6, 113, 120n.
175
eugenics in, 67
good *vs.* evil dichotomy in, 85
low intelligence and crime in,
67–69
punishment in, 129–30
social/political change, in
1960s, 145–46
social programs in, 163
sterilization and chemical castration in, 59
violence in, 133
"Wal-Marting" of rural areas in,
175
Unnever, James D., 136
utility, principle of, 23
utopianism, 163

V

variables, extraneous/intervening, 11
verbal intelligence, criminals and,
77
verification, of theories, 12
Vila, Bryan, 191
violence, criminality and
aggression, personality testing
for, 78
aggression and low arousal, 58
aggression and punishment,
130
aggression and toxic substances,
58–59
aggression in children, research
on, 136

brain disorders, 56–57
collective efficacy and, 96–97
feminist theory and, 166
Freud and, 73–74
radical theory and, 157–58, 161
subculture of violence theory
(Wolfgang and Ferracuti),
132–33
violence-prone personality, theory of, 80
Vold, George B., 44, 115n. 26,
116n. 27, 152
Voltaire, on marriage, 24

W

Walton, Paul, 114n. 1, 158
War on Poverty, 108
Warr, Mark, 28
waterboarding, interrogation *vs.*
torture using, 148
welfare, policy implications of, 70,
108
white-collar crime, 112, 122. *See
also* differential association theory (Sutherland)
conflict theory and, 153
general theory of crime/delin-
quency and, 193–94
left realism and, 168
as replacement discourse, 172
self-control theory and, 138
*Why Do Criminals Offend: A Gen-
eral Theory of Crime and Delinquency* (Agnew), 193–94,
194–95
Why Race Matters (Levin), 70
Wilson, James A., 141n. 50
Wilson, James Q., 101, 127, 141n.
43, 158

Winfree, L. Thomas, 136–37
Wolfgang, Marvin, subculture of
    violence theory by, 132–33
Wood, Peter B., 141n. 50
Woods, Jordan Blair, on queer
    criminology, 177
Wortley, Richard, 79
Wright, John Paul, 41n. 31, 88n.
    83

Y

Yochelson, Samuel, 80
Young, Jock, 114n. 1, 158, 168

Z

Zimbardo, Philip, humanistic psy-
    chological theory by, 80–81,
    84–85
zoonomy, 45